The Northwest Vegetarian Cookbook

THE
Northwest
Vegetarian
Cookbook

200 RECIPES
THAT CELEBRATE
THE FLAVORS OF OREGON
AND WASHINGTON

DEBRA
DANIELS-ZELLER

TIMBER PRESS
Portland · London

To Tom and Jennifer, who light up my life,
and to all the farmers who grow our food.

Frontispiece: Photo courtesy of Winter Green Farm.

Photographs are by the author unless otherwise
indicated.

An earlier edition of this book was published
in 2004 by LOC Press.

Published in 2010 by Timber Press, Inc.

The Haseltine Building
133 S.W. Second Avenue, Suite 450
Portland, Oregon 97204-3527
www.timberpress.com

2 The Quadrant
135 Salusbury Road
London NW6 6RJ
www.timberpress.co.uk

Printed in the United States of America
Text design by Susan Applegate

Library of Congress Cataloging-in-Publication Data

Daniels-Zeller, Debra.
The Northwest vegetarian cookbook: 200 recipes
that celebrate the flavors of Oregon and Washington/
Debra Daniels-Zeller.
    p. cm.
Rev. ed. of: Local vegetarian cooking. © 2004.
Includes bibliographical references and index.
ISBN 978-1-60469-034-7
    1. Vegetarian cookery. 2. Cookery, American—
Pacific Northwest style. I. Daniels-Zeller, Debra.
Local vegetarian cooking. II. Title.
TX837.D223 2010
641.5′636—dc22   2009036882

A catalog record for this book is also available from
the British Library.

Contents ❧

Preface

Eating locally is about synchronizing the food we eat every day with the seasons; it's about buying directly from farmers and feeling connected to the land where our food is grown. Knowing where food—strawberries and asparagus in the spring, apples and squash in the fall—comes from and meeting the growers who harvest it links us to the earth and brings us in tune with seasonal rhythms.

Since the late 1990s, "eat locally" has become the mantra in nearly every community in the Northwest, where I live. More varieties of local fruits and vegetables, along with more shoppers, show up at markets each season. It's exciting waiting for favorite farmers to arrive and discovering what treasures they've brought. Mulberries, blackcaps, creamy tasting papaws—fun and flavorful fruits like these aren't available in chain grocery stores. And as more farmers get into growing year-round, more varieties of fresh food become available in winter; some farmers' markets in Portland and Seattle remain open year-round.

This book offers inspired recipes that celebrate Northwest farms. It focuses on the plant world—vegetables, fruit, beans, nuts, and grains—because that's where my fork is planted. In each of its six recipe sections, it offers profiles of farmers and farms that provide the bountiful harvest we cook with.

- "The Well-Grounded Breakfast" contains pieces about bees (because nothing much happens without them) and two Northwest crops they pollinate—apples and pears.

- "Salads Year-Round" features pieces about farmland preservation and seed production.

- "Seasonal Soups and Homemade Breads" profiles farm restaurants and farmers growing unique crops.

- "Starters and Side Dishes" offers pieces about extending farming seasons and first-generation farmers.

- "Savory Vegetarian Entrées" profiles a bio-dynamic community-focused farm and a farmer who will always be remembered by the farming community.

- "Fresh Fruit Desserts" features profiles about summer tree fruit growers and berry farms.

In the back of the book are guides to Northwest produce and to Northwest beans and grains.

The diverse small farms spanning our Northwest landscape bring us a rich, unique local food supply, worth supporting and preserving for generations to come.

How This Book Was Born

I wasn't raised on a farm, and aside from my father's tiny annual garden I had little contact with food fresh from the earth. I grew up in small towns in Utah, New Mexico, and Colorado, and finally cities in California in the 1950s and '60s, and my mother was a big fan of frozen dinners. When we moved from Cortez, Colorado, to San Diego, our small-town friends joked that we'd be prune pickers. I was so disconnected from the earth, I didn't know whether prunes grew on trees or bushes.

In California I discovered new varieties of fruits and vegetables, and after high school when I visited Oregon, I fell in love with blueberries near the Rogue River. Enchanted with the flavor, I wanted to move to the Northwest. So in the early 1970s I moved to Bellingham, Washington, where I met Tom, now my husband. He was a builder who had worked on a blueberry farm and was living on a five-acre farm on the Mount Baker Highway east of Bellingham. Tom was raising pastured cows, and he had a bumper crop of ripe tomatoes.

We gorged on fresh salads every evening, but later that year the owners sold the farm, and soon we bought a cabin just south of Bellingham. Our land there was covered with evergreens, and we suffered through meals of flavorless store-bought vegetables. When we moved closer to Seattle in the 1980s, I was thrilled by the produce at Pike Place Market. Our love affair with salads picked right back up where it had left off.

When the University District farmers' market opened in 1992, I shopped there on Saturday mornings, and I also joined Puget Consumers' Co-op (PCC Natural Markets), where I heard continual praise for Nash Huber's legendary sweet carrots. Seduced by the freshness and flavor of local market produce, I became committed to having a direct connection to my food supply. My weekly produce purchases inspired recipes for many meals shared with family and friends. For 16 years I also taught vegetarian cooking classes at PCC Natural Markets, and these classes resulted in more than enough recipes for a cookbook. As I contemplated which recipes to include, I realized adding farm stories would enhance the book.

I also gathered some recipes from farm Web sites and adapted them for this book. I'd always imagined farm recipes were passed down from generation to generation like farmland, but I soon discovered that farming leaves little time for creating dishes, and many of our Northwest farmers are first-generation farmers with simple yet delicious recipes that are as basic as adding butter, salt, and maybe a twist of lemon to a freshly steamed vegetable.

About the Farms

Researching information for this book, I visited Oregon and Washington farmers' markets and farms from southern Oregon to northern Washington. Farmers' markets in the Northwest and across the country began multiplying just a few decades ago, and in 2009 Oregon had 90 markets and Washington had 120, with new markets sprouting up each year. Many market information tables offer free directories that list all the markets in the state. In addition to hanging out at markets, I also visited food co-ops to discover local farmers.

In the Ashland Food Cooperative produce

department, I learned about Whistling Duck Farm and the Fry Family Farm. One slightly overcast day, I walked with farmer Vince Alionis around Whistling Duck Farm near Grants Pass, Oregon, and left with a basket of the sweetest tomatoes. Not far from Whistling Duck Farm, in Talent, I inhaled the fragrance of Suzi Fry's beautiful flowers and bonded with Zeus, their farm dog. I savored a delectable berry turnover from the Frys' friends at Pennington Farms, also in Grants Pass.

On my way to Corvallis, I stopped at the Gathering Together Farm restaurant. Over coffee and an old-fashioned potato doughnut, I talked with farmer John Eveland and then walked through the farm fields near the meandering Mary's River. The next day, in Gaston, Oregon, I dined on an exotic smoky frikeh pilaf and savored fresh salad greens after touring Carol and Anthony Boutard's farm.

In Washington, I visited more farms and added stories. At Rockridge Orchards in Enumclaw, I learned about unusual crops like sancho peppercorns and yuzu, a hearty Asian citrus, as I walked through Wade Bennett's bamboo orchards. At Nash Huber's organic farm in Sequim, Kia Armstrong gave me a tour of the fields and I joined the work crew for a lunch of grilled zucchini steaks, carrot hummus, braised greens, and the best blackberry cake I'd ever tasted. A few weeks later, Tom and I went to Nash's semi-annual community barn dance, which raised donations for their farm-to-cafeteria program. I can still see Nash and his wife, Patty, jitterbugging to a Seattle band on the crowed dance floor of Nash's packing shed, decorated with hay bales and vegetables.

The farm profiles in this book highlight a farmer's history, farming techniques, and seasonal challenges and opportunities. One year the pears I'm crazy about are in short supply because the bears had a midnight picnic in the orchard, or the plums I'd hoped for are nonexistent because they didn't get pollinated. From pollination to harvest, these stories shape my menus composed of local foods.

Not all the farms profiled in this book are certified organic, because I wanted the profiles to be representative of our entire local farming landscape. There are various reasons for farmers not getting their farms certified. Some farms use pesticides, while some are just in the process of getting their organic certification, which can take up to three years. Other farms have dropped their organic certification because of the expense and extra work of detailing everything from seed to harvest that organic farms must keep track of to maintain the certification. As a regular market shopper, I've learned to ask farmers about their growing techniques. "Everyone should have their own personal farmer," says Washington farmer Wade Bennett. It's not a bad idea to talk to farmers and if possible visit farms to see how your food is grown.

About Community Supported Agriculture Programs

Many small, diversified farms throughout the Northwest offer a community supported agriculture (CSA) program. In this program, a farm typically offers local food shoppers weekly boxes of fresh fruits and vegetables for a number of weeks for a subscription fee, paid in advance. This system benefits small farms because the advance payment provides capital for operating expenses, and it benefits consumers because the boxes often contain more than you might get for the same amount of money if you were shopping and paying weekly.

The CSA system of marketing direct from farm to table started in the early 1960s in Japan, Germany, and Switzerland and was exported to the East Coast of the United States in the 1980s. Since then, small farms across the country have adopted the CSA model and developed their own versions of the program. CSA members have the opportunity to cultivate relationships with a farmer, have input into what the farmer grows, and learn about farming techniques and crops. CSA newsletters vary from farm to farm. Some feature produce descriptions, including history, nutrition information, and cooking and storage tips. Some also contain farm updates. Recipes are usually included with each box.

One typical example of a Northwest farm offering a CSA subscription is Stoney Plains Organic Farm in Tenino, Washington. They have a no-frills flier that advertises a variety of CSA options with full and partial shares. The full share has enough produce for two to four people, and the partial share is suitable for one or two. The farm selects 6 to 12 items each week (fewer items in spring and more in summer and fall). A sample box might include cauliflower, cabbage, carrots, chard, cucumber, green beans, tomatoes, fennel, and salad mix. Patrick Meyer from Stoney Plains says that the value of getting a CSA box is that members always get the best produce before vegetables are packed for markets.

This CSA program runs for 20 weeks, and subscribers or members pick up weekly produce boxes at one of the markets the farm sells at. Subscribers have the option of getting fresh eggs every week for an additional price—a tempting addition, since eggs disappear quickly at summer markets. This farm also donates 1 percent of its CSA fees to a scholarship fund for agriculture students.

A CSA program at Rama Farm in Bridgeport, Washington, offers one or two layered boxes of luscious apricots, peaches, or nectarines. Rama Farm is a small family farm with a few acres of fruit trees. Their sweet stone fruit attracts many shoppers and is sold out at markets within a few hours, so their CSA program guarantees a supply of their popular fruit. This CSA program is perfect for people who want to freeze or preserve fruit or for two families who want to split a box of juicy, ripe fruit.

Deep Roots Farm in Oregon offers a "Market Advantage CSA," which gives market shoppers the freedom to create their own weekly CSA share with the produce the farm brings to market each week. Nash's Organic Produce in Sequim, Washington, offers "Nash's Farm Bucks" in a farm share program similar to this one. Shares in these CSA programs are purchased for less than their retail value, giving shoppers a savings each time they shop. The average cost of a CSA subscription per week varies from farm to farm, so do the math and determine what produce you want before you buy.

Each CSA subscription is a unique reflection of the farm. Read brochures and talk to farmers, and you can also search online and read the weekly newsletters that some Northwest farms add to their produce boxes. Some farms sponsor farm activities and host potlucks, seasonal gatherings, or autumn harvest celebrations. Other farms mention the possibility of work shares for people who want to work on the farm and learn more about farming or for those can't afford a full share price.

A number of the farms profiled in this book offer CSA programs. The list below is a starting point.

Fry Family Farm, Talent, Oregon
www.fryfamilyfarm.com
Denison Farms, Corvallis, Oregon
www.denisonfarms.com
Gathering Together Farm, Philomath, Oregon
www.gatheringtogetherfarm.com

Winter Green Farm, Noti, Oregon
www.wintergreenfarm.com
Nash's Organic Produce, Sequim, Washington
www.nashsorganicproduce.com

If you want to learn more about CSA availability in your area, check farmers' markets and ask market managers or other market shoppers for recommendations. If a farm has a Web site, check this for past CSA newsletters to get an idea of what you might receive in a CSA box each week.

Acknowledgments ❧

My thanks go out to all the farmers who opened their fields, barns, and houses and generously gave of their time to talk about farming philosophies and techniques, and to share their stories for this book. I'm grateful to the farmers who took time to return emails or phone calls when their time was already stretched and to the farmers who contributed recipes.

In Washington, I'm very grateful to Katsumi Taki at Mair Farm-Taki, Dorie Belisle at Belle-Wood Acres, and the crew at Nash Huber's farm store for supporting and selling so many copies of the first edition of this book. Thanks also to these farmers who shared their time and stories with me: Judy and Wade Bennett of Rockridge Orchards, Nash Huber and Kia Armstrong of Nash's Organic Produce, Patricia and Patrick Meyer of Stoney Plains Organic Farm, Jeff Miller of Willie Green's Organic Farm, Liz Eggers and Michael Hamphel of Grouse Mountain Farm, JoanE McIntyre of Rent's Due Ranch, Jeanette and Jeff Herman of Cliffside Orchards, Dorie and John Belisle of BelleWood Acres, Charlene Byde of Whispering Winds Farm, Michaele Blakely of Growing Things Farm, and Rose and Allan Merritt of the Merritt farm and Rosabella's Garden Bakery.

In Oregon, my appreciation goes out to farmers Vince and Mary Alionis of Whistling Duck Farm, Suzi and Steven Fry of the Fry Family Farm, Cathy and Sam Pennington of Pennington Farms, Diane Wilt of Wilt Farms and the Sunset Valley Organics line, Tom Denison and Elizabeth Kerle of Denison Farms, John Eveland and Sally Brewer of Gathering Together Farm, Frank Morton of Wild Garden Seed at Gathering Together Farm, Charles Duryea of Grateful Harvest Farm, Cheryl Stewart of Columbia Gorge Organic Fruit, Jabrila Via and Linda Davies of Winter Green Farm, and Anthony and Carol Boutard of Ayers Creek Farm.

I'm also very grateful for the many Northwest beekeepers like Roy Nettlebeck and Lewis Morgan and for all the farmers like Wade Bennett, Charles Duryea, and Liz Eggers and all the hobby beekeepers who nurture these tiny-winged pollinators. Thanks to Josh Nettlebeck for the great bee photos.

Other people who contributed beautiful photos to the book include Brad and Sheila Zahnow, Dorie Belisle, and Linda Davies. Also thanks to Morrie Carter for the author photograph.

My warmest thanks to Theo Nestor for helping shape the farm profiles, and to my writing group—Kathy Gehrt, Jan Schwert, Elsie Hulsizer, Sharon Morris, Sheila Kelly, and Wendy Hinman—for smoothing rough edges of many farmer stories. I'm grateful to Lake Boggan for bringing my book to Timber Press and to Lorraine Anderson, who made the manuscript sparkle. Thanks also to everyone at Timber Press for all their support.

Finally, thanks to my husband, Tom, who cheerfully samples all my recipes; to my daughter, Jennifer, for her continual support; and to Wade Bennett for answering my persistent farm questions at the market every Saturday and for making the best raspberry wine.

The Well-Grounded Breakfast

Morning foods in the Northwest are as diverse as our seasonal landscapes. In the summer, we have long days, treasured moments of sun, and a parade of produce that continues through the season. By late summer, wild blackberries are trailing over backyard fences and sweet peaches draw crowds at farmers' markets. The sun may hang around well into fall, but sooner or later our sunny days morph into short, cool, damp ones. And before we know it, berry season is over and fall has arrived, with apples and pears taking a turn at the table. The last of the fresh apples finally run out in the winter, so by the time strawberries show up, local fruit lovers are ready to repeat the show.

Fresh fruit in the morning is refreshing. When selecting fruit, consider the season. Choose melons, berries, and stone fruits in the summer. Switch to plums, apples, pears, and figs in the fall. Seasonal fruit imparts sweet flavors of time and place. In addition to fruit, easy-to-keep foods like grains and dried beans, and seasonal vegetables sold at farmers' markets provide us with different local breakfast options all year.

Northwest farmers' markets are gold mines for fruits, grains, beans, and a tantalizing variety of vegetables. Nash's Organic Produce in Sequim, Washington, sells wheat, rye, and triticale at Seattle farmers' markets. Ayers Creek Farm in Gaston, Oregon, sells hull-less barley and specialty beans at the Hillsdale farmers' market. A number of farmers also sell dried beans that when rehydrated go well on breakfast tostadas or tucked into breakfast burritos. Vegetables, mushrooms, and eggs round out the local cast for warming vegetarian breakfasts.

Whatever you choose, create a morning meal that lures you out of bed. If time is an issue, try make-ahead baked breakfasts or choose smoothies and quick fruit salad options. Whole grains provide energy all morning. One savory winter recipe, Root Harvester's Breakfast—made with buckwheat, parsnips, shitake mushrooms, and eggs—provides an even supply of energy until lunchtime. For those who prefer a sweet-treat breakfast, Northwest farmers contributed recipes for pie, cake, and clafouti made with seasonal fruits. On leisurely mornings, enjoy these treats warm from the oven or scramble some eggs or tofu with sautéed vegetables for a savory meal.

Make breakfast fun, seasonal, and local.

Breakfast in the springtime apple orchard
at BelleWood Acres. Photo by Dorie Belisle.

The Pollination Crew—The Tiniest Farmworkers

We can pick and choose our morning foods in the Northwest, but we wouldn't have as many selections or as much variety year-round if it weren't for the tiniest farmworker—the honeybee. The Northwest fruit and vegetable food chain is dependent on honeybees and wild pollinators. These are the tiny-winged workhorses that help produce bumper crops of apples, pears, and berries, and a wide range of vegetable seeds. Colorful blossoms lure bees to pollinate orchards and fields and set the fruits that fill our breakfast bowls.

Since the early 2000s, bees have made the news worldwide. Their colonies are rapidly declining, and beekeepers are increasingly experiencing phenomena such as colony collapse disorder (CCD), in which bees simply disappear from their hives. More people have begun stopping by beekeepers' booths at farmers' markets with questions about bees, so I spoke with Northwest beekeepers and farmers from Washington and Oregon about these tiny pollinating workers. Each beekeeper emphasized the importance of creating conditions that nurture bees.

In the Northwest, the delicate dance between bees and blooms begins in apple orchards every spring. Skagit County apple grower Allan Merritt of Bow, Washington, told me, "Honeybees emerge from the hive when apple trees begin blooming in the spring. The flowers have 24 to 48 hours to pollinate, and one year the peak for blooms was April 15 but it rained all week, and honeybees don't fly in the rain, so our crop was only 33 percent of what it could have been."

Now consider the southern Oregon pear. The image may evoke the famous Harry & David in Medford, with its high-density pear orchards that produce mountains of fruit sold through its Web site and catalog each year. But many people might be surprised to learn that it takes hundreds of thousands of dedicated honeybees pollinating blossoms to produce the sweet, juicy pears we enjoy.

Throughout the harvest season, floral shapes, fragrances, and a rainbow of colors lure the little pollinators like clever advertisements. Small sustainable farms that grow a variety of crops all summer have blooms that bees can feed from and pollinate. Many farmers cultivate plants with flowers that attract beneficial insects to their fields, so native bees have many opportunities to dine on nectar.

We have about 400 species of bees in the Northwest; some are feral honeybees from swarms that have escaped, but many experts say the feral honeybee population has shrunk dramatically, and some say they've completely disappeared. Other wild bees include alkali, alfalfa leafcutter, horn-faced, mason, and bumble. Some of these bees are much better pollinators, but American farmers depend almost exclusively on honeybees.

With their massive numbers and living in movable hives, honeybees have a long-standing contract with agriculture. They move from orchards to fields throughout the season. After pollinating Northwest fruit tree blossoms in the spring, these bees head for berry blooms.

"You can tell when the raspberries are blooming," farmer Wade Bennett at Rockridge Orchards in Enumclaw, Washington, said to me. "The bees fly in a straight line over the hill right to the flowers." Wade raises his own honeybees to pollinate his orchard fruit, grapes, and berries, and he sells sweet raspberry honey at Seattle farmers' markets.

All bramble fruit or berries depend on bees for abundant crops. Liz Eggers and Michael Hamphel at Grouse Mountain Farm in Washington also raise their own honeybees for orchard fruit. Farmers Vince and Mary Alionis at Whistling Duck Farm in southern Oregon discovered a cooperative way to deal with pollination when their neighbor, Dr. Watson, a local family doctor, decided his family needed a hobby. The Watsons became beekeepers, and now the family's bees are helping berry production at Whistling Duck Farm. Other Northwest farmers trade fruit or vegetables for bees, and some like Jeff Miller at Willie

Green's Organic Farm in Washington rent bees for berries.

Beekeeper Roy Nettlebeck of Tahuya River Apiaries on Hood Canal in Washington keeps his bees in the Olympic Mountains. He was devastated one year when vandals destroyed more than half his beehives, but Roy estimates that he loses only 5 to 10 percent of his hives each year to disease. Roy suspects the pesticides of modern agriculture are to blame for many of the modern problems with bees. So far, his bees have escaped colony collapse disorder.

"Traditionally, beekeepers moved bees to agriculture," Roy told me. "If you had five hundred acres of apples, you brought bees in. From the 1940s to the '90s there weren't many problems with bees, and then they got mites, and man in all his wisdom decided to solve the problem with chemicals."

When mites threatened his bees, Roy researched solutions and discovered Russian honeybees.

Hives from Tahuya River Apiaries in the Olympic Mountains of Washington. Photos by Josh Nettlebeck.

These bees had proved resistant to the mites, so Roy gambled on the Russians. Now he exclusively raises hives of these mite-resistant, obsessive bees that continually groom each other and keep their hives spotless. "The problem with chemical pesticides is resistance," Roy explained.

Pesticide-resistant mites are beekeeper Lewis Morgan's primary bee problem. As he set golden glistening jars of honey on a cloth-covered card table at the Milwaukie, Oregon, farmers' market, he told me that he had started beekeeping when he was a teenager and needed a project for vocational agriculture. "I have mostly Carniolian bees [a subspecies of honeybee] now," he said. Lewis shared a story about losing twenty-two of his forty-four beehives to CCD in 2007. "One morning over half my bees had simply vanished," he told me. Inspecting hive after hive, Lewis found only a few immature bees and queens. He thinks CCD may stem from tainted royal jelly imported from China and sold to bee breeders, who feed it to immature bees and queens in brood packages that beekeepers buy to repopulate hives.

But whether the latest bee plague is a result of pesticides or of bee products from China, declining honeybee populations will eventually affect Northwest fruit yields as long as farmers in the Northwest depend exclusively on honeybees. After asking farmer after farmer about bees on their farms, I discovered that many small farms are also cultivating mason bees and encouraging native pollinators, and these pollinating armies haven't let the farmers down.

At Rent's Due Ranch in Stanwood, Washington, JoanE McIntyre told me they've always had enough wild bees for their organic raspberries and blueberries. Wetlands and wildflowers surround Rent's Due Ranch, and the menu variety attracts native pollinating armies, so they've never experienced a lackluster blueberry crop at Rent's Due Ranch.

At Nash's Organic Produce in Sequim, Washington, farm manager Scott Chichester said, "We promote a diverse landscape and grow many non-crop plants." Scott researches and plants species that lure beneficial insects, and the farm crew keeps blocks of orchard mason bees for the orchard fruit.

At Growing Things in Carnation, Washington, farmer Michaele Blakely explained to me that she grows her organic crops differently from other farmers. Weeds and wildflowers grow between rows of vegetables. The wild blooms attract a variety of pollinators, and they flock to the dining area. "There are many different insects besides bees that pollinate," said Michaele.

In Noti, Oregon, at Winter Green Farm, a certified organic farm that uses biodynamic techniques, farmer Jabrila Via told me that they have plenty of natural pollinators. And at Rama Farms in Bridgeport, Washington, six acres of organic orchards with the sweetest apricots, peaches, and nectarines around are a testament to the strength of wild pollinators thriving on small sustainable farms. Farmer Marilyn Lynn noted, "There are more feral honeybees than people realize, at least in this state."

Our tiniest farmworkers, bees work in orchards and fields with little acknowledgment. For millions of years, bees have pollinated blooms on schedule. The next time you bite into a juicy piece of fruit, along with nodding to local farmers remember to give thanks to the tiniest farmworker.

An ideal breakfast is one we can sit down to and enjoy unrushed, but the reality is that some days our schedules are too hectic for that luxury. Instead of surrendering to a meal replacement bar, consider a quick fruit salad, a fruit smoothie, or an easy make-ahead trail mix.

Seasonal Fruit Salad

One year, I discovered the best strawberries from Grateful Harvest Farm in Junction City, Oregon, at the Eugene farmers' market. Another year, I was hooked on sweet, desert-grown melon from Homestead Organic Produce in Quincy, Washington, at the University District farmers' market. Use whatever seasonal fruit appeals to you. Apricots, nectarines, and blueberries are perfect for summer. Apples, figs, or pears make good fall choices. For the salad dressing, look for local honey and hazelnut butter at most Northwest farmers' markets.

> **1 cup plain yogurt**
>
> **½ tablespoon honey**
>
> **1 tablespoon hazelnut butter (optional)**
>
> **1 tablespoon fresh lime, lemon, or orange juice (optional)**
>
> **1 teaspoon finely chopped lime, lemon, or orange zest (optional)**
>
> **3 to 4 cups chopped seasonal fruit**
>
> **1 tablespoon chopped hazelnuts or walnuts**

1. Mix the yogurt, honey, hazelnut butter, and citrus juice and zest in a blender or food processor until smooth.

2. Pour over the fruit in a large bowl, mix, and garnish with the chopped nuts. **Serves 4**

Simple Soaked Oats

These oats don't need cooking and make a good summer breakfast. For variation, add 1 tablespoon toasted, chopped nuts or ground flaxseed. Some Northwest farms offer flaxseed and some grow and harvest walnuts or hazelnuts.

> **½ cup milk (dairy, soy, or rice)**
>
> **⅓ cup rolled oats**
>
> **1 tablespoon ground flaxseed**
>
> **Fresh blueberries or raspberries or other seasonal fruit**

1. Pour the milk over the oats in a bowl. Cover and soak half an hour at room temperature or in the refrigerator overnight.

2. Stir in the flaxseed and top with the berries. **Serves 1**

Winter Fruit Smoothie

You can use frozen local fruit, preserved from the summer harvest, to make smoothies, or you can use dried fruit such as prunes and apricots. Sometimes I add a cube of frozen orange juice, squeezed from oranges gathered at my father-in-law's house in Santa Barbara. Hazelnut butter can come from a local source in northern Oregon and Washington, but if you can't find any local hazelnut butter, use almond or cashew butter.

10 pitted dried plums or apricots

2 cups boiling water

2 tablespoons hazelnut butter

2 to 4 tablespoons orange juice (optional)

1 tablespoon flaxseed oil

1. Pour the boiling water over the dried fruit in a large bowl. Allow to cool, cover, and place in the refrigerator overnight.

2. Puree all the ingredients in a blender until smooth and creamy. Serve immediately.
Serves 2

Summer Fruit Smoothie with Yogurt

No matter which summer fruit you choose, the flavor blend in this drink is hands-down the best taste of summer. I can easily wake up an hour early for this drink to start my day. My favorite version of this is with pitted sour pie cherries or raspberries. I freeze enough in the summer so that I can make this in the winter.

2 cups fresh or frozen blueberries, raspberries, peaches, or other seasonal fruit

1 small ripe banana (optional)

Juice of 1 orange or 6 ounces plain yogurt

1 to 2 tablespoons hazelnut or almond butter

1 tablespoon flaxseed oil or ground flaxseed (optional)

Puree all the ingredients in a blender until smooth and creamy. Pour into a glass and enjoy.
Serves 2

Raw honey from Fleur de Lew of Boring, Oregon, at the Milwaukie farmers' market

Trail Mix

This is the original fast-food breakfast and hiking snack. Use any kind of dried fruit—apples, nectarines, or apricots.

1½ cups coarsely chopped mixed dried fruit

¼ cup raw hazelnuts or almonds

¼ cup walnuts

2 tablespoons raw sunflower seeds

Mix the fruit, nuts, and seeds in a bowl. Store covered in the refrigerator. **Serves 2**

Japanese agricultural exchange student Tetsushi Hokakoba picking Honeycrisp apples in the fall at BelleWood Acres near Lynden, Washington

Energizing Whole Grains

Whole grains are the keystone of civilizations around the world and have long been a part of farming in the Northwest. Dryland wheat farms have dotted the landscape in eastern Washington and Oregon since the late 1800s. Today, organic farms like Bluebird Grain Farms in the Methow Valley near Winthrop, Washington, are revitalizing farmland. Nutritionally balanced soils support a rotation of grain crops alternated with red clover, buckwheat, and peas. Strategic planting allows grain growers Sam and Brooke Lucy optimum seed germination that produces vibrant crops of rye, hard red and soft white wheat, and emmer (an ancient type of wheat). Bluebird Grain Farms sells grains online and at Seattle farmers' markets.

Apple Pie Oatmeal

This recipe combines fresh apples, cinnamon, and nutmeg with steel-cut oats and takes about 12 minutes to cook. You can substitute other grains such as millet or buckwheat but the cooking time is 15 to 20 minutes for these grains.

1 to 2 apples (any variety), cored and diced

2 cups water

1 cup steel-cut oats

½ teaspoon cinnamon

¼ teaspoon nutmeg

Salt

Butter (optional)

Milk (dairy, soy, or rice)

1. Bring the apples and water to a boil in a small to medium saucepan over high heat.

2. Add the oats, cinnamon, and nutmeg, reduce the heat, and simmer until the oatmeal has absorbed the water and is thick, about 12 minutes.

3. Mix in salt to taste. Add some butter and milk if desired. **Serves 2**

Whole-Grain Porridge

For a speedy whole-grain breakfast, use a spice grinder to grind grains. Emmer is an ancient variety of wheat first cultivated in the Middle East. Spelt and kamut are alternative grain options for this recipe.

½ cup ground wheat, emmer, spelt, or kamut

½ cup water

½ cup milk (dairy, soy, or rice)

⅛ teaspoon nutmeg

⅛ teaspoon salt

⅛ cup chopped dates or other chopped dried fruit

Milk to taste (optional)

1. Grind the whole grain in a spice or coffee grinder until its consistency is like coarse cornmeal.

2. Combine the ground grain, water, milk, nutmeg (if desired), salt, and chopped dried fruit in a small saucepan and bring to a boil over medium heat.

3. Stir, reduce heat, and simmer until the grain is soft and has absorbed all the liquid, about 5 minutes, adding more water as needed.

4. Serve and pour milk over the porridge if desired. **Serves 2**

Toasted Three-Grain Cereal

This warming, nutty, three-grain cereal is just the ticket for those cold mornings when it's hard to get started.

- ⅓ cup each: raw buckwheat, millet, and steel-cut oats
- 1¼ cups water
- 1 cup milk (dairy, soy, or rice)
- ½ teaspoon cinnamon
- ½ teaspoon nutmeg
- ⅛ teaspoon salt
- ⅓ cup chopped dried fruit (apricots, cherries, plums, or nectarines)
- 2 to 4 tablespoons chopped walnuts, toasted

1. Toast the buckwheat in a hot skillet over medium heat. Stir for a few minutes, then add the millet and oats and continue to dry-roast the grains until lightly browned and fragrant, about 5 minutes. Remove from the heat.

2. Combine the water and milk in a small saucepan and add the grains, cinnamon, nutmeg, salt, and fruit. Bring to a boil over medium heat, reduce the heat, and simmer until all the liquid has been absorbed, 15 to 20 minutes.

3. Garnish with toasted walnuts and serve with additional milk if desired. **Serves 2**

Nutty Amaranth, Teff, and Steel-Cut Oats

This is a substantial hot cereal with a variety of grains. Amaranth is a hearty, nutritious grain loaded with calcium. The plant grows well in western Washington and Oregon, though most farms cultivate it for the greens, not the seeds. Teff also contains calcium, and the grains are so tiny that 150 could fit inside one kernel of wheat.

- 2 tablespoons hazelnut butter
- 1 cup water
- 1 cup vanilla soy or rice milk
- ⅓ cup each: amaranth, teff, and steel-cut oats
- ½ teaspoon vanilla extract
- 1 sweet-tart apple or pear, peeled, cored, and cut into tiny chunks
- ⅛ teaspoon salt
- Maple syrup
- 2 tablespoons chopped hazelnuts, toasted
- Fresh seasonal berries or dried fruit

1. Combine the hazelnut butter and water in a steep-sided container and blend with a hand blender until creamy.

2. Place in a small saucepan and add the soy or rice milk, amaranth, teff, oats, vanilla extract, apples or pears, and salt. Bring to a boil over medium heat.

3. Reduce the heat to a simmer and cook until the grains are soft and all the liquid has been absorbed, about 30 minutes, adding more water if necessary.

4. Top with the maple syrup, chopped nuts, and fruit. **Serves 2**

Pancakes and Sweet Toppings

Using alternative flours in recipes provides an opportunity to experience how different grains react with liquid and fat, and how these flour-liquid-fat combinations alter taste and texture. Pancake recipes that incorporate low- or no-gluten flours need additional binding ingredients (arrowroot powder, tapioca flour, or potato starch) to produce a wheatlike texture. Look for alternative flour and binding ingredients at food co-ops and natural food stores.

Most fruit-based toppings can be sweet without adding lots of sugar. A few exceptions are cranberries and quince, two mouth-puckering fruits that can be sweetened with apples, pears, honey, or sugar.

Light Lemony Oatcakes

These crepelike pancakes are perfect for rolling up your favorite fruit fillings.

1 cup vanilla soy or rice milk

1 tablespoon fresh lemon juice

1 heaping tablespoon rolled oats

2 teaspoons baking powder

½ teaspoon baking soda

1 teaspoon finely chopped lemon zest

⅛ teaspoon salt

1½ tablespoons tahini

1 tablespoon maple syrup or honey

1. Combine the soy milk and lemon juice in a small bowl and set aside.

2. Grind the oats into flour in a spice grinder or blender. Combine the oat flour, baking powder, baking soda, lemon zest, and salt in a large bowl and mix well.

3. Combine the soy milk–lemon juice mixture with the tahini and maple syrup or honey in a

blender, or with a hand blender in a deep-sided bowl, and blend until smooth and creamy.

4. Stir the wet ingredients into the dry ingredients. The mixture will be quite thin.

5. Heat a nonstick or lightly oiled griddle over medium heat and spoon about ¼ cup batter per pancake onto the griddle. When bubbles form and break, turn carefully and cook until lightly browned.

6. Top the pancakes with Strawberry-Plum Sauce or Raspberry-Orange Sauce (recipes later in this section). **Makes 10 3-inch pancakes**

Buckwheat Pancakes

The assertive taste of buckwheat is balanced in these pancakes with banana, which also helps to bind this gluten-free flour. For a substantial breakfast, serve these with scrambled eggs, fried tofu or smoked tempeh strips, and fresh seasonal fruit.

1 heaping cup buckwheat flour

2½ teaspoons baking powder

1 tablespoon sugar

⅛ teaspoon salt

1 cup carob or chocolate soy or rice milk

1 teaspoon vanilla extract

1 medium-sized ripe banana, mashed (about ½ cup)

2 tablespoons finely chopped walnuts (optional)

1. Combine the buckwheat flour, baking powder, sugar, and salt in a large bowl and mix well.

2. Mix the soy or rice milk, vanilla extract, and banana in a blender, or with a hand blender in a deep-sided bowl, until smooth.

3. Combine the wet ingredients with the dry ingredients in a blender and blend until smooth.

4. Heat a nonstick or lightly oiled griddle over medium heat and spoon about ¼ cup batter per pancake onto the griddle. Sprinkle with chopped walnuts if desired. When bubbles form and break, turn carefully and cook until lightly browned. **Makes 10 3-inch pancakes**

These go well with Apple-Cranberry Topping (recipe later in this section).

Blueberry Hotcakes

Tapioca flour is the binding ingredient in these gluten-free hotcakes. You can also use the same amount of arrowroot powder or potato starch instead of tapioca flour.

½ cup each: rice and millet flour (or 1 cup of either flour)

4 teaspoons tapioca flour

½ tablespoon baking powder

½ teaspoon baking soda

¼ teaspoon salt

1 medium-sized ripe banana, mashed (about ½ cup)

1 cup apple juice

1 cup fresh blueberries

1. Combine the rice and/or millet flour, tapioca flour, baking powder, baking soda, and salt in a large bowl and mix well.

2. Mix the mashed banana and apple juice in a blender, or with a hand blender in a deep-sided bowl, until smooth.

3. Stir the wet ingredients into the dry ingredients. Gently stir in the blueberries.

4. Heat a nonstick or lightly oiled griddle over medium heat and spoon about ¼ cup batter per pancake onto the griddle. When bubbles form and break, turn carefully and cook until lightly browned. **Makes 10 3-inch pancakes**

These go well with Blueberry Topping (recipe follows).

Blueberry Topping

Have a double dose of blueberries with this topping on blueberry hotcakes. For variation, blend ripe, peeled peaches, apricots, or nectarines.

2 cups fresh blueberries

Puree the blueberries in a blender until smooth. Serve fresh. Store in a covered container in the refrigerator for a few days. **Makes 1 cup**

TIPS FOR PERFECT PANCAKES

- Sift or mix together dry ingredients, making sure there are no small lumps.
- Beat liquid ingredients separately. Egg replacer and liquids should be well blended.
- After combining dry and liquid ingredients, use the batter immediately since the leavening process begins once the ingredients have been combined. Double-acting baking powder means the leavening begins when the powder and other dry ingredients are combined with a liquid and acts again when the dish is heated.
- Use less salt with alternative grain flours because wheat-free pancakes need additional leavening to rise, and both baking powder and baking soda contain sodium.
- Cook pancakes on a preheated nonstick or lightly oiled griddle. The griddle is ready when water dripped onto it sputters.
- Measure ¼ cup batter for a 3-inch pancake. Pour the batter at intervals over the hot surface.
- When bubbles appear all over the surface and then break, flip the pancake and cook the reverse side. The first side will take a few minutes longer than the second to cook.
- Serve pancakes as soon as they come off the griddle.

Rows of blueberry bushes at Cascadian Home Farm

Strawberry-Plum Sauce

Some berry farmers sell red currants in the summer, and I buy enough of these tart, colorful summer gems to freeze and use throughout the year as a lemon substitute in various recipes. This is a fresh sauce, sweetened with strawberry jam, but you can use another fruit jam to vary the flavor. I like to use Italian plums for this recipe.

> 8 small ripe plums, pitted and halved (about 1 cup)
>
> 2 tablespoons red currants or fresh lemon juice
>
> 2 tablespoons fruit-sweetened strawberry jam

1. Puree the ingredients in a blender until smooth and creamy.

2. Serve immediately or refrigerate and serve later. Store in a covered container in the refrigerator for a few days. **Makes 1 cup**

Raspberry-Orange Sauce

Agar (or agar agar) is a thickening agent made from a red seaweed and is used to make a Japanese dessert that resembles Jell-O. Look for agar flakes in natural or Asian food stores. This sauce is best eaten warm because it thickens as it cools. But reheat it and you'll have a wonderful syrup again.

> 1 cup raspberries, fresh or frozen
>
> Juice and zest of 1 orange (about ¼ cup juice)
>
> 2 tablespoons fruit sweetener
>
> 1 tablespoon agar flakes

1. Combine all the ingredients in a small saucepan and slowly bring to a boil over medium heat, stirring frequently.

2. Reduce the heat and simmer until the sauce thickens, about 5 minutes. Serve warm, or refrigerate and reheat to serve later. Store in a covered container in the refrigerator for up to a week. **Makes 1 cup**

Apricot-Hazelnut Topping

Apricots and hazelnut butter give this topping a compelling flavor and creamy consistency. If you're near the Corvallis farmers' market, look for Filberts R Us or stop at Hazelnut Hill just outside of town. To find hazelnut butter in Seattle or Bellingham, stop at farmers' markets and look for Holmquist Orchards. This topping also makes a good sauce for fruit salads.

> Apricot nectar or apple juice
>
> 10 dried apricots
>
> 1 to 2 tablespoons hazelnut butter

1. Pour the juice over the apricots in a glass measuring cup to make 1 cup and soak overnight.

2. Mix the apricots and the juice with the hazelnut butter in a blender until smooth and creamy. Store in a covered container in the refrigerator for up to a week. **Makes 1 cup**

Apple-Cranberry Topping

Chunky, warm apples simmered with cranberries— sweet and tart flavors are blended together into one mouth-watering sauce. You can use dried pie cherries in this recipe if you don't have any cranberries.

> 1½ cups peeled, chopped apples (such as Granny Smith, Fuji, Winesap, or McIntosh)
>
> ¼ cup dried cranberries
>
> 1 cup apple cider or apple juice
>
> 2 tablespoons apple cider vinegar
>
> 2 tablespoons fruit sweetener or honey
>
> 1 teaspoon cinnamon
>
> ½ tablespoon arrowroot powder

1. Combine all the ingredients in a medium saucepan and stir until the arrowroot has dissolved.

2. Bring the mixture to a boil over medium heat, reduce the heat, cover, and simmer until the apples are very tender, about 12 minutes. Serve over hot pancakes. **Makes 1¾ cups**

More farms like Bluebird Grain Farms are providing locally grown and ground flour for Northwest farmers' market shoppers. Each batch of flour has a different moisture content after it's ground, making it sometimes tricky to bake with whole-grain flour. That's why bakers rely on weight rather than dry-cup measurements when baking. Pay attention to the way each batter is described in baking recipes to understand how it should look before baking.

Maple Pumpkin Bread

Baked pumpkin and maple syrup combine to give this autumn quick bread a moist, sweet taste. For this bread, I usually bake a whole small sugar pie pumpkin (the kind you use to make pumpkin pie). Try poking it with a fork, setting it on a cookie sheet, and baking it at 350°F. Try substituting other varieties of squash such as acorn, butternut, or sweet dumpling.

2½ cups whole wheat pastry or barley flour

1 tablespoon baking powder

1 teaspoon cinnamon

½ teaspoon nutmeg

¼ teaspoon cloves

⅓ cup butter

1½ cups baked sugar pie pumpkin, scooped out of the shell

1 cup maple syrup

1 cup currants, raisins, or chopped dried apricots

½ cup dried cranberries or cherries

¾ cup chopped walnuts or pecans, lightly toasted

1. Preheat the oven to 350°F and lightly oil 2 9-by-5-inch loaf pans.

2. Combine the flour, baking powder, cinnamon, nutmeg, and cloves in a large bowl and mix well. Cut in the butter with a fork or pastry blender until well blended.

3. Mix the pumpkin and maple syrup in a separate bowl until smooth. A hand blender in a deep-sided bowl works well for this.

4. Stir the wet ingredients into the dry ingredients until the mixture has the consistency of very thick cookie dough. Add a bit more flour if necessary. Fold in the fruit and nuts.

5. Spoon the batter into loaf pans and bake for 45 minutes or until a tester or toothpick comes out clean.

6. Let the bread cool in the pans on a cooling rack for 15 minutes. Run a knife around the edges of the pans, invert them over the cooling rack, and gently tap them until the loaves come out. Serve warm. Store in a covered container at room temperature for up to 5 days or freeze.

Makes 2 9-by-5-inch loaves

- Preheat the oven before baking. Setting the baking sheet on a pizza stone in the oven helps the batter cook evenly as the top browns.
- Have all the ingredients at room temperature. Cold dough and batter can cook unevenly and take longer to bake.
- Lightly oil a baking dish or line it with parchment paper before baking.
- Combine dry and wet ingredients separately and then blend wet into dry.
- Stir the ingredients gently for only about 15 strokes. Do not overmix, as this will develop the gluten and produce tough bread or rubbery cake.
- Cake, muffin, and quick bread batter should be fairly thick. Look for a consistency like oatmeal or even almost like cookie dough. If a batter is too thin, it will not bake correctly and will never get completely done.
- As soon as the batter is mixed, spoon it into a prepared baking pan and put it in a preheated oven. Baking soda and baking powder begin acting as soon as they contact moisture. Double-acting baking powder reacts again when heat is applied.
- Refrain from opening the oven door until the bread is within 5 to 10 minutes of being done. If the heat in the oven escapes, the quick bread will cook unevenly.
- To determine when bread is done, insert a toothpick or wire cake tester into the center. If the tester comes out clean, the bread is done. Let the bread or cake sit for 15 minutes before removing it from the pan.
- To remove bread from a pan, slide a knife around the edges, invert the pan over a cooling rack, tap the bottom lightly, and shake gently.

Cheryl's Nut Cake

Cheryl Harrison from Skagit Valley Co-op in Mount Vernon, Washington, shared this favorite recipe. Cheryl uses grape seed oil or melted butter for this cake, but you can also try using hazelnut oil from Holmquist Orchards in Lynden, Washington. This cake is mildly sweet for breakfast. You can also add 1/4 cup cocoa powder to the dry ingredients and make a chocolate nut cake.

> **2 cups ground hazelnuts or walnuts**
>
> **1½ cups whole wheat pastry or unbleached flour**
>
> **½ cup ground oats, oat bran, or oat flour**
>
> **2 tablespoons baking powder**
>
> **1 teaspoon baking soda**
>
> **7 ounces silken tofu (about 1 cup) or 2 eggs, beaten**
>
> **½ cup grape seed oil or melted butter**
>
> **1 teaspoon vanilla extract**
>
> **⅔ cup honey**
>
> **1 cup soy milk or milk**

1. Preheat the oven to 350°F and oil a 9-by-13-inch baking pan.

2. Grind the nuts into meal in a food processor or blender. Combine the nut meal, flour, oats, baking powder, and baking soda in a large bowl and mix well.

3. Mix the tofu or eggs with the oil, vanilla extract, honey, and milk in a blender, or in a bowl with a mixer. Stir the wet into the dry ingredients to make a thick but pourable batter.

4. Pour the batter into the prepared baking pan and bake until the cake is golden brown and tests done, 30 to 40 minutes. **Makes a 9-by-13-inch cake**

Fresh Pear or Apple Cake

This delicious cake recipe comes from Cheryl Stewart of Columbia Gorge Organic Fruit in Oregon. Serve this for brunch and add a dollop of whipped cream to each serving. I have used melted butter instead of oil in this recipe, but the cake comes out a little heavier. Try a combination of apples and pears or toss in ½ cup dried cherries or chopped apricots from the summer harvest.

> 4 cups fresh apples or pears, cored and diced
>
> 2 cups sugar
>
> ½ cup canola oil
>
> 1 cup chopped walnuts or pecans
>
> 2 eggs, beaten
>
> 2 teaspoons vanilla extract
>
> 2 cups sifted flour
>
> 1 teaspoon baking soda
>
> 1 teaspoon baking powder
>
> 2 teaspoons cinnamon
>
> 1 teaspoon salt

1. Preheat the oven to 350°F (325°F for a glass cake pan), and oil and flour a 9-by-13-inch cake pan.

2. Combine the fruit and sugar in a large bowl and mix well.

3. Add the oil, nuts, eggs, and vanilla extract to the fruit-sugar mixture. In another bowl, sift the flour, baking soda, baking powder, cinnamon, and salt together and stir into the fruit-sugar mixture. Blend well but don't overmix the batter.

4. Pour the batter into the prepared pan and bake until the cake tests done, about 1 hour. **Makes a 9-by-13-inch cake**

Pear Clafouti

This delicious baked French pancake is perfect for fall mornings. It was adapted from a recipe by Jeanette Herman of Cliffside Orchards in Kettle Falls, Washington. You can substitute Bosc pears, try different varieties of apples, or sprinkle a few huckleberries over the pears before baking. Refrigerate this breakfast dessert if you aren't going to eat it right away. It will keep for about four days, refrigerated.

> 4 ripe Bartlett pears, peeled, cored, and cut in half
>
> 3 eggs, beaten
>
> ½ cup sugar
>
> ⅓ cup flour
>
> ¾ cup whole milk (or half milk and half cream)
>
> 1 teaspoon vanilla extract
>
> 1 tablespoon brandy (optional)
>
> Salt
>
> Powdered sugar or crème fraîche

1. Preheat the oven to 350°F and oil or butter a 9- or 10-inch-round pan.

2. Lay the pears cut side down in the pan.

3. Combine the eggs and sugar in a large bowl and beat until foamy and thick. Add the flour and continue to mix until a smooth batter forms. Add the milk, vanilla extract, and brandy if desired. Sprinkle in a pinch of salt and mix well.

4. Pour the mixture over the pears and bake until browned on top, about 30 minutes.

5. Serve with a sprinkle of powdered sugar or a dollop of crème fraîche. **Serves 4**

Ginger-Peach Scones

Peaches and ginger naturally go together, and from southern Oregon to northern Washington local peaches are a favorite summer treat. Mair Farm-Taki, near Yakima, Washington, grows both peaches and ginger. Pennington Farms in Grants Pass, Oregon, sold a nectarine jam that makes a perfect sweet topping for these scones. For a leisurely summer breakfast, bake these scones ahead and freeze, then thaw and heat them wrapped in foil in a 350°F oven for about 10 minutes.

½ cup rolled oats

2 cups whole wheat pastry or barley flour

1 tablespoon baking powder

⅓ cup sugar

¼ cup cold butter

1 teaspoon grated fresh ginger

1 medium-size ripe banana, mashed

5 tablespoons milk (dairy, soy, or rice)

½ teaspoon vanilla extract

1 medium-large peach, peeled and chopped (about ¾ cup)

¼ cup chopped candied ginger

¼ cup chopped walnuts

¼ teaspoon cinnamon mixed with 1 tablespoon sugar

1. Preheat the oven to 375°F and line a baking sheet with parchment paper.

2. Grind the oats into flour in a spice grinder or blender. Combine the oat flour, whole wheat pastry flour, baking powder, and sugar in a large bowl and mix well. Cut in the butter with a fork or pastry blender or with your fingers until the mixture resembles a coarse meal.

3. Squeeze the ginger pulp between your fingers to express the juice into the mashed banana. Mix the banana, milk, and vanilla extract in a blender, or with a hand blender in a steep-sided bowl, until smooth and creamy.

4. Stir the wet ingredients into the dry ingredients. Gently stir in the peaches, candied ginger, and walnuts until the mixture is sticky, not quite a formed dough. With your hands, form the mixture into a dough by turning it a few times, adding more flour (a few tablespoons) if necessary.

5. Turn the dough onto a lightly floured board and knead it gently until it sticks together. Pat it into a 9-inch round and cut it in half. Cut each half into six wedges and place them 1 inch apart on a baking sheet. Sprinkle with cinnamon sugar.

6. Bake until lightly browned, about 18 minutes. Remove from the oven and cool slightly before removing the scones to a cooling rack. Store in a covered container at room temperature for up to 3 days or freeze. **Makes 12 scones**

Apple Crumble Pizza Pie

When I was young, my Aunt Margie loved pie for breakfast. Mom told me it was because Aunt Margie was from Maine, and I used to imagine all the lucky children in Maine eating pie instead of oatmeal for breakfast. But you don't have to be from Maine to enjoy Rose Merritt's delicious apple pie recipe for breakfast. And if you don't have a pizza pan, Rose says to roll the dough into a 14-inch circle, place it on a cookie sheet, and turn up the edges.

1 cup sugar, evenly divided

2 teaspoons cinnamon, evenly divided

½ teaspoon nutmeg

½ cup cold butter

¾ cup flour (all-purpose or unbleached)

Pastry for an 8- or 9-inch piecrust

1½ cups cornflakes, crushed

6 to 7 Jonagold apples, peeled, cored, and cut into ½-thick slices (about 8 cups)

1. Preheat the oven to 450°F. Lightly spray or wipe oil on a pizza pan.

2. Mix ½ cup sugar, 1 teaspoon cinnamon, and the nutmeg in a small bowl and set aside. In another bowl, use a pastry blender or fork to cut the butter into the remaining sugar, cinnamon, and flour. Mash together until crumbly and set aside. This is the crumble topping.

3. Roll the pastry out 1 inch larger in diameter than your pizza pan. Ease this dough onto the pan and flute (turn up) the edge. Cover the crust with a thin layer of crushed cornflakes.

4. Beginning at the edge, cover the crust with the apples, overlapping slices. Sprinkle the sugar-cinnamon-nutmeg mixture over the apples and top with the crumble topping.

5. Bake for 10 minutes, then reduce the heat to 400°F and bake until the edges are golden brown and the apples are tender, 30 to 40 minutes. Serve warm. **Serves 6 to 8**

Apples in bins for packing at BelleWood Acres. Photo by Dorie Belisle.

Cherry-Apple Oatmeal Breakfast Cookies

With oats, nuts, and dried fruit, these cookies make an easy breakfast option when made in advance. You can find dried fruit at farmers' markets or dry your own apples or cherries using a dehydrator or in the oven at very low heat.

1½ cups rolled oats

1½ cups whole wheat pastry or barley flour

½ cup shredded coconut

½ cup brown sugar

½ tablespoon baking powder

½ cup melted butter

½ cup maple syrup

½ tablespoon vanilla extract

½ cup chopped walnuts or hazelnuts, toasted

½ cup dried sour cherries

½ cup chopped dried apples

1. Preheat the oven to 375°F and line a baking sheet with parchment paper.

2. Combine the oats, flour, shredded coconut, brown sugar, and baking powder in a large bowl and mix well.

3. In another bowl, combine the butter, maple syrup, and vanilla extract. Stir the wet into the dry ingredients. Blend in the walnuts and dried fruit.

4. Scoop up a teaspoon of the dough and form into a ball. If the dough sticks to your hands, oil your hands a little and then handle the dough. Each cookie should be about the size of a large marble.

5. Place the dough on the prepared baking sheet and when the sheet is full, flatten the cookies with the oiled bottom of a glass or your hand. Bake until lightly browned, 12 to 16 minutes.

6. Remove from the oven and let cool slightly before removing to a cooling rack. The cookies become crisp as they cool. Store in a covered container at room temperature for up to a week or freeze. **Makes about 45 cookies**

FOOD FOR THOUGHT: CLIFFSIDE ORCHARDS

Farmers plant their roots in a variety of ways. Jeanette Herman of Cliffside Orchards worked in eastern Washington orchards decades ago because she enjoyed the freedom of seasonal work. In the 1970s, she lived in a house with 12 other people in Humboldt County, California, and came to Washington every year to prune trees and work in the orchards. She met her husband, Jeff, in the orchards, and they bought farmland 80 miles north of Spokane. At their farm today, the Hermans grow apples, pears, peaches, nectarines, and cherries on nine acres. In midsummer they bring their harvest 350 miles over the Cascades to Seattle farmers' markets, where eager shoppers look for their juicy stone fruit, crisp apples, and sweet pears.

Hazelnut Breakfast Biscotti

The breakfast cookie has arrived! My mother always had a few biscotti with her morning coffee, so enjoy them first thing in the morning or save them for an afternoon treat. These twice-baked Italian cookies can be baked up to a day ahead the first time, then sliced and baked again.

2 cups unbleached flour

1 cup whole wheat pastry flour

1 teaspoon each: baking powder and baking soda

Zest of 1 lemon, finely chopped

1 cup chopped hazelnuts, lightly toasted

½ cup butter

1 cup sugar

2 eggs, beaten

¼ cup fresh lemon juice

½ tablespoon vanilla extract

1. Preheat the oven to 350°F.

2. Combine the flour, baking powder, baking soda, lemon zest, and hazelnuts in a large bowl and mix well.

3. In a separate bowl, cream the butter and sugar together and blend in the eggs. Mix in the lemon juice and vanilla extract. Stir the wet into the dry ingredients, adding enough flour for a very stiff dough, if necessary.

4. Divide the dough in half and roll into 14-inch logs. Place on an ungreased baking sheet, flatten the tops of the logs, and bake until lightly browned on the bottom, about 25 minutes. Turn the oven off. Remove the logs from the oven and let them cool completely.

5. After at least ½ hour has elapsed, reheat the oven to 325°F. When the logs are cool, slice ½ inch thick at approximately a 45° angle. Lay flat on a baking sheet or pizza screen. Bake until lightly browned, about 25 minutes. If using a baking sheet, turn halfway through baking to ensure even browning. Store the biscotti in a covered container at room temperature for up to a week or freeze. **Makes about 3 dozen**

TIPS ON TOASTING NUTS

- To toast raw nuts in the oven, set the temperature to 325°F. Spread the nuts in a single layer on a baking sheet and bake for 10 to 12 minutes. Pine nuts and pecans take less time than walnuts, hazelnuts, and almonds.
- To toast nuts in a skillet, turn the heat to medium. Use a heavy skillet. Cast iron is ideal. Add the nuts, stir, and toast until they have a nutty aroma and taste toasted.

Corn Biscuits

Fresh corn from the cob tastes best in this reinvented version of my grandmother's biscuits. Use white or yellow corn, whichever is your favorite. For a lighter biscuit, use half unbleached flour.

- 1 cup milk (dairy, soy, or rice)
- ½ tablespoon fresh lemon juice or rice vinegar
- 1¾ cups whole wheat pastry flour
- ¾ cup cornmeal
- 4 teaspoons baking powder
- ½ teaspoon baking soda
- ½ teaspoon salt
- ¾ cup corn (fresh off the cob, or frozen)
- ¼ cup melted butter
- 1 tablespoon maple syrup or honey

1. Preheat the oven to 450°F and oil a baking sheet or line it with parchment paper.

2. Combine the milk with the lemon juice in a small bowl and set aside.

3. Combine the flour, cornmeal, baking powder, baking soda, and salt in a large bowl and mix well. Stir in the corn. Add the butter and maple syrup to the milk–lemon juice mixture.

4. Make a well in the center of the dry ingredients and add the liquid ingredients. Stir until a soft dough forms. Add enough flour to make a stiff dough, like a cookie dough consistency.

5. Drop the dough from a spoon onto the prepared baking sheet. Bake until the biscuits are lightly browned on top, about 15 minutes. Serve warm. Store in a covered container at room temperature for up to 3 days or freeze. **Makes 9 large or 12 small biscuits**

Summer at Whistling Duck Farm in southern Oregon

Hot and Hearty Breakfast Entrées

There are times when nothing but a filling hot breakfast will do. When you get into the breakfast doldrums, tempt yourself with scrambled tofu or try a breakfast burrito.

Breakfast Burritos

You can make these burritos the night before for a quick breakfast. Store the burritos in the refrigerator until you're ready for them. Heat them for a few minutes in the microwave or for 10 minutes at 350°F in a conventional oven. Use canned or soaked, cooked, and refried dried beans.

- ½ **pound firm or extra-firm tofu, drained**
- 1 **tablespoon extra virgin olive oil**
- 1 **small yellow onion, chopped**
- ½ **medium red or green bell pepper, chopped**
- 6 **whole wheat tortillas**
- 1 **cup chopped zucchini or other summer squash**
- 1 **to 2 cloves garlic, pressed**
- ½ **tablespoon arrowroot powder**
- ½ **tablespoon nutritional yeast**
- 2 **tablespoons salsa**
- 1 **tablespoon chopped fresh basil, or 1 teaspoon dried**
- ⅛ **teaspoon turmeric**
- ¼ **teaspoon salt**
- 1 **cup refried beans**
- ½ **cup grated sharp cheese (optional)**
- **Salsa**

1. Preheat the oven to 350°F.

2. Lay the tofu on a plate and place about five plates on top to squeeze out the excess water. Let the tofu sit this way while you prepare the vegetables.

3. Heat a heavy 10-inch skillet over medium heat. Add the oil, onions, and bell pepper and stir. Reduce the heat, cover, and sweat the onions and peppers until the onions are soft, about 10 minutes, stirring occasionally.

4. While the vegetables cook, wet a clean kitchen towel (not terry cloth) and lay it on a pie tin. Lay the tortillas on the towel, cover with the towel, and set in the oven for about 10 minutes.

5. Add the zucchini and garlic to the skillet. Stir and cook for 1 minute. Crumble the drained, pressed tofu over the vegetables. Sprinkle the arrowroot and nutritional yeast over the tofu. Stir and cook on medium heat for a few minutes. Blend in the salsa, basil, turmeric, and salt. Cook until the tofu is heated through, about 7 minutes.

6. While the tofu cooks, heat the refried beans on low in a small saucepan for a few minutes.

7. Remove the tortillas from the oven. Lay them flat and spread 1 heaping tablespoon of refried beans on one side. Top with 3 tablespoons of the tofu-veggie mixture and with cheese if desired. Spoon on salsa to taste. Fold the bottom of the tortilla over the filling, then roll up and serve.

Makes 6 burritos

Root Harvester's Breakfast

This is a favorite family recipe from Vince and Mary Alionis of Whistling Duck Farm near Grants Pass, Oregon. They've enjoyed this recipe so often, they recited the ingredients to me in unison.

- 2 cups water with ⅛ teaspoon salt added
- 1 cup raw buckwheat
- 1 to 2 tablespoons olive oil
- 1 small onion, diced
- ½ red or yellow bell pepper, diced (optional)
- 2 or more garlic cloves, minced
- 1 medium parsnip, diced
- 4 or 5 chanterelle or shitake mushrooms, sliced
- 2 eggs, whisked with a little milk
- Grated cheese (optional)

1. Bring the water and buckwheat to a boil in a medium saucepan over medium heat and then reduce the heat and simmer until the buckwheat beings to thicken, about 15 minutes.

2. While the buckwheat cooks, heat a heavy skillet over medium heat and add the oil, onion, and bell pepper. Stir and cook the onion and pepper until soft, then stir in the garlic and parsnip and continue cooking until the parsnip is soft. Add the mushrooms and cook until the mushrooms are soft.

3. When the vegetables are cooked, stir in the eggs until cooked. Serve topped with cheese if desired. **Serves 4 to 6**

Scrambled Tofu with Wild Mushrooms

A little arrowroot powder sprinkled onto the tofu as it cooks creates an egglike consistency. Nutritional yeast, found in natural food stores, lends a cheesy flavor without the cheese.

- 1 pound firm or extra-firm tofu, drained
- 1 tablespoon extra virgin olive oil
- 1 medium onion, diced
- 2 cloves garlic, minced
- 1 cup sliced mushrooms (porcini or hedgehogs are best, but you can also use cremini or portobellos)
- 1 tablespoon nutritional yeast
- 1 tablespoon arrowroot powder
- ¼ teaspoon turmeric
- Generous pinch of red pepper flakes
- ½ teaspoon salt
- ¼ cup chopped cilantro or parsley

1. Lay the tofu on a plate and place about five plates on top to press out the excess water. Let the tofu sit this way while you prepare the onions, garlic, and mushrooms.

2. Heat a heavy skillet over medium heat. Add the oil and onions and stir. Reduce the heat, cover, and sweat the onions until soft, about 10 minutes, stirring occasionally.

3. Remove the lid and add the garlic and mushrooms. Cover and cook until the mushrooms are slightly soft.

4. Crumble the drained, pressed tofu over the onions, garlic, and mushrooms. Sprinkle the

nutritional yeast, arrowroot, turmeric, and pepper flakes over the tofu. Stir and cook on medium heat until the tofu is heated through, about 7 minutes.

5. Blend in the salt and serve sprinkled with chopped cilantro or parsley. **Serves 2**

Spinach and Egg Cheese Squares

This baked dish is perfect for a brunch or a leisurely morning meal. I love the prewashed baby spinach from local farms like Willie Green's Organic Farm in Monroe, Washington. Green garlic is available in the spring. If the season is past, use about ¹⁄₂ cup sliced green onions or diced shallots. Look for smoked tempeh strips and silken tofu in natural food stores.

- **1 tablespoon ghee (clarified butter)**
- **4 tempeh strips**
- **1 green garlic, sliced**
- **1¼ cups ricotta cheese or 1 package silken tofu**
- **2 cups grated sharp Cheddar or aged Gouda**
- **2 eggs, beaten**
- **⅓ cup flour (whole wheat pastry, barley, or unbleached white)**
- **2 tablespoons salsa**
- **6 cups washed and chopped spinach**

1. Heat a heavy skillet over medium heat. Add the ghee and tempeh strips. Cook until the strips are browned and crispy and then remove. Add the garlic and stir and cook until slightly wilted, adding a little water if necessary to prevent sticking.

2. Preheat the oven to 350°F. Lightly oil (with butter or ghee) a 7-by-9-inch baking dish.

3. Combine the ricotta and cheese in a large bowl and mix well. In another bowl, combine the beaten eggs and barley flour and mix well. Stir in the garlic, salsa, spinach, and the cheese mixture. Spread in an 8-by-8 or 9-inch baking dish. Crumble the tempeh over the mixture.

4. Cover and bake for 30 minutes. Remove the cover and continue to bake until golden brown, about 10 minutes. Cut into squares. **Serves 4**

Why Local Matters: Northwest Apples and Pears

Every autumn, fresh crisp apples and juicy pears take over our local farmers' markets in the Northwest. At Seattle's University District market, Cliffside Orchards from Kettle Falls, Washington, sells 16 different kinds of organic apples, a few varieties of pears, and stone fruits. A few stalls down, Grouse Mountain Farm, a small two-acre farm in Chelan that grows stone fruits in the summer, offers a selection of heirloom organic apples, pears, Asian pears, and even a few kinds of quince.

Farmers' markets have helped revive sagging apple and pear sales with wide varieties of autumn tree fruit and lots of samples to taste, but the past few decades have been tough for many Northwest apple and pear growers. Changing foreign trade agreements, the influx of foreign fruit, and low wholesale prices have forced many apple growers to change their tactics so they can reverse the decline in their share of sales.

One farmer who has had to adapt with the times is Skagit Valley apple grower Allan Merritt. "It was costing more to grow the fruit than the money it brought in," said Allan about the struggles with the crashing apple economy that he and his wife, Rose, confronted in the latter part of the 1990s. Generating more "value-added" or processed farm products is one strategy that Allan and Rose have embraced at the bakery–gift shop they built on their farm and that Rose manages.

I visited Rosabella's Garden Bakery on the Merritt farm, about 15 minutes northeast of Mount Vernon on Farm to Market Road, on a cold and drizzly day in early autumn. A perfect day for apple pie and coffee, I thought as I pulled into the place. Allan was setting out boxes and baskets filled with apples on the large covered porch in front of the bakery. "There used to be farms everywhere you looked around here," Allan recalled. He grew up in the Skagit Valley and remembers riding the school bus with Judy Jenson, a girl down the road whose family now makes Golden Glen Creamery cheese on their farm. "Farming has changed in 30 years," said Allan. "In the 1990s there were 25 apple growers around here; now we're down to 3."

For more than 35 years, Allan grew apples, pears, plums, berries, and flowers on their 40-acre farm. He rented bees from their neighbor in the spring, sold apples and pears to the wholesale market in the fall, and made a living. He remembers the Alar scare of the late 1980s as something the apple industry quickly bounced back from. It was trade with China in the 1990s that spurred the collapse of the Northwest apple economy, he told me. That's when Allan's annual income losses began accumulating.

"China changed the game," said Allan. "They grow more apples and sell them cheaper than we can. They aren't allowed to sell their fresh apples here, but competition from them to sell juice concentrate is heated and that industry has disappeared for us." Apple growers had always depended on selling imperfect fruit to processors—it amounted to about 30 percent of their income—but in the '90s, China, Argentina, and Brazil captured the low bid for the fruit concentrate industry. The world supply of fruit concentrate was overloaded, and with tighter border security since 9/11 farmers have also had to deal with a shortage of farmworkers.

But these global changes didn't stop the Merritts. They studied how small farms across the country managed to survive in economic downturns, and Rose decided to gamble their savings when she drew up plans for a bakery and farm store in a rustic barn structure. She wanted the barn to look as if it had always been part of the landscape, and as soon as it was built, she started turning Allan's apples into pies, tarts, and cider doughnuts. And she didn't stop there. She added berry and apple preserves, salsas, cider, and even a wine with their Rosabella's label. To support other local artisans and farmers, she brought in as many locally made products as her budget allowed, and spring through fall, she arranged and sold freshly cut flowers.

Rosabella's Garden Bakery on Allen and Rose Merritt's apple farm

Inside the bakery, the yellow 1950s Formica table took me back in time as I read the farm news while sipping a latte and savoring a caramel apple tart. When I finished, I strolled through the little store with kitchen knickknacks and farm products everywhere. When I found a four-pack of Skagit Fresh Sparkling Fruit Juices with a picture of a farm and berries on the label, Allan shared the story with me.

He and two other farmers decided to turn their apples and berries into beverages, so the farmers pooled their resources, developed flavor combinations, and formed the Skagit Fresh Natural Beverage Company. Then they got a grant from the United States Department of Agriculture to market their sparkling beverages. Little by little they picked up accounts in one of the worst economic downturns in this country. Gradually, many Washington grocery and natural food stores from Bellingham to Seattle picked up this unique Skagit Valley product.

The Merritts aren't the only Northwest apple and pear growers who have diversified and processed their crops into what farmers call value-added products. Northeast of Bellingham, in the shadow of Mount Baker on Ten Mile Road, John and Dorie Belisle have been growing apples and pears at BelleWood Acres since the early 1990s. They moved here from Florida to grow apples, Dorie told me. "We were just looking for a quiet lifestyle, growing apples," she said.

But it wasn't exactly the quiet life she'd originally imagined. They planted the orchards and started selling their apples in 1996, and three years later, Dorie became involved with her neighbors when they formed a neighborhood watershed

community group. They worked to preserve farmland and watersheds while supporting fish habitat along Ten Mile Creek. "It was fun; I got to know my neighbors," Dorie explained.

While Dorie and her neighbors focused on helping farming and fish to co-exist, the Belisles' apple harvest grew. They built a cider barn and added a dehydrator. They opened a farm store and later put in a commercial kitchen for pies and cookies. In the fall, during apple harvest, tour buses come and go. Dorie leads farm tours, and inside the store, customers sample apple slices and buy local honey, sachets of lavender, and knickknacks. Outside, fresh fruits and vegetables from the farm are available.

Today, most of their harvest is sold wholesale to a distributor that carries their apples to grocery stores from Bellingham to Seattle. "With apples, it's hard to get a bigger piece of that retail dollar," said John. "There is a lot of competition within our own state."

Competition for sales is something the Stewart family has felt every day since getting into the juice business. In 1975, Cheryl Stewart moved with her husband and sons from California to a 95-acre farm in Hood River, Oregon, and in 1989 they transitioned their farm to organic. "We struggled that first year and learned by trial and error," said Cheryl.

Her sons suggested making juice because there weren't any local organic juices on the market at that time. So the Stewarts added a packinghouse, called it Columbia Gorge Organic Fruit, and jumped into the juice market. Columbia Gorge Organic Fruit became the first major brand of local organic juices.

"Nature's in Portland and PCC Natural Markets in Seattle were our first customers," said Cheryl. Organically Grown Company (an Oregon and Washington distributor) is another a longtime customer that has picked up and delivered fruit to the Stewart farm for years.

The farm grew, and the Stewarts now cultivate 20 kinds of apples and 12 to 14 types of pears, as well as cherries, nectarines, and peaches on their now 200-acre farm that produces most of the fruit for Columbia Gorge Organic juices. The Stewarts' organic smoothies and juice blends now sit alongside national brands like Odwalla in natural food stores from Washington to California.

Whether we frequent farmers' markets or grocery stores, abundant selections of local apple and pear varieties surround us. Feed your own inner fruit explorer.

Farm sign at BelleWood Acres

Gathering Together Farm
www.gatheringtogetherfarm.com
Philomath, OR
GF Sweet
Slice
Cucumber's
$ 2.25/#
CERTIFIED ORGANIC PRODUCE

Gathering Together Farm
www.gatheringtogetherfarm.com
GF Siletz
Tomatoes
$ 3.50/#
CERTIFIED ORGANIC

Salads Year-Round

Salads add a touch of freshness to any meal. In the Northwest, our maritime climate and long growing season make fresh local produce for salads easy to find most of the year.

Look for salad possibilities as produce parades through its yearly cycle. In the spring, dandelion greens, pea vines, asparagus, and strawberries lead the way. Throughout the summer, greens, cucumbers, radishes, and tomatoes are fresh from gardens and fields. Usual and unusual vegetables fill farmers' market tables and shoppers' baskets. In midsummer, red currants, berries, and cherries add sweet and tart tones and warm colors. In the fall, shredded beets, sliced pears, toasted hazelnuts, and farmstead Gorgonzola top greens and tantalize palates. In the winter, shredded carrots, daikon radishes, and red and green cabbage add a fresh crunch to whole grain or bean-based salads.

Add acidic tones of vinegar or citrus with a bit of oil and just about anything locally cultivated and harvested can be called a salad. From simple tossed greens to more substantial fare like coleslaw or potato and pasta salads, fill your salad bowl with local flavors.

For oils, in Washington try the locally produced hazelnut oil from Holmquist Orchards in Lynden, or use a good quality extra virgin olive oil. For citrus and vinegars, check out farm booths at your local market. You may find lemons at the Saturday Portland farmers' market. In Seattle, some farmers at markets sell yuzu, a small yellow winter-hearty citrus similar to the lemon. Various farm booths sell farm-made vinegar. One of my favorites is rosemary-infused raspberry vinegar from Rent's Due Ranch in Stanwood, Washington. Another favorite is a naturally fermented berry-apple cider vinegar from Rockridge Orchards in Enumclaw, Washington.

Farm CSA newsletters offer plenty of ideas for creative Northwest salads. One intriguing recipe from Nash's Organic Produce in Sequim, Washington, is for French Breakfast Radish and Carrot Salad. Another recipe worth checking out is the one for Fennel-Orange Salad, inspired by a recipe I discovered in the Gathering Together Farm CSA newsletter on their Web site. Both recipes are included in this section, along with profiles of these two farms.

Summer salad staples: Siletz tomatoes and cucumbers from Gathering Together Farm at the Corvallis farmers' market

The farm stories in this section explore how Northwest farmers are not only saving farmland but also saving and growing their own seed. With a long, fairly mild growing season, the Northwest is one of the best places to grow seed crops, yet not every farmer grows his or her own seed. At Nash's farm, a variety of seed crops are cultivated, including carrots, spinach, cabbage, broccoli, and kale. At Gathering Together Farm, 50 different kinds of organic lettuce seed are grown and sold through their farming seed partners, Wild Garden Seed.

Northwest Salad Greens and Embellishments

Everybody knows the ubiquitous iceberg lettuce, the kind preferred by large-scale growers for decades because it packs like a cannonball for long-distance travel. Iceberg grows in warmer zones, but Crispino is the Northwest version. The "Ozzie and Harriet salad of my youth," says farmer Frank Morton of Wild Garden Seed. All crunch and zero flavor, the pale green orb is dismissed by nutritionists but still garners fans. If you're hungry for the lettuce of your youth, check farmers' markets, because some Northwest farmers sell it.

Frank Morton knows that nostalgia lurks in many of us, and Wild Garden Seed produces Crispino seeds to satisfy that craving. Visit the Gathering Together Farm store in Philomath, Oregon, to pick up a seed booklet or check out the Wild Garden Seed Web site at www.wildgardenseed.com. To cultivate diversity in your own garden, try Wild Garden Seed spring, summer, or fall seed mixes. More adventurous gardeners and chefs should try "Morton's Secret Mix." Who can resist the enticing description of reds, greens, darks, splashes, blushes, crisps, heads, and tongues?

I can't. Let green salads be a parade of produce in the summer. Check "A Guide to Northwest Produce" in the back of the book for full descriptions of salad greens available at Northwest farmers' markets. And dress up your salads with the following additions:

Vegetables—You can add just about any vegetable to a salad. Gather ideas from farmers at the market before trying unfamiliar vegetables. Don't forget to toss in a few raw cruciferous vegetables such as cabbage, bok choy, broccoli, Brussels sprouts, cauliflower, collards, kale, kohlrabi, rutabaga, and turnips. These nutritional powerhouse vegetables have anticarcinogenic properties. Other vegetables like carrots, beets, and red bell peppers contain a variety of nutrients and add color for visual appeal. Grate, or cut into diagonals, tiny cubes, julienne strips, or batons to add textural variety to your salads.

Dried fruit—Raisins, blueberries, cherries, cranberries, and even chopped apricots are great in salads. You can soak and then drain them or just toss them in from the bag.

Edible flowers—In the spring you can buy edible flowering plant starts at farmers' markets. Or wait till summer, when you can find various edible flowers next to salad greens at markets. Some can come from your own yard but make sure they're edible before you harvest flowers and top your salad with them. Edible flowers include violets, nasturtiums, roses, borage flowers, lemon blossoms, and acacias.

Nuts—Walnuts grow well in the Northwest, and many people don't realize that 99 percent of U.S. hazelnut (also called filbert) crops are grown in Oregon's Willamette Valley. Some hazelnut orchards like Filberts R Us in Corvallis, Oregon, and Holmquist Orchards in Lynden, Washington, have been around since the 1920s. Freddy Guys Hazelnuts and Oregon Walnuts are sold at Portland farmers' markets. And Grouse Mountain Farm in Chelan, Washington, sells giant super-sweet walnuts at the Seattle University District farmers' market in the fall. Toasted or raw, nuts add crunch to salads.

Pickles—Whether you like cucumber chips, dill pickles, or mixed vegetable pickles, you can count on finding some kind of pickled vegetable at many farmers' markets. Farmers may make and sell their own, or vendors may buy cucumbers from local farmers and make them into pickles.

Holmquist Hazelnut Orchards truck in Everson, Washington, near the Canadian border

Saving Farmland, Saving Seeds

Our salad bowls may be filled with diverse offerings from farmers' markets, but we wouldn't have such produce abundance if farmers didn't have access to farmland and seeds. Dedicated to preserving both, Washington farmer Nash Huber received the prestigious Land Steward of the Year Award from the American Farmland Trust in 2008. Nash, 67, was the first vegetable farmer and the first farmer from the Northwest to receive the award, which has been presented annually since 1997 to a farmer or farm family for leadership in farmland protection.

At the crowded event in Seattle where Nash was presented with this award, a letter of congratulations from Senator Maria Cantwell was read and many longtime friends and associates of Nash's took the stage and told stories about how instrumental he was in forming the PCC Farmland Trust and how much he had given the community. When Nash got up to speak, he described where he'd come from and what fueled his passion for farmland preservation. Nash grew up on a farm in Illinois. His parents and grandparents on both sides had been farmers—"all the way back," he said. When he was young, in the 1950s, farms grew a variety of crops with livestock and grass. An average farm size was about a hundred acres. "We didn't call it organic then," Nash explained. "That's just the way we farmed."

But agriculture changed after World War II. Farms grew and began specializing in one or two crops, using pesticides and chemical fertilizers. A drought in 1953 drove a lot of Illinois farmers out,

and by the 1960s many farms had already converted to single-crop farms of a thousand or more acres. Nash left his family's farm, got a degree in chemistry, and worked for an agribusiness company before he was drawn to Washington's Olympic Peninsula in 1968 and back to farming.

His first challenge was access to land. "Farmland was all locked up," he said. "Farmers had inherited it and passed it on in families. It wasn't hard to rent a piece of land, but how do you farm organically with a year-to-year lease? We just went out there on faith and did it."

Nash started his farm by growing hay and raising bees on a few acres. Eventually, he bought a dozen acres and leased additional farmland, and in 1979 his farm was the fourth in the state to be certified organic. He built a packing shed and sold produce at his farm stand and farmers' markets, to restaurants, through wholesale accounts, and eventually to PCC Natural Markets in Seattle. PCC promoted Nash's produce, especially his carrots, which became so popular that customers began asking for these sweet treasures by name.

The future looked promising for Nash's farm, but dark clouds lurked on the horizon. In the late 1990s, Delta Farm, a farm that bordered Nash's, was divided up for development and offered for sale. Nash had increasingly seen farmland around him swallowed up by development. He'd had enough, and when Joe Hardiman, the produce buyer for PCC Natural Markets, visited the farm and saw the "For Sale" sign, Nash wondered out loud if PCC had what it took to save this fertile land.

Hardiman took Nash's challenge to PCC board members, who quickly set up a nonprofit fund, borrowed from the bank, and purchased the farm. The PCC Farmland Fund (later restructured as the PCC Farmland Trust) collected donations from PCC shoppers and obtained local business loans. PCC's newspaper, *The Sound Consumer*, ran articles about the importance of farmland preservation, and these stories rallied community support for local farms. In 2001 (just four years later), the mortgage for Delta Farm was paid off. Today, Nash leases 74 acres of the 97-acre farm, and the remaining land is protected with conservation easements from the Washington Department of Fish and Wildlife.

The PCC Farmland Trust "really came through and saved me," said Nash. "Relationships are important, and that's the way it has to be. PCC

FOOD FOR THOUGHT: CONSERVATION EASEMENTS TO PROTECT FARMLAND

According to the American Farmland Trust, the nation's leading advocate for farm and ranchland protection, 86 percent of our nation's fruits and vegetables are cultivated near urban areas where farmland is at risk for development. Conservation easements can protect water quality, wildlife habitat, and migration routes, and limit development. These easements are legal agreements between a landowner and a land trust or government agency that monitors and protects the natural values of the property for future generations. Easements provide tax incentives to landowners who agree to permanent restrictions on land uses. These easements are passed on in perpetuity and can be donated by landowners or purchased by a trust.

Delta Farm, rescued from development by PCC Farmland Trust and now farmed by Nash Huber

had faith in our farm when others were skeptical."

To satisfy the growing demand for his produce, Nash needed more land, and from 2001 to 2003 his farming operation grew from 25 to 400 acres comprised of a patchwork of parcels, all within a few miles of his packing shed. Aside from the 12 acres Nash owns, the remainder is tied up in leases that span from 3 to 30 years. The PCC Farmland Trust is one of eight landlords for all this acreage, and in 2009, only 60 percent is protected by conservation easements. The remaining fertile land remains at risk for future development.

"The whole drive for us is to have a stable land base so our crew has a farming future," Nash explained. "Without farmland, farmers don't have a farming future."

And without access to seeds that work for this region, farmland loses its meaning. Small-scale seed production evolved as another passion for Nash when he tried to order his usual carrot seed one year and was told that the variety had been discontinued. Nash had grown these carrots year after year, and customers were crazy about the sweet carrot flavor. Besides, the carrot variety "has strong tops and you can machine harvest it,

Nash's vintage flatbed Ford and packing shed

and it holds in the winter," Nash explained. When it was discontinued, he realized that he needed to grow some seed.

Luckily, Nash had saved enough carrot seed to plant a crop and take it to seed. From planting to seed, the whole process takes about two years. When the flowers dry and the carrots in the ground become thick and woody, the crop is ready to harvest. The seeds are winnowed from the dry pods, then sifted through screens and saved for the following season. Nash studied growing, harvesting, and saving seeds and incorporated seed crops into his farming plan. Then he began sharing his techniques with other farmers.

Nash shared this carrot-seed story at an educational farm walk sponsored by Tilth Producers of Washington in the late summer of 2008. Eighty-five people, mostly farmers, showed up to learn about grain and seed production. As we gathered around and began jotting notes, Nash said, "Growing seed doesn't really pay, but it's something we [small farmers] need to do to maintain open-pollinated varieties."

He explained that the Northwest was once home to many seed companies, and these local companies fostered relationships with farmers in the area who knew which seeds worked. Providing seed for crops that grew well in the Northwest was a priority. But then seed companies started consolidating, and each time seed companies merged, the variety available declined. "Now we have a couple of multinational companies," Nash said, referring to the large companies that tend to favor hybrid plant varieties.

"With an OP [open pollinated variety], anybody can take that baby and go somewhere else," Nash said. "The pink elephant in the room is ownership and how you get paid for your work. That's why the trend is toward hybridization."

One farm visitor asked how seed growing fit in with the overall farm operation. "It fits in like everything you do on a farm. After you do it for a while, you inherently learn when something has to happen in the overall farming operation. You rank things that happen according to your life passion and you just do it," said Nash. He keeps doing what he loves, and the local food movement is that much stronger for his efforts.

Vinaigrette Variations and Dressings

Cookbooks often advise cooks to keep a variety of oils on hand, but you don't need anything more for salads than good-quality flaxseed oil, extra virgin olive oil, and of course a local hazelnut oil. Holmquist Orchards in Lynden, Washington, makes a great hazelnut oil. For the best flavor, buy extra virgin or expeller-pressed oils. As for vinegar, check farmers' market selections. Some of my favorite local vinegars are raspberry, lavender, and apple cider vinegar. And finally, when adding herbs, don't overlook cilantro, rosemary, and thyme to alter flavors.

Willie Green's Cranberry-Cilantro Vinaigrette

Jeff Miller of Willie Green's Organic Farm in Monroe, Washington, started out specializing in growing greens for restaurants. A former chef, he knew how to connect with chefs, and when his first crop of greens sprouted, he had eight different Seattle-area restaurants to sell them to. This recipe uses farm-fresh cilantro and is perfect over tender baby greens as well as crisp romaine leaves.

¼ cup seasoned rice vinegar

½ teaspoon minced garlic

¼ cup (or more) fresh cilantro

¼ cup dried cranberries

¾ cup extra virgin olive oil

Salt

Whisk the vinegar, garlic, cilantro, and cranberries in a blender until well blended. Slowly pour in the oil and continue blending until smooth. Add salt to taste. Store in a covered container in the refrigerator for up to a week. **Makes 1 cup**

Willie Green's Sun-dried Tomato–Balsamic Vinaigrette

This is another favorite salad dressing from farmer Jeff Miller at Willie Green's Organic Farm. To soften sun-dried tomatoes, pour boiling water to cover and let the tomatoes sit for 20 minutes. Drain the water and save it to cook grains or add to a soup.

3 tablespoons soaked and softened sun-dried tomatoes

½ cup extra virgin olive oil

½ cup balsamic vinegar

¼ cup red wine vinegar

1 teaspoon minced garlic

1½ teaspoons minced shallot

1 teaspoon summer savory, finely chopped

1 teaspoon basil, finely chopped

Combine all the ingredients in a shaker bottle and shake, then let marinate at room temperature for 2 hours, shaking every 30 minutes. Store in a covered container in the refrigerator for up to a week. **Makes 1¼ cups**

Balsamic Vinaigrette

This deep-flavored vinaigrette goes well on simple greens with grated carrots or finely chopped spring turnips. In late summer use it on romaine with shredded beets. The quality of balsamic vinegar used in this dressing makes a world of difference. High-quality salad dressings make high-quality salads. Agave nectar, a natural sweetener, can be found in natural food stores.

2 tablespoons extra virgin olive oil

2 tablespoons balsamic vinegar

½ teaspoon Dijon mustard

½ teaspoon sugar or agave nectar

2 cloves garlic, pressed

Pinch of salt and freshly ground pepper

Whisk together the oil, vinegar, mustard, sugar or agave nectar, and garlic in a small bowl. Add the salt and pepper. Store in a covered container in the refrigerator for a few weeks. **Makes ¼ cup**

FOOD FOR THOUGHT: TRUSTWORTHY LOCAL FOOD CONNECTIONS

In 2006, farmer Jeff Miller at Willie Green's Organic Farm could hardly keep up with the demand for his spinach after a national spinach recall left no corporate baby spinach in grocery stores. When news about tainted foods like spinach and tomatoes spreads across the country, farmers' markets experience a surge in new customers. People are comfortable about food purchases when they know the farmer who grew it. Farmers' markets and CSA programs give people front-row tickets to local food connections.

Spinach-Basil Dressing

With the abundance of spinach available in the Northwest during the summer months, try this unusual green dressing to top your salad. Locally produced flaxseed oil can be found at natural food stores and co-ops.

1 cup fresh spinach leaves, packed

¼ cup fresh basil leaves, packed

2 green onions, chopped

3 tablespoons extra virgin olive oil

1 tablespoon flaxseed oil

2 tablespoons brown rice vinegar

1 teaspoon honey

Pinch of cayenne

Salt and freshly ground pepper

Mix the spinach, basil, green onions, oils, vinegar, honey, and cayenne in a blender or small food processor until smooth and creamy. Add salt and pepper to taste. Store in a covered container in the refrigerator for up to a week. **Makes 1 cup**

Spicy Creamy Lemon Dressing

More home gardeners and some farmers are starting to grow Meyer lemons. Raintree Nursery in Morton, Washington, sells young Meyer lemon trees. They advise bringing the tree inside during the winter months, so that means growing it in a large moveable planter. If you don't want to grow lemons but still want local possibilities, look for Meyer lemons at the Saturday Portland farmers' market fall through winter from Gus and Barbara Eberhardt of Raynblest Farm in Elkton, Oregon.

2 tablespoons extra virgin olive or hazelnut oil

2 tablespoons fresh lemon juice

1 tablespoon rice vinegar

1 tablespoon aioli or mayonnaise

1 teaspoon honey

Pinch of cayenne

Salt

Whisk together the oil, lemon juice, rice vinegar, aioli, and honey in a small bowl. Add the cayenne and then add salt to taste. Store in a covered container in the refrigerator for up to a week. **Makes ¼ cup**

Creamy Cucumber Dressing

When cucumbers come into season, they are suddenly everywhere at Northwest farmers' markets. This recipe is a great way to use cucumbers. I have also made this dressing with a few tablespoons of Gorgonzola blended in.

1 cup peeled, seeded, and roughly chopped cucumber (about ½ a medium cucumber)

2 tablespoons aioli or mayonnaise

2 tablespoons fresh lemon juice

1 teaspoon finely chopped lemon zest

2 tablespoons hazelnut oil or extra virgin olive oil

1 teaspoon finely chopped fresh dill

Salt and freshly ground pepper to taste

Water as needed

Combine the cucumber, aioli or mayonnaise, lemon juice and zest, oil, dill, and salt and pepper in a blender or with a hand blender and puree until smooth and creamy. Thin with water to the desired consistency. Store in a covered container in the refrigerator for up to a week. **Makes 1½ cups**

Lemon-Tahini Dressing

The 1970s are gone, but I still love some of the popular foods from that decade like lemon-tahini dressing. It is perfect over crunchy romaine, and it also makes an interesting alternative dressing for potato salad.

- ¼ cup raw tahini
- Juice and finely chopped zest from one large lemon
- 1 tablespoon white miso
- 2 cloves garlic, pressed
- 2 tablespoons finely chopped fresh cilantro or parsley
- Pinch of cayenne
- Water as needed

Whisk together the tahini, lemon juice and zest, miso, and garlic in a small bowl. Mix in the cilantro or parsley and cayenne and thin with water to the desired consistency. Store in a covered container in the refrigerator for up to a week. **Makes ½ cup**

Orange-Hazelnut Dressing

This is a sweet-sour dressing that goes well on simple fruit salads and green salads. Why not try it with slices of fall pears, spinach, and Gorgonzola cheese? If you can't find hazelnut oil at your farmers' market, try a natural food store. This dressing can also be made with flaxseed or olive oil.

- 2 tablespoons hazelnut oil
- 2 tablespoons orange juice
- 1 teaspoon finely chopped orange zest
- Pinch of salt and freshly ground pepper

Whisk together the oil, orange juice, and zest in a small bowl. Add the salt and pepper. Store in a covered container in the refrigerator for up to a week. **Makes ¼ cup**

Crunchy Salad Additions

Sometimes a salad doesn't seem complete without the crunch of croutons, roasted nuts, or seeds. Packaged croutons often taste stale and may contain questionable preservatives. Making your own crunchy additions is easy. Toasting nuts or seeds ensures they are fresh and will go well with the greens you purchased from the market. They keep well in the refrigerator for a week or more.

Spicy Toasted Hazelnuts

Hazelnut and filbert *are two names for the same nut; the trees are members of the birch family. Like apples, hazelnuts of different varieties have unique flavors. Some types are sweeter than others. Barcelona, an old-fashioned variety, is grown at Filberts R Us, a seven-acre farm in Corvallis, Oregon, that has been in existence since the 1920s. Duchilly is another popular variety, grown by Holmquist Orchards and sold at the Bellingham and Seattle farmers' markets.*

> 1½ cups raw hazelnuts
>
> 1 tablespoon extra virgin olive oil
>
> ½ teaspoon cumin
>
> ¼ teaspoon salt
>
> Cayenne

1. Preheat the oven to 350°F. Spread the hazelnuts on a baking sheet and bake until browned, 8 to 10 minutes.

2. Drizzle the oil over the nuts. Sprinkle the cumin, salt, and cayenne over the nuts. Stir until well distributed, return to the oven, and bake for 2 more minutes. Cool and store in a covered container in the refrigerator for up to a few weeks. **Makes 1½ cups**

Spicy Toasted Seeds and Nuts

These spicy nuts are a fun way to dress up green salads. I've added them to rice and quinoa-based salads with great results, too. I use hazelnuts and walnuts from the farmers' market in this mix, along with pumpkin and sunflower seeds purchased from the bulk bins at a natural food store.

> 1 cup roughly chopped walnuts, or ½ cup walnuts and ½ cup hazelnuts
>
> ½ tablespoon tamari
>
> 1 teaspoon chili powder
>
> ⅛ teaspoon cayenne
>
> ½ cup raw pumpkin seeds
>
> ½ cup raw sunflower seeds

1. Preheat the oven to 325°F. Combine the nuts, tamari, chili powder, and cayenne in a bowl and mix well, until the nuts are coated.

2. Spread the nuts on a baking sheet and bake for 6 minutes. Remove and mix in the pumpkin and sunflower seeds. Return the nuts and seeds to the oven and bake until toasted, 3 to 5 minutes. Cool and store in a covered container in the refrigerator for a few weeks or freeze for longer storage. **Makes 2 cups**

Herbed Croutons

You can vary the herbs in this recipe. Instead of basil and marjoram, try sage or crumbled rosemary or simply leave out the herbs and make them with garlic and a little salt and pepper. Use any type of locally made artisan bread. I often find dried herbs at various farm booths at farmers' markets in the spring or fall when farmers have less produce to put on tables.

5 slices of bread, ½ inch thick, hard crusts removed

¼ cup safflower oil

3 cloves garlic, pressed

1 teaspoon dried basil

½ teaspoon dried marjoram

¼ teaspoon freshly ground pepper

Salt

1. Preheat the oven to 300°F and cut the bread into small cubes.

2. Whisk the oil, garlic, basil, marjoram, pepper, and salt to taste in a medium bowl until blended. Add the bread and toss until all the cubes are coated with oil.

3. Spread on a baking sheet and bake for 10 minutes. Turn the cubes and return to the oven for about 2 more minutes. Remove and let cool.

Makes about 3 cups

Heirloom tomatoes from Grouse Mountain Farm at the University District farmers' market in Seattle

Vegetable-Based Salads

Vegetable salads like coleslaw and potato salad are potluck and picnic favorites as well as comfort foods. Look beyond these classics and you'll find a world of fresh vegetables waiting to be combined in unique ways and garnished with the acidic bite of citrus or vinegar that defines a salad. Search out the best ingredients from local farms. You won't be sorry.

Lemon Cucumber Salad

Lemon cucumbers are an heirloom cucumber variety that makes an appearance at many Northwest farmers' markets. The unique cucumber is named for its round yellow appearance, not its flavor. This is another recipe treasure adapted from Nash's CSA newsletter.

3 tablespoons apple cider vinegar

3 tablespoons hazelnut or extra virgin olive oil

1 teaspoon diced fresh jalapeno, with seeds for a spicier salad

Salt and freshly ground pepper

3 lemon cucumbers, thinly sliced (about 1½ cups)

1 cup shredded carrots

4 cups cut or torn romaine lettuce

1. Whisk together the vinegar, oil, jalapeño, and salt and pepper to taste in a medium-size bowl.

2. Add the cucumbers and carrots to the bowl and allow to marinate for 10 minutes.

3. Divide the romaine lettuce onto four plates. Top each salad with cucumbers and carrots. Drizzle the remaining dressing over the salads. **Serves 4**

Fennel-Orange Salad

This recipe is adapted from one I found in a Gathering Together Farm CSA newsletter online. In midsummer, the fennel at Gathering Together Farm imparts a light licorice perfume to the air. The buzzing bees, the warm sun, and the gentle breeze invite farm restaurant visitors to slow down and enjoy the day.

1 fennel bulb, diced

1 bunch arugula, torn or cut into pieces

¼ cup orange juice

1 tablespoon fresh lemon juice

2 to 3 tablespoons extra virgin olive oil

Salt and freshly ground pepper

½ cup chopped walnuts (optional)

1. Combine the diced fennel and arugula in a salad bowl.

2. In a smaller bowl, whisk together the orange juice, lemon juice, and oil. Pour the dressing over the fennel and arugula and toss. Season with salt and pepper to taste and sprinkle with walnuts if desired. **Serves 4**

Carrot and Raisin Salad

From Bellingham to Ashland, you can find farmers at markets selling sweet, crunchy carrots. Many growers claim to have the sweetest at the market. I like to sample them all because the flavors can vary widely and every one is better than supermarket offerings, which often have bitter tones. In the winter when local parsnips are sweet, add grated parsnips to the mix.

- ¼ cup aioli or mayonnaise
- 1 tablespoon honey or agave nectar
- 1 tablespoon white miso
- 1 teaspoon finely chopped lemon zest
- ¼ teaspoon nutmeg
- ¼ teaspoon freshly ground pepper
- 3 cups grated carrots
- ¼ cup fresh lemon juice
- ⅓ cup dried cherries or raisins
- ¼ cup toasted coconut (optional)

1. Whisk together the aioli or mayonnaise, honey or agave nectar, miso, lemon zest, nutmeg, and pepper in a small bowl until smooth and creamy.

2. Place the carrots, lemon juice, and cherries or raisins in a medium-size salad bowl. Pour the dressing over the mixture and blend. Serve garnished with toasted coconut if desired. **Serves 4**

French Breakfast Radish and Carrot Salad

This salad was adapted from a recipe in a CSA newsletter from Nash's Organic Produce. A pinch of fresh dill and a squeeze of lemon can also work in this recipe. Blanch the fava beans before adding them or just slip them out of the pod, measure, and add them fresh to the salad.

- 3 tablespoons red wine vinegar
- 3 tablespoons extra virgin olive oil
- 2 cloves garlic, pressed
- ½ teaspoon honey
- 12 radishes, sliced
- 2 cups matchstick-sliced carrots
- 4 cups spicy greens salad mix, torn into bite-size pieces
- 1 cup fava beans
- Salt and freshly ground pepper

1. Combine the vinegar, oil, garlic, and honey in a shaker bottle and shake until well blended. Combine the radishes and carrots with the oil-vinegar mixture in a bowl.

2. Distribute the salad greens onto four plates. Spoon the radish-carrot mixture over the greens and sprinkle the fava beans on top. Drizzle with any remaining vinaigrette and season with salt and pepper to taste. **Serves 4**

Coleslaw

Cabbage lovers in the Northwest can rejoice because farm-fresh cabbage is available most of the year. And many locally grown cabbage varieties are tastier than cheap grocery store cabbage. For this recipe, I use traditionally made apple cider vinegar from Rockridge Orchards in Enumclaw, Washington. For ginger flavor variation, add ginger juice (squeezed from 1 tablespoon of grated ginger.)

½ cup aioli or mayonnaise

2 tablespoons apple cider vinegar

1 tablespoon ketchup

½ tablespoon chopped bottled hot peppers (optional)

Pinch of salt

2 medium Granny Smith apples, peeled and shredded

2 tablespoons fresh lemon juice

4 to 4½ cups thinly shredded green cabbage

¼ cup chopped dried fruit such as apricots, figs, or sour cherries

1. Whisk together the aioli or mayonnaise, vinegar, ketchup, hot peppers if desired, and salt in a small bowl. Toss the shredded apples with the lemon juice.

2. Combine the apples, cabbage, and dried fruit in a large bowl. Toss and mix well, and blend in the dressing. **Serves 6**

Spicy Spinach and Red Cabbage Salad

A version of this salad served in a class I took in the 1990s has remained a favorite memory. Check farmers' markets for sun-dried tomatoes. I found them at the University District farmers' market in the spring from Mair Farm-Taki, a farm near Yakima, Washington. A number of farmers at Northwest farmers' markets sell spinach, arugula, and red cabbage.

¼ cup sesame seeds

¼ cup toasted sesame oil

½ cup fresh lemon juice

1 teaspoon honey

¼ teaspoon crushed red pepper flakes

1½ tablespoons sun-dried tomato bits

1 bunch spinach, torn into bite-size pieces

1 bunch arugula, torn into bite-size pieces

2 cups finely shredded red cabbage

¼ cup crumbed feta cheese

1. Toast the sesame seeds in a heavy skillet over medium heat until they smell fragrant and toasted, then crush them with a mortar and pestle or in a spice grinder.

2. Whisk together the oil, lemon juice, honey, pepper flakes, and tomato bits in a small bowl. Allow the dressing to sit for about 1 hour while the tomatoes rehydrate.

3. Place the spinach, arugula, and cabbage in a large salad bowl. Drizzle with the dressing and toss gently. Sprinkle with the sesame seeds and feta cheese. **Serves 4**

Warm Potato Salad

At the Wednesday Corvallis, Oregon, farmers' market in midsummer, I bought young sweet-tasting potatoes called Colorado Reds from Gathering Together Farm (GTF). The first week I bought them, they were sweet and light pink in the middle. A few weeks later, the flesh was all white but still had a great flavor and texture for potato salad. Go forth and find your own favorite potatoes for this recipe, adapted from a GTF newsletter.

2 pounds medium-size red potatoes (about 6), cut into bite-size chunks

1½ cups peas

6 tablespoons extra virgin olive oil

¼ cup red wine vinegar

2 teaspoons Dijon mustard

1 teaspoon honey or agave nectar

1 teaspoon salt

¼ teaspoon celery seed

Cayenne (optional)

1 cup finely chopped celery

½ cup sliced green onions

1. Steam the potatoes until just barely tender, 12 to 14 minutes. In another pan, steam the peas until tender, 2 to 4 minutes. Do not overcook. Drain both and place in a bowl.

2. In a smaller bowl, whisk together the oil, vinegar, mustard, honey or agave nectar, salt, celery seed, and a pinch of cayenne, if desired. Pour over the potatoes and peas. Add the celery and green onions. Mash a few potatoes and blend to create a creamier consistency. **Serves 4**

FOOD FOR THOUGHT: THE VENERABLE CABBAGE

Cabbage has been cultivated for more than 4,000 years and domesticated for about 2,500 years. Cabbage cultivation spread throughout Europe, adapting to colder climates well because the cabbage could be stored in cold cellars over the winter when people had little else to eat. Compact-headed cabbage was developed during the Middle Ages. Cabbage was brought to the Americas by Jacques Cartier in 1536 and has been a popular food crop ever since. Farmers' markets offer numerous opportunities to sample different cabbage varieties from summer through winter.

Pickled Onions and Turnips

These onions and turnips are perfect alongside tomatoes not only on salads but also on sandwiches. The red in the onions turns the vinegar and turnips pink after a few hours of soaking.

2 large red onions, sliced

1 cup sliced turnips (no need to peel)

3 cups boiling water

1 cup rice vinegar

1 to 3 teaspoons sugar

⅛ teaspoon salt

1 sprig of thyme

A few crushed peppercorns

½ to 1 cup water

1. Place the onions and turnips in a strainer and pour the boiling water over them.

2. Transfer the onions and turnips to a medium-size bowl. Add the vinegar, sugar, salt, thyme, and peppercorns. Stir and add enough water to cover the vegetables. Marinate for 1 hour.

3. Pour into a glass container and store covered in the refrigerator for up to 2 weeks. **Makes about 2 cups**

Balsamic Marinated Beets

At many Northwest farms, work crews harvest a variety of beets summer through fall. From the first tender young beets to mature roots in winter, beets are perfect jewels on Northwest salads. In the winter when I don't have fresh basil, I add a sprig of rosemary or thyme instead to make these beets for salad toppers.

2 cups sliced raw beets

1 or 2 green onions, thinly sliced

2 tablespoons chopped fresh basil

½ cup balsamic vinegar

¼ teaspoon salt

¼ teaspoon freshly ground pepper

1. Steam the beets until fork-tender, about 5 minutes.

2. Combine the beets in a bowl with the green onions, basil, vinegar, and salt and pepper. Stir, let cool, and refrigerate covered for a few hours before eating. **Makes 2 cups**

Pasta, Grain, and Bean Salads

Give hearty whole-meal salads a Northwest touch with fresh vegetables from the market. These salads go well with light soups and warm crusty bread. Feel free to alter salads with alternative vinegars or oils. Substitute seasonal vegetables or switch varieties of beans and whole grains. These edible artistic creations can change with your mood, pantry supplies, or fresh vegetables from your CSA box.

Basil-Carrot Pasta Salad

Garden-fresh herbs and toasted hazelnuts make this an all-star standout at summer gatherings.

¼ cup aioli or mayonnaise

2 tablespoons fresh lemon juice

1 tablespoon rice vinegar

1 tablespoon white miso

2 cloves garlic, pressed

1 tablespoon fresh marjoram leaves

1 tablespoon chopped bottled hot peppers

Salt

2 cups shell or bow tie pasta

1 medium-size carrot, grated

¼ cup finely chopped sweet or red onion

2 tablespoons marinated sun-dried tomatoes

¼ cup finely chopped fresh basil

½ cup coarsely chopped hazelnuts, toasted

1. Whisk together the aioli or mayonnaise, lemon juice, vinegar, miso, garlic, marjoram, and peppers in a small bowl. Add salt to taste.

2. Add the pasta and 1 teaspoon of salt to a large pot of boiling water and cook according to the package directions. Do not overcook. As soon as the pasta is done, drain and rinse it with very cold water to stop the cooking process.

3. Mix the cooled pasta with the carrot, onion, sun-dried tomatoes, and basil in a large bowl. Gently stir in the dressing. Refrigerate for 1 hour before serving. Garnish with toasted hazelnuts.

Serves 4

FOOD FOR THOUGHT: FARM FIELDS AS HABITAT

Farm fields provide habitat for wildlife and birds. According to Skagitonians to Preserve Farmland, half a million ducks and more than 13,000 trumpeter swans, 30,000 snow geese, bald eagles, peregrine falcons, and migrating songbirds are supported on Skagit Valley farmland. On the North Olympic Peninsula, 10 percent of Nash Huber's 400-acre farm is devoted to wildlife habitat. Birds, bees, and animals are critical for fruit and seed production. Without them, many plants would lose their ability to regenerate.

Buckwheat and Roasted Vegetables with Balsamic Vinaigrette

Sweet roasted Northwest vegetables help tame the assertive flavor of buckwheat, which pairs well with quality balsamic vinegar. Dehydrate pitted pie cherries from your own trees or from your favorite cherry farmer at the summer market.

- 2 medium white or red potatoes, cut into small chunks
- 1 yam, peeled and cut into small chunks
- 1 medium onion, cut into chunks, or 1 cup diced shallots
- 1 medium carrot or parsnip, cut into ½-inch slices
- 10 cloves of garlic (about 1 head), peeled
- 2 tablespoons ghee (clarified butter)
- 2 tablespoons balsamic vinegar
- ½ teaspoon chipotle chile powder
- ½ teaspoon salt
- 1 cup stock or water
- ½ cup toasted buckwheat (kasha)
- 3 tablespoons balsamic vinegar
- 2 tablespoons extra virgin olive oil
- ½ teaspoon sugar
- 2 cloves garlic, pressed
- Pinch of cayenne
- ⅓ cup dried cherries
- 2 cups finely shredded green cabbage and/ or carrots
- ½ cup chopped walnuts, toasted
- ⅓ cup finely chopped curly or flat-leaf parsley
- Salt

1. Preheat the oven to 350°F. Place the potatoes, yam, onion, carrot or parsnip, and garlic in a glass baking dish and stir in the ghee and vinegar. Spread out in a single layer and sprinkle with chipotle powder. Roast the vegetables until they are fork-tender, about 1 hour. Stir halfway through roasting. Sprinkle with the salt.

2. Bring the stock or water to a boil in a small saucepan. Add the buckwheat, stir once, reduce the heat, and simmer covered for 20 minutes. Let the buckwheat sit for 5 minutes after cooking. Fluff with a fork.

3. Whisk together the vinegar, oil, sugar, garlic, and cayenne in a small bowl. In a large bowl, combine the roasted vegetables, buckwheat, cherries, and cabbage and/or carrots. Pour the vinaigrette over and toss. Serve warm or refrigerate and enjoy later.

4. Right before serving, blend in the toasted nuts and garnish with the parsley. Season with salt to taste. **Serves 4 to 6**

Rice, Wheat Berry, and Parsley Salad with Lemon-Tahini Dressing

Wheat berries add a chewy texture to this whole grain salad that sparkles with parsley. Nash's Organic Produce in Sequim grows and sells wheat berries at many Seattle markets. You can also try emmer, an ancient wheat relative, available at the University District market from Bluebird Grain Farms. Raw peas and corn are also tasty additions to this summer salad.

2¼ cups water

Pinch of salt

½ cup wheat berries, rinsed

1 cup basmati rice, rinsed

1 each: red and green bell pepper, seeded and finely chopped

1½ cups finely chopped parsley, curly or flat leaf

¼ cup tahini (raw or toasted)

¼ cup fresh lemon juice

3 tablespoons tamari

1 tablespoon honey or agave nectar

1½ tablespoons rice vinegar

1. Bring the water to a boil in a medium saucepan. Add the salt and wheat berries. Cover, reduce the heat to a simmer, and cook for 30 minutes, then add the rice and simmer until both grains are tender, about 45 minutes. Check 10 minutes before the grains have finished cooking to see if they require more water. To check, gently pull the grains away from the sides of the pan with a fork. If you don't see any liquid, add ¼ cup water and continue cooking until the grains are done.

2. Remove from the heat and let the grains sit for 5 minutes before fluffing with a fork. When the grains have cooled, gently mix with the peppers and parsley in a medium bowl.

3. Whisk together the tahini, lemon juice, tamari, honey or agave nectar, and vinegar in a small bowl. Gently stir the dressing into the grains. Cover and refrigerate before serving. **Makes 4 to 6 servings**

Kia Armstrong with organic leeks and fennel on Nash Huber's farm

Wild Rice, Barley, Squash, and Cranberry Salad

This rice salad is perfect for fall holiday gatherings. Look for local hazelnuts and wild rice from Freddy Guys Hazelnuts in Monmouth, Oregon. They are regular vendors at the Saturday Portland farmers' market. Ayers Creek Farm near Gaston, Oregon, sells organic Arabian blue barley that needs to be soaked overnight before cooking. If you can't find wild rice or barley from local sources, check for them in natural food stores. The best way to serve this salad is warm. It makes a great main dish and also works well as a side dish next to stuffed squash or potato gratin.

Juice of 1 orange

2 tablespoons balsamic vinegar

2 tablespoons extra virgin olive oil

¼ teaspoon crushed red pepper flakes

½ teaspoon salt

1 tablespoon grated fresh ginger

2 cups water

½ cup wild rice

½ cup hulled, soaked barley

Pinch of salt

1 or 2 tablespoons extra virgin olive oil

1 large onion, chopped

1 medium delicata squash, seeds removed and cut into bite-size pieces

1½ cups grated carrots blended with 1 tablespoon fresh lemon juice

⅓ cup dried cranberries

½ cup chopped hazelnuts or pecans, toasted

⅓ cup finely chopped parsley

1. Whisk together the orange juice, vinegar, oil, pepper flakes, and salt in a small bowl. Squeeze the juice of the ginger into the dressing, discarding the pulp, and blend in.

2. Bring the water to a boil in a medium saucepan. Add the wild rice, barley, and salt. Reduce the heat, cover, and simmer until the grains are done, about 55 minutes. Both will be slightly chewy. Remove from the heat, let sit 5 minutes, and fluff with a fork.

3. Heat a heavy skillet over medium heat. Add the oil and onion, stir to coat the onion, then reduce the heat, cover, and sweat the onion until soft. Remove the cover and continue to cook until the onion is caramelized (browned). While the onion cooks, steam the delicata squash until fork-tender, about 7 minutes.

4. Mix together the cooked grains, onion, delicata squash, carrots, and cranberries in a large bowl. Gently mix in the salad dressing. Right before serving, stir in the hazelnuts and parsley.

Serves 6 to 8

Millet, Quinoa, and Chickpea Salad

This is a simple grain-and-bean salad, infused with lemon and enhanced with Northwest spinach. Some small farms in the Northwest are bringing more unique grains like quinoa and beans like garbanzos to farmers' markets. Carrots, green onions, and spinach can be found in markets from Ashland to Bellingham. Make most of this salad ahead of time, then mix in the spinach and place the tomatoes around the edge right before serving.

¼ cup brown sesame seeds

½ cup millet

½ cup quinoa

2 cups water

¼ teaspoon salt

1 cup cooked chickpeas (garbanzos) or drained, canned chickpeas

2 cups grated carrots

½ cup thinly sliced green onions

¼ cup fresh lemon juice

Zest of 1 lemon, finely chopped

¼ cup extra virgin olive oil, or hazelnut oil

3 tablespoons chopped fresh basil

2 cloves garlic, pressed

½ teaspoon sugar

¼ teaspoon cayenne

½ teaspoon salt

1 small bunch fresh spinach, rinsed well and drained, torn into small pieces

1½ cups chopped tomatoes

1. Preheat the oven to 325°F. Toast the sesame seeds in a heavy skillet over medium heat until dry, aromatic, and a few shades darker. When cool, grind them coarsely with a mortar and pestle or spice grinder and set aside.

2. Rinse the millet and quinoa, and then stir and toast the grains in the skillet over medium heat until lightly toasted, about 7 minutes.

3. Bring the water and salt to a boil in a medium saucepan. Add the grains, stir once, cover, and cook until both grains are slightly chewy and tender and all the liquid is absorbed, about 25 minutes. Check the water level at 20 minutes and add a small amount more if necessary. Remove from the heat and let sit for 5 minutes before fluffing the grains with a fork.

4. Combine the grains, chickpeas, carrots, and green onions in a large bowl. In a small bowl, whisk together the lemon juice and zest, oil, basil, garlic, sugar, cayenne, and salt. Stir gently into the whole-grain mixture.

5. Right before serving, blend in the spinach. Place the tomatoes around the outside of the salad. Sprinkle the ground sesame seeds over the top. **Serves 6**

Lentils and Braised Winter Greens with Lemon-Ginger Vinaigrette

This is a perfect Northwest autumn or winter salad. Dehydrated sour cherries from summer's harvest wake up whole grains in the winter. Dried cherries found in grocery stores are rarely organic, are of lower quality, and usually contain added sugar. If you don't have sour cherries, cranberries will do. You can roast the garlic up to three days ahead of making this salad. Store roasted garlic in the refrigerator until you're ready to use it.

- 1 head garlic
- 1 tablespoon safflower oil
- 1 tablespoon chopped bottled hot peppers
- 2 tablespoons each: fresh lemon juice, sherry vinegar, and extra virgin olive oil
- 1 tablespoon finely chopped lemon zest
- 1 teaspoon honey
- ½ teaspoon salt
- 1 tablespoon grated ginger
- 1 cup vegetable stock or broth
- 1 cup water
- ½ cup brown rice
- ¾ cup French lentils, rinsed
- 2 cups cut-up, steamed delicata squash
- ¼ cup dried cherries or cranberries
- 1 tablespoon extra virgin olive oil
- 1 medium red onion, chopped
- 2 cups chopped braising greens (kale, collards, or chard)
- 2 to 4 tablespoons water or white wine
- ⅓ cup chopped hazelnuts, toasted

1. Preheat the oven to 350°F. Cut the top off of the head of garlic and lay the head on a piece of foil. Drizzle the oil over the garlic head. Wrap it in foil and bake until very tender, about 45 minutes. Let the garlic cool.

2. Press the roasted garlic out into a small bowl. Blend the garlic with the peppers, lemon juice, vinegar, oil, lemon zest, honey, and salt. Squeeze the ginger over the other ingredients, discarding the pulp, and whisk together until smooth.

3. Bring the stock and water to a boil in a medium saucepan. Add the rice, reduce the heat, cover, and simmer for 20 minutes. Add the lentils, bring to a second boil, reduce the heat, and continue to simmer until done, about 40 minutes.

4. When the rice and lentils are done, strain and combine with the squash and dried cherries or cranberries in a large bowl. Pour the dressing over and blend.

5. Heat a heavy skillet over medium heat. Add the oil and red onion. Stir and cover, cooking on low until the onions are tender. Add the braising greens and water or wine. Cover and cook until the greens are very tender, about 20 minutes.

6. Mix the warm greens into the rest of the salad. Sprinkle the hazelnuts on top and serve.

Serves 4 to 6

Lentil Salad with Spicy Lime Vinaigrette

Chili powder, cardamom, cilantro, lime juice, and mirin (a sweet rice wine) dress up the lentils in this salad. Make this salad in the summer when peppers and corn are in season. Look for lentils in natural food stores, and while you're there, find mirin in the international aisle. This salad is even better the second day, after the flavors have married.

3 tablespoons fresh lime juice

1 tablespoon mirin (sweet rice wine)

½ teaspoon salt

¼ cup extra virgin olive oil

1½ teaspoons chili powder

¼ teaspoon ground cardamom

¼ cup chopped cilantro

1 heaping cup French lentils, rinsed

3 cups water

1 tablespoon extra virgin olive oil

1 large onion, chopped

1 red pepper, seeded and chopped

1 jalapeño, seeded and minced

2 cups corn, freshly cut off the cob

Salt and freshly ground pepper

½ cup finely chopped parsley (optional)

⅓ cup chopped walnuts, toasted

1. Combine the lime juice, mirin, salt, oil, chili powder, cardamom, and cilantro in a small bowl and whisk together.

2. Bring the lentils and water to a boil in a medium saucepan over high heat, then reduce the heat and simmer until the lentils are soft but not overcooked, about 40 minutes. Drain and run under cold water to stop the cooking process.

3. Heat a heavy skillet over medium heat. Add the oil, onion, red pepper, and jalapeño. Reduce the heat, cover, and sweat the vegetables until tender. Remove the cover and continue to stir and cook until the onions are lightly browned. Blend in the cooked lentils and corn, cover, and cook until the corn is tender, about 5 minutes.

4. Place the mixture in a large bowl, pour the dressing over it, and blend in. Add salt and pepper to taste. Refrigerate before serving. Right before serving, blend in the parsley if desired. Garnish with the walnuts. **Serves 6**

Black Bean, Corn, and Couscous Salad

Black beans and corn are an easy pairing in late summer when corn is in season. Fresh corn makes a world of difference in the flavors of this salad. This versatile hearty dish goes well with a lighter salad like coleslaw and warm corn tortillas or braised greens and cornbread. (See "Northwest Beans and Grains" in the back of the book for dried bean cooking instructions.)

3 tablespoons apple cider vinegar

2 tablespoons extra virgin olive oil

1 tablespoon lime juice

1 teaspoon sugar

2 teaspoons chili powder

½ teaspoon cumin

¼ teaspoon cayenne

1 cup whole wheat couscous

1 cup boiling water

1½ cups cooked black beans

1 fresh jalapeño, seeded and minced

3 cloves garlic, peeled and sliced

1 cup fresh corn, raw or lightly steamed

1 red onion, finely chopped

¼ cup pimento-stuffed olives (optional)

Salt

¼ cup chopped cilantro

1. Whisk together the vinegar, oil, lime juice, sugar, chili powder, cumin, and cayenne in a small bowl.

2. Pour the boiling water over the couscous in a medium-size bowl, cover, and let sit for 5 minutes. Fluff with a fork.

3. Combine the couscous with the beans, jalapeño, garlic, corn, red onion, and olives, if desired, in a large salad bowl. Season with salt to taste, if olives are not used. Pour the dressing over and toss. Serve warm or refrigerate and serve later. Garnish with cilantro before serving.

Serves 6

Spicy Bean and New Potato Salad

New potatoes are the first potatoes of the season and can be found at any Northwest farmers' market. White or cream-colored beans work well in this salad. Stoney Plains of Tenino, Washington, sells dried beans at the Olympia and Seattle farmers' markets. Ayers Creek Farm of Gaston, Oregon, sells dried beans at the Hillsdale farmers' market.

½ cup fresh lime juice

¼ cup light sesame oil

1 teaspoon sugar

½ teaspoon salt

2½ cups halved or quartered new potatoes

1 cup cooked beans (anything but fava or black beans)

1 tablespoon light sesame oil

1 large red onion, sliced in slivers

1 red pepper, seeded and sliced into strips

1 teaspoon each: coriander, turmeric, cumin, and chili powder

¼ teaspoon each: cardamom, cinnamon, and cayenne

⅛ teaspoon ground cloves

2½ cups grated carrots

½ cup raisins or currants

½ cup chopped walnuts, toasted

½ cup chopped cilantro

1. Whisk together the lime juice, oil, sugar, and salt in a small bowl.

2. Steam the new potatoes until fork-tender, about 5 minutes. Remove from the heat and run under cool water in a strainer. Combine the potatoes and cooked beans with the dressing in a large bowl, tossing gently.

3. Heat a heavy skillet over medium heat. Add the sesame oil, onion, pepper, and spices. Stir and cook on medium low heat until the onion and pepper are tender but not wilted and overcooked, 5 to 7 minutes. Remove from the heat and let cool slightly.

4. Add the onion and pepper along with the carrots and raisins or currants to the salad mixture and mix well. Serve slightly warm or refrigerate and serve later. Mix in the walnuts and cilantro just before serving. **Serves 6**

Italian White Bean Salad with Yellow, Red, and Green Peppers

Cannellini beans are found at some farm booths at farmers' markets. Willie Green's and Stoney Plains are two organic Washington farms that sell dried beans in Seattle. You can use garbanzos or another light-colored bean if you want. Many Northwest farmers sell sweet and hot peppers in the summer.

1 cup dried cannellini beans, soaked for at least 6 hours

2 bay leaves

3 cups water

1 each: red, yellow, and green bell pepper

5 tablespoons extra virgin olive oil

¼ cup fresh lemon juice

1½ tablespoons tomato paste

1 teaspoon honey or agave nectar

2 tablespoons chopped fresh basil

1 tablespoon fresh oregano

1 teaspoon fresh thyme

½ teaspoon salt

¼ cup finely minced red onion

¼ cup finely chopped parsley

Freshly ground pepper

1. Cover the beans and bay leaves with the water in a medium saucepan, bring to a boil over high heat, reduce the heat, partially cover, and simmer until the beans are tender, 1 to 1½ hours. Prepare the rest of the salad and dressing while the beans cook. Drain the beans, remove the bay leaves, and run cold water over them to stop the cooking process.

2. Place the three peppers on a screen over a grill and turn them until the skins are charred and blistered. If you don't have a grill, place the peppers on a baking sheet under the broiler, turning them frequently until blackened. Place the peppers in a paper bag until cool, peel the skins off, seed, and cut into thin strips.

3. Whisk together the oil, lemon juice, tomato paste, honey or agave nectar, basil, oregano, thyme, and salt in a small bowl, until the tomato paste is well blended.

4. Mix the beans with the peppers, onion, and parsley in a large bowl. Toss with the dressing and add freshly ground pepper to taste. Serve warm or at room temperature. **Serves 4**

Marinated Beans

These beans make a great side dish. They can also be used to add flavor, texture, and protein to green salads. Use dried or shell beans that hold their shape well, such as garbanzos (chickpeas), kidney beans, Great Northern beans, or scarlet runner beans. You can also use half fresh green beans that have been steamed.

3 tablespoons sherry or balsamic vinegar

2½ tablespoons extra virgin olive oil

½ teaspoon sugar

2 to 4 cloves garlic, pressed

1 teaspoon chopped fresh rosemary

½ teaspoon salt

Pinch of crushed red pepper flakes

2 cups cooked and cooled beans

¼ cup chopped fresh chives

1. Whisk together the vinegar, oil, sugar, garlic, rosemary, salt, and pepper flakes in a small bowl.

2. Stir the marinade and beans together in a medium bowl. Marinate for at least 1 hour. Mix in the chives right before serving. **Makes 2 cups**

Green beans at the Eugene farmers' market

Black-Eyed Peas and Collard Greens with Sun-dried Tomato Dressing

If you want local dried beans and can't find black-eyed peas, use a different bean; anything but black beans (which turn everything dark) will do. Most dried beans have to be soaked overnight. Collard greens, tart apples, and celery make this a late summer or autumn salad. If you don't like collards, use a mild variety of kale.

1 teaspoon fennel seeds

¼ cup finely chopped sun-dried tomatoes, soaked overnight

¼ cup extra virgin olive oil

2 tablespoons mirin (sweet rice wine)

2½ tablespoons brown rice vinegar

1 tablespoon chopped bottled hot peppers

2 or 3 cloves garlic, pressed

½ teaspoon salt

1 cup dried black-eyed peas, rinsed

3 cups water

1 large tart apple, peeled and cored

1 tablespoon fresh lemon juice

1 tablespoon extra virgin olive oil

1 large onion, chopped

1 large bunch collard greens, removed from stems, rolled tightly, and cut into thin strips

1½ cups finely chopped celery

½ cup crumbled feta cheese or chopped cheese curds

1. Heat a skillet over medium heat. Add the fennel seeds, stir, and toast until the seeds darken and are very aromatic, about 5 minutes. Remove from the heat and grind to a fine powder with a suribachi (Japanese grinding bowl).

2. Drain the sun-dried tomatoes and mix with the ground fennel, oil, mirin, vinegar, peppers, garlic, and salt in a blender. Allow the mixture to sit for 1 hour.

3. Bring the black-eyed peas and water to a boil in a medium saucepan over high heat. Reduce the heat, partially cover, and simmer until tender, 45 to 60 minutes. While the beans cook, prepare the rest of the ingredients.

4. Grate the apple and blend with the lemon juice in a small bowl. Heat a heavy skillet over medium heat. Add the oil and onion, stir, reduce the heat, cover, and sweat the onion until soft. Add the collard greens, stir, cover, and cook until very tender. You may have to add a bit of water.

5. When the black-eyed peas are done, drain and combine with the other ingredients, including the celery and dressing, in a large bowl. Garnish with the feta cheese or chopped cheese curds. Serve warm or cold. **Serves 4 to 6**

Sowing the Seeds of Farm Synergy

Near the end of summer at Gathering Together Farm in Philomath, Oregon, flowers were in bloom and from the road all seemed quiet and peaceful. But beyond the road, this farm hummed with activity. Behind the farm restaurant, a woman sliced lemons for lunch, and farther back near the packing shed, workers prepped freshly harvested vegetables and filled boxes destined for farmers' markets, restaurants, and wholesale orders. A woman in a yellow tank top and shorts breezed out of the barn, hopped in the cab of a flatbed truck with a few beehives in the back, and called out, "I'm doing bees today." As she drove off, another flatbed carrying ten or more farmworkers cruised by in the other direction. In the restaurant kitchen, pans clanged and a restaurant worker belted out a blues tune.

Gathering Together Farm is owned and farmed by John Eveland and his wife, Sally Brewer. John and Sally partner with seed growers Frank and Karen Morton, who produce seeds for the farm's vegetables grown on this 50-acre certified organic farm. The land is laid out in odd-sized land parcels along the Mary's River, and the farm has an inviting rustic store with a casual restaurant. Between produce sales at the store, farmers' markets, wholesale orders, and a 300-member CSA program, Gathering Together Farm feeds a community of people, all eager for locally grown food treasures.

The farm is a field of chores in motion; even the quiet field behind the restaurant is a workforce of honeybees pollinating fragrant fennel blossoms and gathering nectar. Every farmworker, down to the tiny honeybee, keeps the wheels of Gathering Together Farm on track. In fact, keeping everybody on the farm motivated and moving in the right direction is one of the things that farmer John told me he likes best about farming.

John and Sally started Gathering Together Farm in 1987 with three other people on 20 acres of land. A year later, the other families had dropped out, and John and Sally farmed vegetables on 7 acres. A fourth-generation farmer from Iowa, John grew up on a corn and soybean farm. He'd been a counselor and had owned and run a vegetarian restaurant called Nearly Normal's in Corvallis, Oregon. Sally had grown up on a vegetable farm in New Hampshire, and Sally and John grew and sold produce to First Alternative Food Co-op in Corvallis, Northwest-based Organically Grown Company, and local restaurants like Nearly Normal's. They also sold their harvest at the Corvallis farmers' market.

In the farm's early days, John and Sally met Frank and Karen Morton, who had recently moved to the area to farm. Frank had grown a diversity of vegetables since 1980 and was thinking about starting a seed business because he was interested in saving seeds. In 1987, the Mortons bought a farm and called it Shoulder to Shoulder, just five miles up the Mary's River from Gathering Together Farm.

The Mortons sold salad greens to restaurants,

and Frank started his seed production company, Wild Garden Seed, as a joint venture between the two farms. Most of the seed crops are grown at Gathering Together Farm and are processed, packaged, and sold commercially and used for the farm's vegetables. The Mortons, their two sons, and a few other workers make up Gathering Together Farm's seed production crew.

Wild Garden Seed officially merged with Gathering Together Farm in 2000 to create one farm business, and a few years later, Wild Garden Seed was covered under the Gathering Together Farm organic certification. Since organic farms are required to use organic seed when available, this farm merger made getting high-quality organic seed much easier for Gathering Together Farm.

"We are much better working together than independently," Frank said to me. "Growing organic food and seed within the same system makes sense." Gathering Together Farm can harvest greens like lettuce and kale and still get plenty of seeds from those crops. They also save tomato, cabbage, melon, and broccoli seeds from year to year. Growing seeds boosts the farm's bottom line. "We supply Gathering Together Farm with about $1,000 worth of seed every year, and that seed might have cost the farm $3,000 to buy," explained Frank.

During harvest season, Gathering Together Farm harvests more than a hundred varieties of 40 different vegetables. The seed production crew collects seed from crops like chard, kale,

Tractor and greenhouse at Gathering Together Farm

and collards during the second year of growth, but lettuce is their main seed crop, with about 50 different varieties.

A lettuce seed crop takes six months from germination to maturity and faces many challenges along the way. Transplanted to fields in February, the lettuce plants will reach two to six feet high in late summer. Frank continually monitors fields for disease and disease-resistant plants. If the crops have successfully dodged disease and pests, the next obstacle is on the way. As soon as the tender seedpods emerge, deer appear. An organic solution of raw eggs mixed with water is sprayed on each pod, and the deer beat a hasty retreat to find a meal elsewhere.

When the pods are ready to harvest, workers pull the plants, roots and all, from the ground and stack them on water permeable cloth to dry. They cover the crop with lightweight landscape fabric but always end up sharing some of the harvest with the birds that show up. Once the seeds are dry, workers knock them with sticks and winnow away the chaff and fluff similar to that of an aged dandelion. They dry their seed crop during fall and winter. All of the seed produced by Wild Garden Seed is open pollinated and untreated.

Frank Morton also runs a plant-breeding program and produces naturally disease-resistant plant varieties for farmers who don't use chemical fertilizers and pesticides. One thing Frank really likes doing on the farm is scouting for odd plants, rare crosses and those with different traits from others. He tags and sets aside various plants for his plant-breeding program. (Lettuce is self-pollinating, so cross-pollination with wind or insects that generates new lettuce varieties is unusual.)

Frank selects plants for taste, color, size, and vigor and continually monitors the fields for disease-resistant plants that make an organic farmer's life easier.

Gathering Together Farm's first original lettuce came from an accidental cross of heirloom lettuce seeds. Now Wild Garden Seed sells lettuce seed from original lettuce varieties that originated on Gathering Together Farm. The farmers work with Oregon State University, which sends professors and students out to study the vegetable and seed systems.

"We live in a good seed and vegetable production zone," Frank told me. Wild Garden Seed sells seeds all over the world through its Web site and through organic seed companies. Their seed is geared to small, diverse organic farms. Now they're sharing their techniques with other farmers throughout Oregon. "We're developing a program called the Family Seed Project, to train growers to produce their own seed," said Frank.

Back at the farm store, the Wild Garden Seed catalog of organic seed for salad greens and herbs tantalizes home gardeners. Even nongardening types reach for it, tempted to try cultivating the Gathering Together Farm treasures of greens in their own gardens.

The lunch crowd drifted in for pizza baked in the earth oven. A Gathering Together Farm salad listed on the menu was made with the farm's salad blend, Siletz tomatoes, fresh mozzarella, basil leaves, and a parsley vinaigrette. I ordered it, and when the salad arrived, it glistened with the vinaigrette and with the story behind the vibrant lettuce leaves on the plate.

Seasonal Soups and Homemade Breads

Nothing says comfort like the fragrance and flavor of homemade soup made with fresh vegetables. In the Northwest, we're fortunate to have a wide diversity of produce for our seasonal soups. From tomatoes, basil, corn, and eggplant in the summer to squash, leeks, kale, and potatoes in winter, Northwest soup combinations are endless.

Soup is typically layered, but it doesn't have to be complicated or time consuming. Anyone can learn to combine flavors to make a great soup. Over the years, I've learned a few tips and shortcuts.

First, use a good-quality heavy soup pot, not an old thin aluminum one. The bottom of an inferior pan thins unevenly over time and eventually burns the bottom layer, and burned soup is impossible to repair. Slow cooking in a Crock-Pot is another option. Soup can simmer all day long and be ready when you are.

Second, start with fresh vegetables and use a stock to give soup depth, but if you don't have time to make stock, add stock essentials such as carrots, celery, onions, and chopped parsley to blend in the flavors that stock contributes. Stocks aren't hard to make; if you want an abbreviated version, check out my Rich and Savory Quick Stock in this section. It takes only 20 minutes. Another idea is to make stock when you have more time and freeze it in a plastic container (glass will break) for future convenience.

Creating great soup is part artistry, part skill, and a little luck. It's also fun, because you can correct mistakes and adjust flavors unless you've added too much salt or burned your creation. One quick trick for a bland soup is to add a squeeze of lemon, then taste and balance this citrus with a little sweetener like a pinch of sugar or a drizzle of honey.

Plan ahead and consider ingredient combinations. Spice and herb combinations put a signature on soup and make it unique. Imagine the herbs and flavors together, like fennel or rosemary and tomatoes. Or consider how fresh ginger adds zing to sweet winter squash. Blend in a sweet-tart apple and these flavor tones step into the picture. Hazelnut butter, a Northwest treasure, adds a satisfying mouth-feel without adding any cream. Season with salt and freshly ground pepper, and adjust the sweetness to balance the ginger. Innovation through experimentation— that's what soup is about.

Pumpkins and farm tractor in Snohomish County, Washington. Photo by Sheila and Brad Zahnow.

Take a few ingredients, combine them with a broth, and it's soup. For an easy recipe check out farmer Judy Bennett's Pumpkin Soup or try my adaptation of a recipe discovered on the Winter Green Farm Web site—Potato-Leek Soup with Parsley. You can follow the recipes in this chapter as they are written or look for seasoning inspiration and create your own great soup recipes.

Soup for All Seasons

Tailor your soup to the season. For example, make asparagus soup in the spring or a black bean, salsa, and corn soup with tortillas in late summer. In the winter, take a pass on expensive imported fresh red peppers and go for locally raised squash, carrots, or beets. Here in the Northwest, we're fortunate to have a great selection of produce just hours away from the farm where it grew.

Autumn

As the days grow short, the chill of autumn sets in, and for many people, warmer, heavier foods are more appealing. Squash, beans, and whole grains define autumn soups. Choose from Northwest fall produce such as potatoes, parsnips, turnips, rutabagas, apples, and young braising greens. Onions, garlic, celery, and carrots are also plentiful. Fresh tomatoes disappear in autumn, so if you want local tomatoes later in the year, blanch and freeze or can summer's crop.

For a tangy balance, add vinegar to your autumn soup. I like raspberry vinegar from Rent's Due Ranch or apple cider from Rockridge Orchards. You can also get a slightly sour addition with tart apples. These are perfect partners for winter squash or beets.

Winter

Onions, garlic, potatoes, and squash stored from the fall harvest offer building blocks for some of the best winter soups. And these thick, hearty soups are nourishing for the body and comforting for the soul as the short days give way to cold winter nights. This is the time of year when the fragrance of savory slow-simmered soup fills the kitchen. From December through March, make soups with roots and hearty greens. Parsnips, beets, and Jerusalem artichokes also inspire new soup creations. Both parsnips and kale become sweeter after the first frost. Black truffles are in season and contribute an intriguing wild mushroom flavor when finely grated and stirred in just before serving. Try adding some to potato-leek soup. Slice artisan bread and farmstead cheese and you have a perfect winter meal.

Spring

In early spring, local produce variety is low, but options are still there if you look for the farmers who sell overwintered vegetables like carrots, cauliflower, and potatoes. Some growers, like Wade Bennett of Rockridge Orchards in Enumclaw, Washington, cultivate early spring crops of hearty Asian greens and bamboo. Also, foragers like Jeremy Faber at Foraged and Found in Seattle sell foraged wild greens like dandelions and nettles at markets, to restaurants, and in some grocery stores.

Beets, carrots, and potatoes can be kept in cool places, like a garage, over the winter and used in the spring. Stored onions and garlic are eager to begin growing and often sprout green shoots. Don't throw away the whole bulb, because these bitter-tasting shoots can be pulled or cut out. Check your stored potatoes often. If they begin to sprout, cut out the sprouts and discard them, and then use the potatoes right away. Or steam them, put them in the refrigerator, and use them later.

The first local asparagus means spring has definitely arrived, and soon the seasonal parade ushers in garlic greens (one of the luxuries of the Northwest), baby turnips, tiny beets, and sugar snap and English peas. These first arrivals are our assurance that the treasure trove of summer is just around the corner.

Summer

Summer soups embrace weekly produce selections, offering a greater diversity of vegetables in a lighter base. Okra, sugar snap peas, bok choy, green beans, eggplant, fennel, heirloom tomatoes, and fresh herbs of all kinds are a just few of the market finds that add to the summer soup pot. Summer soups are light and often serve as accompaniment to a substantial salad. When the sun brightens long summer days, enjoy a relaxing soup and salad dinner outside.

Don't miss a week at the market in the summer, because some of the best produce might be available for only a week or two. If you do miss something like baby okra, something else like Japanese eggplant can inspire you. Northwest farms produce a smorgasbord of fruits and vegetables, and many farmers change their lineup a little each year. In any season, search out the most flavorful vegetables and use simple seasonings and maybe a squeeze of lemon or a drizzle of local raspberry vinegar to balance flavors.

FOOD FOR THOUGHT: PESTICIDE-LADEN PRODUCE

If you can't afford to eat everything organic, consider moving away from the fruits and vegetables that are contaminated with the most pesticides. The Environmental Working Group (www.ewg.org) lists the following produce as being laden with high levels of pesticides:

apples	pears
celery	potatoes
cherries	raspberries
grapes, imported	spinach
hot peppers	strawberries
peaches	

Farm to Restaurant: Sowing a New Road

Northwest restaurants have been enthusiastic local farm customers since the 1990s, and now Northwest farmers are bringing the restaurant to the farm. In the summer of 2008, I talked with two Northwest farmers—Jeff Miller and John Eveland—about restaurants on their farms.

In Monroe, Washington, at Willie Green's Organic Farm, Jeff Miller enthusiastically discussed plans for building and opening a restaurant on his farm. "We'll have tours and guest chefs, and all the food will come from our farm or other local farms," Jeff told me. "Farm and restaurant—it's a natural extension."

This natural extension has already arrived at Gathering Together Farm in Philomath, Oregon, where farmers John Eveland and Sally Brewer started their farm, added a farm store, and then opened a restaurant. The store showcases the farm's organic produce and doubles as a casual dining area. In the kitchen, chefs transform the farm's fruit and vegetables into exceptional pastries, salads, soups, pizzas, and intriguing main dishes. Though meat is on the menu, there are plenty of meat-free options to tempt vegetarians.

Store and restaurant are open spring through late fall, and the restaurant is also open for special holidays like Valentine's Day. You can stop for breakfast on Saturdays or lunch Tuesday through Saturday, make plans for a Thursday or Friday night dinner, or phone in reservations for one of the monthly dinners that feature local wines.

Spring through fall, the aroma of pizza baked in an earth oven on the covered deck during lunch tantalizes palates. Inside the farm store, tables with neat wooden chairs fill the room, and along the walls, refrigerated cases boast vibrant produce, locally made cheese, and bottles of local wine. Shelves show off jars of hot peppers, pasta sauce, and preserves, all made with Gathering Together produce. At the pastry counter, freshly baked treasures like almond rhubarb coffee cake, cherry scones, and blueberry turnovers tempt customers. And life is too short to pass up the old-fashioned potato doughnuts. Even delivery truck drivers stop to enjoy hot coffee and pastries created by Bobbie Lee Woutersz, the farm's baker and pastry chef.

Farm chef JC Mersmann creates compelling menus that shift as the harvest calendar surges forward. His kitchen crew cooks up gems like Summer Squash Enchiladas, Purple Potato Salad with Glazed Baby Carrots, and Mary's River Crepes—farmer John's famous rice flour crepes filled with summer squash, broccoli, and ricotta cheese. The menu offers flavors of the farm's harvest, tucked into composed and tossed salads and simmered in soups like Caramel Eggplant, a decadent-tasting creamy soup with sweet caramelized onions. And who can resist sweet endings like pie cherry sorbet or blueberry cake topped with blueberry ice cream and drizzled with blueberry sauce? "The swinging door to the kitchen is never idle," John told me, smiling.

John Eveland is no stranger to restaurants.

Before he and Sally started their farm, he owned a vegetarian restaurant in Corvallis. But John's fourth-generation farming roots took over, and he was drawn back to his first love—farming. The restaurant seemed a natural progression for this farm.

By contrast, organic farmer Jeff Miller didn't start out with farming roots. His winding road to organic farming started in Pittsburgh, Pennsylvania, where as a young boy he dreamed about becoming a chef, not a farmer. Jeff told me that his father "always had a well-trimmed lawn but had no interest in growing food," so Jeff never thought about a farming career. But he was always cultivating something. "I grew vegetables in the basement when I was young," he told me. "Wherever I lived, I had a garden."

After high school, Jeff attended the New York Culinary Institute of America and then returned to Pittsburgh as a chef. Eventually he moved to San Francisco and cooked for several four-star restaurants, including the famous Stars. While he was there, Jeff was impressed by the quality and quantity of organic produce moving through the kitchen doors. In the early 1980s, one of Jeff's friends returned from a trip to Seattle and mentioned that there weren't any farmers selling specialty vegetables to restaurants there.

Greenhouse at Gathering Together Farm

Tired of the administrative aspects of a chef's work, Jeff began to dream about having his own organic farm. As he formulated his farm plan, he spent time observing an urban farm in Berkeley that grew salad greens.

In the late 1980s, Jeff cashed in a life insurance policy, packed some specialty lettuce seeds, hopped on his motorcycle, and headed north to Washington to become a farmer. He leased land near Woodinville and called his farm Willie Green's Organic Farm—Willie for his grandfather and Green's for the specialty greens he began growing. When his lettuce crop came up, Jeff headed to Seattle and got eight different accounts right away. "I was a chef, so I knew how and when to talk to chefs," he explained.

Romanesco cauliflower (also known as Romanesco broccoli) at the University District farmers' market from Willie Green's Organic Farm

In 1996, Jeff bought a 24-acre farm 35 miles northeast of Seattle. Outside Monroe, the farm is just across the Skykomish River in the Tualco Valley. He grew unique lettuce varieties and eventually added vegetables like Brussels sprouts, carrots, turnips, and sugar snap peas. Over the years, Jeff bought and leased more farmland and now cultivates diverse row crops and a variety of berries, including golden raspberries and mulberries. In addition to selling to restaurants and other wholesale accounts, Jeff sells his organic produce at nine Seattle farmers' markets and through his CSA program.

Nowadays, Jeff oversees transplanting, growing, and harvesting as he fields phone calls for orders and discusses crop plans with his farm manager. At the farm, workers pluck, pull, and cut vegetables in the fields, then transport them to a greenhouse, where they're washed and prepped for market. Bins of tender young greens take a turn in a gigantic lettuce spinner that dries the leaves. Then they go in a chiller, where fans dry any remaining moisture, leaving the greens with a crisp bite. Produce is packed, stacked, and trucked to Seattle. When they don't have to pack and load trucks for markets the next day, the workers weed, fertilize, and plant new seeds for crops. They build trellises for peas and beans, and transplant starts to the fields. Moving from restaurant to fields to restaurant brings the farm's focus back to Jeff's other passion—cooking.

"You've got to love the farm lifestyle," Jeff said, his eyes brimming with culinary possibilities.

His enthusiasm is contagious, but being new to farming can be a challenge. One of Jeff's biggest risk factors has been the weather, like the black clouds that rolled in so quickly in 2006 that the crew had little time to react before marble-sized hail suddenly pummeled Jeff's fields for 15 minutes. The crop of peas, destined to be a bumper crop, was a mass of severed vines. Jeff's market tables were almost bare for weeks, but eventually they recovered, along with Jeff's cheflike confidence.

When I visited in early summer 2008, Jeff detailed his farm restaurant plans. "It will be a two-story structure—a restaurant and lounge with rustic post-and-beam construction and landscaping that features native plants. Guests will tour the farm before dinner and see where their food comes from. It's going to be first class all the way," he told me proudly.

Jeff's restaurant dream conjures up images of Gathering Together Farm's Friday night dinners. Before the meal, customers tour the farm on John Eveland's vintage red flatbed truck, learning about organic crops and seed growing and seeing the biodiversity on the farm, from Monarch butterflies to organic crops and songbirds. This is first class in action—a simple farm dinner where word is spread about sustainable farms and local food.

Savory Soup Stock

A good stock can improve any soup by providing the background flavor for the ingredients. Commercial broth or stock can work in a pinch, and you can always leave it out and use water, but making the real thing is easy and doesn't really take long. Be creative when making soup stock. Save a variety of vegetable scraps in the freezer—onion skins, sweet potato peels, mushroom stems, celery tops, and other produce discards can be stored in plastic bags there until you need them. Whenever you have time, make soup stock. Cool and freeze it in pint-size containers until you're ready to use it. Simply thaw it in the refrigerator the day before using it.

Soup stock basics

- Save vegetable scraps in labeled plastic bags in the freezer for easy stock making.
- Don't be tempted to use any vegetable discards that are over the hill or moldy. Place bendable carrots on the compost heap, not in the soup pot.
- Roughly cut all vegetables to the same size, about 1-inch pieces. This brings out the flavor of the vegetables and strengthens the stock flavor.
- Start with 6 cups of cold water. Add all ingredients, bring to a boil, then simmer for 35 to 40 minutes.
- Strain the stock after it has finished cooking and discard the cooked vegetables. Never let the stock sit, because certain vegetables and herbs can turn it bitter and cause the soup to have a slightly off taste.
- If you want a stronger flavor, after straining reduce the stock by simmering it until it reaches the desired strength.
- Store stock in a covered container in the refrigerator for up to one week. Freeze in a plastic container for longer storage.

Vegetables, herbs, and other additions to soup stocks

Beans—Use green beans or leftover cooked dried beans for a hearty flavor. You can also add dried lentils—about ¼ cup. These, like the other vegetables, are strained out before the stock is used.

Carrots—Cut up the tops as well as the bottoms. Carrots and their tops give stock a sweet, earthy flavor.

Celery—A basic addition to soup stock. If you don't have celery, use about ½ teaspoon celery seed. You can also use raw celery root pieces and skins or leftover cooked celery root.

Corn—Use the inner husks, the cob (cut into 2-inch pieces), and the corn kernels (fresh, frozen, or leftover). The cobs add a deep, rich flavor.

Dried herbs—Classic additions include 1 or 2 bay leaves, basil, marjoram, and a pinch of thyme. Other herbs that lend specific flavors include sage, rosemary, cilantro, and fennel.

Fresh herbs—Add about three times the amount of fresh as you do dried herbs.

Garlic—Fresh or roasted garlic adds a rich,

deliciously sweet flavor. Squeeze the entire bulb of roasted garlic. For fresh garlic, add about three peeled cloves.

Jerusalem artichokes—Also called sunchokes, raw or cooked these are always good earthy-flavored additions.

Kombu—This is a sea vegetable that enhances flavors. You can either leave it whole or cut it into smaller pieces.

Miso—Miso is a fermented soy product traditionally used in Japan. White miso is better for vegetable and summer soups. It imparts a light, sweet flavor. For full-bodied soups, add brown or red miso. Add about ¼ cup of either variety to the soup stock. Since miso is salty, don't add any salt when adding miso.

Mushrooms—Save the stems and use them for an earthy-flavored stock. You can also add dried mushrooms (about ½ to 1 ounce). A few shiitake or porcini give a unique flavor to the soup stock.

Onions—Red and yellow onions contribute a sweet flavor to the stock. Onion skins make a nice brown broth, but too many in the stock may leave a bitter taste.

Parsley—Use parsley generously, about a handful for a pot of stock. Parsley is rich in nutrients as well as flavor.

Pepper—Any type of pepper can make a good addition. Black peppercorns, a pinch of cayenne, a jalepeño, or just ¼ teaspoon chipotle chile powder add a bit of spice.

Potatoes—Cooked potatoes can fall apart and cloud the stock, which won't be a problem if you are making a thick, creamy soup, but if you want a clear stock, stick to washed, raw potato skins.

Salt—Natural sea salt is less processed and contains more minerals. This is the preferred choice for vegetable stock as well as anything else you prepare.

Squash—Winter squash adds a sweet flavor; summer squash imparts a much lighter taste for summer months.

Sweet potatoes and yams—Both add color and an earthy, deep flavor to stocks. Use the skins as well as raw pieces. Leftover baked sweet potatoes, like potatoes, cloud the stock but are excellent for a rich taste.

FOOD FOR THOUGHT: BLOGGING FARMERS

Some Northwest farmers are blogging about what's happening on the farm. Check out www.freshlydougvegetables.blogspot.com to learn about Snohomish County, Washington, farmers Doug and Charlene Byde. They logged 30 years of organic gardening experience before starting their 18-acre certified organic farm in Stanwood, Washington, in 2004. With a goal of offering reasonably priced organic produce, they christened their farm Whispering Winds and started offering their "Freshly Doug Vegetables" through a CSA program in 2005.

Northwest Vegetarian Soup Stock

All of the vegetables for this stock can be found at farmers' markets in the Northwest. Kombu, a sea vegetable found on the international aisle of natural food stores, and lentils give this stock a deep, savory taste. You don't have to use the kombu, but it adds minerals and flavor. You can make a richer-tasting stock by browning the mushrooms and garlic in butter before adding the water and other vegetables. You can also roast the vegetables with a little oil for about an hour at 350°F before making the stock, for a deeper flavor. Fresh herbs lose their flavor in stock, so use dried herbs instead. Use this stock as a base for soups and stews or as a cooking liquid for grains.

- 6 cups water
- 1 strip kombu, cut into small pieces (optional)
- 3 stalks celery, cut into 1-inch pieces
- 2 carrots, cut into 1-inch pieces
- 1 yellow onion, sliced (for a darker stock, use the onion skins)
- 1 handful parsley, chopped
- 4 mushrooms, any variety, sliced (optional)
- ¼ cup lentils, rinsed
- ¼ teaspoon dried thyme
- 1 teaspoon dried oregano
- 1 teaspoon dried basil
- 3 to 4 cloves garlic, peeled and sliced
- ½ teaspoon crushed red pepper flakes
- Salt

Combine all the ingredients in a large soup pot and bring to a boil over medium heat. Reduce the heat, simmer for about 30 minutes, strain, and cool. **Makes 6 cups**

Rich and Savory Quick Stock

An easy way to make a flavorful stock is to use light or brown miso. Onion, garlic, and herbs can be obtained locally. When I can't find local onions, I use leeks or shallots. Simmer this stock while you sauté vegetables before making a soup or pilaf.

- 4 cups water
- 1 onion with skin, roughly cut
- 3 cloves garlic, sliced
- ½ teaspoon each: dried sage, rosemary, and thyme
- 2 tablespoons brown or barley miso
- ¼ teaspoon pepper

Combine all the ingredients in a large soup pot and bring to a boil over medium heat. Reduce the heat, partially cover, simmer for about 20 minutes, strain, and cool. **Makes 4 cups**

Garlic-Mushroom Soup Stock

This savory stock makes a rich-tasting soup and also makes an excellent cooking liquid for grains. Foragers and wild food gatherers like Chef Louis Jeandin in southern Oregon and Donna Weston near Seattle gather and sell fresh and dried mushrooms at local markets. Delicata is a flavorful, easy-to-cut variety of winter squash.

- 6 cups water
- 1 onion, chopped
- 3 stalks celery, cut into 1-inch pieces
- 2 heads garlic, cloves separated, peeled, and crushed
- 1 ounce dried mushrooms (I prefer porcini but any variety will do)
- 1 cup cubed winter squash with seeds (I prefer delicata but any variety will do)
- ½ tablespoon tomato paste
- ½ teaspoon dried rosemary
- 1 teaspoon dried basil
- ¼ teaspoon cayenne
- ½ teaspoon salt or ¼ cup brown miso

Combine all the ingredients in a large soup pot and bring to a boil over medium heat. Reduce the heat, simmer for about 30 minutes, strain, and cool. **Makes 6 cups**

Whispering Winds Farm in Stanwood, Washington, where Doug and Charlene Byde grow "Freshly Doug Vegetables." Photo by Sheila and Brad Zahnow.

Hearty Stews and Soups

Loaded with vegetables, grains, and beans, hearty soups with local ingredients are pure comfort food during the rainy autumn and winter months. Simply serve with hunks of crusty artisan bread and/or a simple salad. To enjoy these soups in spring and summer, make them lighter by cutting back on the beans and grains and adding more seasonal produce to the mix.

Curried Lentil Soup

This soup is great any time of year, but celery makes an appearance at Northwest farmers' markets in late summer or early fall. Its local flavor is a bonus because grocery store celery is all crunch and zero flavor. Look for celery at a market near you to make this quick, tasty soup. You can substitute red lentils here; they take only 20 minutes to cook. The spices are better when they are freshly ground, but you don't have to use freshly ground spices to make this soup.

- 1 tablespoon extra virgin olive oil or safflower oil
- 1 teaspoon each: coriander, turmeric, cumin, chili powder
- ¼ teaspoon each: cardamom, cinnamon
- ⅛ teaspoon each: cloves, cayenne
- 1 large onion, chopped
- 1 stalk celery, chopped
- 1 carrot, sliced
- 3 or 4 cloves garlic, minced or pressed
- 1 heaping cup brown or green lentils, rinsed
- 4 to 5 cups stock or water
- 2 medium-large potatoes, cut into small chunks
- 1 large baked sweet potato, skin removed, or 1 cup winter squash
- Salt
- ¼ cup fresh lemon juice
- ⅓ cup finely chopped cilantro

1. Heat a heavy soup pot over medium heat. Add the oil and spices and sauté for 1 minute. Stir in the onion, reduce the heat, cover, and cook until the onion is soft. Blend in the celery, carrot, and garlic. Stir and cook for a few minutes.

2. Add the lentils and stock or water. Bring the soup to a boil. Reduce the heat and simmer, partially covered, for 30 minutes.

3. Add the potatoes, cover, and simmer until the potatoes are soft, about 30 minutes.

4. Puree 1 cup of soup with the sweet potato or squash in a blender or with a hand blender. Return to the pot and add salt to taste. Cook for about 5 more minutes. Remove from the heat, stir in the lemon juice, and serve garnished with the cilantro. **Serves 4**

Creamy Double Garlic–Chipotle Lentil Soup

I make this soup, a garlic lover's delight, every fall after buying braided garlic garlands from JoanE McIntyre of Rent's Due Ranch at the University District market. I buy a few so I can hang them up and snip off garlic heads all winter. Roast the garlic while you prepare the rest of the soup. The roasted garlic blends perfectly with smoky chipotle chiles, and red lentils give the soup a creamy texture. Look for the mild-tasting elephant garlic near regular garlic. The season for it is fall and if you can't find any, use a few additional cloves of regular garlic.

2 heads garlic

2 tablespoons extra-virgin olive oil or safflower oil, divided

1 large onion, chopped

3 cloves elephant garlic, peeled and sliced

1 cup red lentils, rinsed

1 or 2 medium carrots, sliced

3 medium potatoes, cut into small chunks

3 chipotle chile peppers

1 28-ounce can diced tomatoes

4 cups water

Salt

½ cup chopped flat-leaf parsley or cilantro

1. Preheat the oven to 350°F. Cut the tops off of both heads of garlic and lay the heads on a piece of foil. Drizzle 1 tablespoon of the oil over the garlic heads. Wrap them in foil and bake until very tender, about 45 minutes. Let the garlic cool before pressing it out into a small bowl.

2. Heat a heavy soup pot over medium heat. Add 1 tablespoon olive oil and the onion, stir, reduce the heat, cover, and sweat the onions until they are soft. Stir in the elephant garlic and cook over medium heat, stirring constantly, until the onions and elephant garlic are lightly browned, 7 to 10 minutes.

3. Add the lentils, carrots, potatoes, chipotle peppers, tomatoes, and water to the soup pot. Bring to a boil, reduce the heat, and simmer until the lentils are falling apart, about 30 minutes.

4. Add the roasted garlic to a cup of the soup in a small, steep-sided container and puree it with a hand blender, then stir it back into the soup pot. Remove the chile pods and season to taste with salt. Garnish with the parsley or cilantro. **Serves 4**

Savory Split Pea and Celeriac Soup

With the texture of potatoes and the taste of celery, celeriac or celery root adds an earthy character to autumn and winter soups. Celeriac used to be a fairly common vegetable in the United States and has recently made a comeback at markets. Look for celeriac in late summer through fall. In midwinter you can sometimes find celeriac on tables next to other winter roots. Once you cut and peel it, plunge the white flesh into water with a little lemon juice or vinegar added to keep it from browning, because otherwise it will turn brown almost immediately. If you don't have shallots, use onions.

2 tablespoons extra-virgin olive oil or safflower oil

1½ cups chopped shallots

4 cloves garlic, minced or pressed

¼ teaspoon cayenne

5 cups soup stock or water

1 bay leaf

1 strip kombu, cut into small pieces (optional)

1 heaping cup split peas, rinsed

¼ cup brown rice (long or short grain)

3 or 4 stalks celery, chopped

2 medium carrots, sliced

1 medium celeriac (about ¾ pound), peeled and cut into bite-size chunks

½ tablespoon sugar

2 tablespoons fresh lemon juice

Salt

⅓ cup finely chopped parsley

1. Heat a heavy soup pot over medium heat. Add the oil and shallots. Stir, reduce heat, cover, and sweat the shallots until they are soft, about 10 minutes. Add the garlic and cayenne. Stir and cook until the shallots are caramelized (browned), about 5 minutes.

2. Add the soup stock or water, bay leaf, kombu, split peas, rice, celery, and carrots. Bring to a boil, then reduce the heat and simmer for 30 minutes.

3. Stir the celeriac and sugar into the soup. Continue to cook until the peas are soft and the rice is cooked, about 30 more minutes. Blend in the lemon juice and salt to taste. Garnish with the chopped parsley. **Serves 6**

Split Pea Dal Soup

Dal is a spicy Indian dish made with lentils. This soup incorporates seasonal vegetables that add a layer of local flavor. Try corn, beans, peas, summer squash, cauliflower, carrots, or winter squash for the seasonal vegetables.

1½ tablespoons extra virgin olive oil or safflower oil

1 large onion, chopped

1 fresh jalapeño, seeded and minced

2 cloves elephant garlic, or 4 cloves regular garlic, peeled and sliced

2 or 3 medium-size rutabagas or turnips, peeled and sliced

1 teaspoon each: turmeric, coriander, and garam masala

1 tablespoon sugar

1 cup yellow split peas

4 to 5 cups water

2 cups seasonal vegetables, cut into bite-size chunks

Salt

1 cup milk (dairy, soy, or rice)

¼ cup fresh lemon juice

Plain yogurt, goat or cow (optional)

⅓ cup chopped cilantro (optional)

1. Heat a heavy soup pot over medium heat. Add the oil, onion, jalapeño, and garlic. Stir and cook until the onion is soft. Stir in the rutabagas or turnips, spices, sugar, and split peas. Stir to coat the vegetables, then add the water and seasonal vegetables.

2. Cover, bring to a boil, reduce the heat, and simmer for 40 minutes. Add salt to taste and stir in the milk. Remove from the heat and stir in the lemon juice. Add a dollop of yogurt and garnish with cilantro if desired. **Serves 6**

Black-Eyed Pea Chili

My grandmother and mother believed that eating black-eyed peas on New Year's Day was good luck for the coming year. Don't wait for New Year's to make this savory chili! Black-eyed peas don't have to be soaked before cooking, but overnight soaking makes them more digestible. If you want local beans and can't find black-eyed peas at the market, look for pinto, white, flageolet, or cannellini beans.

3 tablespoons extra virgin olive oil or safflower oil

1 large onion, chopped

1 or 2 fresh jalapeños, seeded and finely chopped

1 tablespoon chili powder

1 teaspoon ground cumin

½ teaspoon dried oregano

3 cloves garlic, pressed

1 carrot, sliced

1½ cups dried black-eyed peas, soaked overnight and drained

3 cups water

1 15-ounce can diced tomatoes

⅛ cup tomato paste

2 tablespoons brown rice vinegar

1 tablespoon sugar

Salt

½ cup shredded aged Cheddar cheese

Chopped cilantro, diced avocado, chopped green onions (optional)

1. Heat a heavy soup pot over medium heat. Add the oil, onion, and jalapeños. Stir, cover, reduce the heat to low, and cook until the onions are soft.

2. Add the chili powder, cumin, oregano, garlic, carrot, black-eyed peas, water, tomatoes, and tomato paste. Mix well and bring to a boil. Reduce the heat, cover, and simmer until the black-eyed peas are tender, about 1 hour.

3. Add the vinegar, sugar, and salt to taste. Simmer for 15 minutes. Garnish with the Cheddar cheese. Sprinkle the cilantro, avocado, or green onions over the top if desired. **Serves 4 to 6**

TIPS ON HANDLING FRESH SHELL BEANS

Fresh shell beans are spring and summer treats. They look like dried beans but they are more fragile and require greater examination before you buy them because they get old within a week. Cranberry, fava, and edamame (green soybeans) are the most common. Store them in the refrigerator for only a few days. Cook them slowly and gently in broth or with herbs for an hour. Don't boil them or they may become tough.

Baked Bean Stew

My only experience with baked beans as a child was from a can, but a growing number of farms throughout Washington and Oregon cultivate and sell fresh and dried shell beans perfect for this baked bean recipe. This soup goes from homey to elegant when you garnish servings with finely chopped parsley, grated carrots, and a sprinkling of chopped, toasted pecans.

1 tablespoon extra virgin olive oil or safflower oil

1 large onion, chopped

¼ to ½ teaspoon crushed red pepper flakes (optional)

1 or 2 stalks celery, cut into ½-inch pieces

1 carrot, chopped

5 cups water

1½ cups white beans, washed, soaked overnight, and drained

1 cup acorn or butternut squash, baked, skin removed

¼ cup molasses

1½ tablespoons Dijon mustard

3 tablespoons tamari

4 cups cut-up seasonal vegetables (use potatoes, carrots, corn, winter or summer squash, peas, peppers, parsnips, or turnips)

¼ cup finely chopped parsley (optional)

¼ cup grated carrots (optional)

¼ cup chopped pecans, toasted (optional)

1. Heat a heavy soup pot over medium heat. Add the oil, onion, pepper flakes, celery, and carrot. Stir and cook until the onion begins to brown, about 5 minutes. Add the water and beans. Bring the water to a boil. Reduce the heat and simmer until the beans are tender, about 1 hour.

2. Combine the squash, molasses, mustard, and tamari in a blender and puree until smooth. Stir into the soup. Add the vegetables and cook until they are tender, about another 15 minutes. Add water to thin if necessary. Garnish with parsley, carrots, and pecans if desired. **Serves 6**

Squash at the BelleWood Acres farm store in Lynden, Washington

Autumn Harvest Soup

I invented this soup when I received two sugar pie pumpkins in my winter CSA box one week. Onion, garlic, fennel, carrots, and turnips were also in the box. I chose French lentils as an ingredient because they are easy to cook and don't lose their shape when simmered for a long time. Substitute gray, brown, or green lentils if you can't find the French variety.

1 small sugar pumpkin (about 2 cups cooked pumpkin)

2 tablespoons extra virgin olive oil or safflower oil

1 large onion, chopped

4 cloves garlic, pressed or minced

1 cup chopped or sliced fennel

3 carrots, sliced

3 turnips, cut into small chunks

3 small potatoes, cut into small chunks

1½ cups cut-up cauliflower

½ cup French lentils

1 28-ounce can tomatoes (whole, diced, or ground)

3½ cups water

2 teaspoons dried basil

¼ teaspoon cayenne

1 teaspoon sugar

½ cup sliced olives

2 cups cut-up turnip greens

Salt

Feta cheese, crumbled (optional)

1. Poke holes in the pumpkin with a fork, place it on a small baking sheet, and bake at 350°F until tender, about 1 hour. Let cool before cutting it open and removing the seeds.

2. While the pumpkin bakes, heat a heavy soup pot over medium heat. Add the oil and onion. Cover and sweat the onion until soft. Add the garlic and fennel. Stir and cook for a few more minutes. Blend in the carrots, turnips, potatoes, cauliflower, lentils, tomatoes, water, basil, cayenne, and sugar. Bring to a boil, then reduce the heat and simmer for 1 hour.

3. Scrape the pumpkin away from the skin, add the pumpkin to the soup, and stir in with the olives and turnip greens. Cook the soup until the greens are soft. Add salt to taste. Garnish with feta if desired. **Serves 6**

TIPS ON USING FENNEL TO FLAVOR SOUPS AND STEWS

Eat and enjoy all the parts of fennel, from the bulb to the feathery leaves. Fennel has a light licorice or anise flavor that becomes more delicate as it cooks. You can transform almost any dish that calls for celery when you substitute fennel. You can also use dried fennel seed to impart a slightly licorice flavor to any dish. Toast a teaspoon of dried fennel seed in a frying pan over medium heat. Stir until the seed changes color and smells fragrant. Crush these toasted seeds with a mortar and pestle. Add ½ teaspoon at a time to recipes. Sample the dish, then add more fennel if desired.

Potato, Fennel, and Tomato Soup

An overabundance of fennel one autumn led to this fennel and potato soup. Tomatoes are an easy pairing with fennel, and yogurt adds a tangy flavor with a creamy texture. Look for fresh mozzarella at the farmers' market. A few small chunks blended in add an unexpected texture surprise. Serve this soup with crusty artisan bread.

2 tablespoons extra virgin olive oil or safflower oil

1 large onion, chopped

1 tablespoon chopped bottled hot peppers

2½ cups chopped fennel bulb

4 to 5 cloves garlic, pressed or minced

1 tablespoon sugar

4 small red potatoes, cut into chunks

1 tablespoon dried basil

1 28-ounce can diced tomatoes

2 cups water

1 6-ounce container plain yogurt

1 to 1½ cups diced mozzarella cheese

Fennel leaves

1. Heat a heavy soup pot over medium heat. Add the oil, onion, and peppers. Stir, cover, and sweat the onion until soft. Add the fennel and garlic, stir, and cook until the fennel is soft. Add the sugar, potatoes, basil, tomatoes, and water. Reduce the heat and simmer for 1 hour.

2. Once the heat is turned off, blend in the yogurt. Place mozzarella chunks in the bottom of each bowl before filling with soup. Garnish with fennel leaves before serving. **Serves 4 to 6**

TIPS FOR CREAMIER SOUP

Adding cream or sour cream to soup is an easy way to make the soup taste rich. You can also make a creamy-tasting soup without the cream. If using a blender, puree only 1 cup at a time; if you try to puree too much hot liquid, it can spurt out of the blender and burn someone.

- Add ¼ cup quick-cooking oats to a soup like broccoli or carrot. Puree the oats with the cooked vegetables.
- Puree ½ cup leftover potatoes, sweet potatoes, beans (not black beans), squash, or cooked whole grains with a small amount of soup. Stir the puree back into the soup pot.
- Puree ¼ cup raw tahini, cashew butter, or hazelnut butter with 1 cup of soup. Stir the puree back into the soup pot.
- Remove 1 cup of the soup and puree it. Stir the puree back into the soup pot.
- Sprinkle 1 tablespoon rice flour over the simmering soup and stir until the soup thickens.
- Blend 1 cup nonfat yogurt into the finished soup.

Old-Fashioned Navy Bean and Vegetable Soup

This soup incorporates many late summer and fall produce selections. White beans or navy beans, take your pick—they both work. If you want to make this soup in a Crock-Pot, add all the ingredients except the miso and the greens and cook on high for an hour. Then turn the heat to low and cook for 8 hours. Add the greens and cook until tender, 5 to 15 minutes. Just before serving, stir the miso into 1 cup of the soup, blend, and stir it back into the soup.

1 cup white or navy beans, sorted, rinsed, soaked, and drained

6 cups water or vegetable stock

1 strip kombu, cut into small pieces (optional)

2 to 4 cloves garlic, pressed

2 teaspoons each: dried basil and oregano

1 teaspoon fennel seed

¼ to ½ teaspoon crushed red pepper flakes

1 bay leaf

2 carrots, diced

3 stalks celery, chopped

2 small red or white potatoes, cut into small chunks

1 cup delicata squash, cut into small chunks (no need to peel)

1 tablespoon extra virgin olive oil or safflower oil

1 medium onion, chopped

2 tablespoons barley or brown miso

2 cups seasonal greens, torn into small pieces (collards, chard, or kale)

Goat cheese, crumbled (optional)

1. Combine the beans, water, kombu, garlic, basil, oregano, fennel seed, red peppers, bay leaf, carrots, celery, potatoes, and squash in a heavy soup pot. Bring to a boil, then reduce the heat, partially cover, and simmer until the beans are tender, about 1 hour.

2. Heat a heavy skillet over medium heat. Add the oil and onion. Reduce the heat, cover, and sweat the onion until soft. Remove the cover and cook the onion until lightly browned.

3. Stir the onion into the soup and continue to simmer until the beans are done. Remove the bay leaf. Puree 1 cup of soup from the pot with the miso using a hand blender. Return to the pot, add the greens, and cook until the greens are tender. Add more water if the soup is too thick. Garnish with goat cheese if desired. **Serves 6**

Mushroom-Barley Soup with Merlot

Made in a Crock-Pot or on the stovetop, this easy, warming soup is perfect on a cool autumn evening. Make and use the Garlic-Mushroom Soup Stock from this section or buy an organic packaged variety from the store. The recipe calls for tamari, but you can also use Bragg Liquid Aminos, a soy-based flavoring with a less fermented flavor than tamari. Look for both in natural food stores.

6 cups mushroom stock

2 or 3 small potatoes, cut into small chunks

1 carrot, sliced

1 parsnip, sliced

1 stalk celery, sliced

½ cup naked (or hull-less) barley, rinsed

½ teaspoon freshly ground pepper

2 tablespoons extra virgin olive oil or safflower oil

1 large onion, chopped

4 cups sliced cremini mushrooms

2 tablespoons flour (whole wheat, spelt, or kamut)

1 cup milk (dairy, soy, or rice)

1 to 2 tablespoons tamari

1 cup Merlot

1 cup finely chopped parsley

1. Combine the mushroom stock, potatoes, carrot, parsnip, celery, barley, and pepper in a heavy soup pot. Bring to a boil, reduce the heat, cover, and simmer.

2. Heat a heavy skillet over medium heat. Add the oil and onion, stir, reduce the heat, cover, and sweat the onion until soft. Add the mushrooms, stir, and cook until the mushrooms are soft and the onions are lightly browned.

3. Sprinkle the flour over the mushrooms and onions. Stir until the flour blends in and is completely coated with oil. Gradually blend in the milk and stir until thickened. Add the tamari.

4. Combine the onion-mushroom mixture and the Merlot with the soup stock. Pour the soup into a Crock-Pot and set on low for 8 hours, or cook it on the stovetop until the barley is tender, about 1 hour. Serve garnished with chopped parsley. **Serves 6**

Lighter Soups

Whether you want a light soup on center stage or as a supporting actor, seasonal vegetable-based soups are perfect options for easy dinners. making and eating vegetable soup on a regular basis is one way to get children to appreciate a wider variety of vegetables. You can enjoy these soups when you want something less filling, and you can also make them more substantial by adding beans or root vegetables, or pureeing a leftover baked potato or sweet potato with a little of the soup and adding it back into the pot.

Judy Bennett's Pumpkin Soup

Most farm recipes are simple and homespun, and this easy soup is no exception. "Anyone can make it," says Judy Bennett of Rockridge Orchards, who recites the ingredients to farm booth customers at the Ballard farmers' market in the fall. I estimated the proportions for this recipe, but you can adjust the amounts yourself and make this rich soup for as many as you want. Judy uses a Cinderella pumpkin for her version, but you can also use a sugar pie pumpkin or a buttercup squash for that perfect squash flavor.

2 cups cooked pumpkin, skin removed

1 cup cream

1 cup water

Salt and freshly ground pepper

1. Combine the pumpkin, cream, and water in a blender.

2. Heat the mixture in a soup pot until warm. Add salt and pepper to taste and serve. **Serves 2**

Creamy Ginger-Pumpkin-Apple Soup

Northwest farm fields are dotted with pumpkins in the fall. Who can resist them? Cutting a thick-skinned squash or pumpkin may seem daunting, but you can take the easy way out: just poke it with a fork and bake the entire pumpkin at 350°F for an hour. Hazelnut butter gives this soup a creamy texture and a sweet nutty flavor; if you don't have any hazelnut, try almond butter.

1 tablespoon extra virgin olive oil or safflower oil

1 red onion, chopped

½ teaspoon cayenne

1 medium-size rutabaga, chopped

1 apple, cored and roughly chopped

2 to 3 cups water

2 cups cooked sugar pumpkin, skin removed

1 tablespoon grated ginger

1 or 2 tablespoons hazelnut butter

Salt

¼ cup cilantro (optional)

1. Heat a heavy soup pot over medium heat. Add the oil, red onion, and cayenne. Stir and cook until the onion is soft. Add the rutabaga and apple, stir to coat, and add the water. Bring to a boil, then reduce the heat and simmer until the rutabaga is soft, about 10 minutes.

2. Add the pumpkin. Squeeze the juice from the ginger into the mixture (discard the ginger pulp). Cook for another 10 minutes. Cool slightly, then puree 2 cups at a time in a blender with the hazelnut butter. Return to the pot, add salt to taste, and gently heat. Add more water to thin to the desired consistency. Garnish with cilantro if desired. **Serves 4**

TIPS ON PREPARING COOKED PUMPKIN

Instead of reaching for a can of pumpkin, prepare your own cooked pumpkin. Follow these steps:

1. Buy sugar pie pumpkins to bake with because they have great flavor and texture. Select one small enough to fit in your oven.
2. Forget about wielding a big carving knife to saw through a tough skin. Set the oven to 350°F. Stab the pumpkin with a fork a number of times and place it on a baking sheet. Bake for 1 hour.
3. Check the pumpkin with a fork, and if the fork pulls out easily, the pumpkin is done. Let it cool, and then remove the seeds and scoop out the flesh to use in pies, breads, soups, or stews.
4. Freeze the pumpkin you don't use in a plastic freezer container. You can always add pumpkin or squash from the freezer to thicken soups or stews.

Potato-Leek Soup with Parsley

A soup recipe similar to this one appeared in the CSA program newsletter from Winter Green Farm. Farm Web sites with such newsletters often illuminate life on the farm as well as providing great recipes. Originally a summer soup made with green onions, the soup called out for leeks when green onions faded from market tables. Timeless soups evolve with the seasons.

- **3 potatoes, diced (peel only if skins look damaged)**
- **2 leeks, thinly sliced**
- **3 tablespoons butter**
- **4 cups vegetable stock or water**
- **2 medium carrots, grated**
- **1 cup finely chopped greens (kale, beet, or chard)**
- **½ teaspoon salt**
- **Freshly ground pepper**
- **1 teaspoon dried basil**
- **2 tablespoons fresh lemon or lime juice**
- **1 teaspoon honey or agave nectar**
- **1 cup finely chopped parsley**

1. Sauté the potatoes and leeks in butter in a heavy skillet over medium heat until the potatoes have absorbed all the butter or are lightly browned.

2. While the potatoes cook, bring the stock to a boil in a heavy soup pot over medium heat. Add the carrots, greens, salt, pepper, and basil. Reduce the heat, simmer, and then add the potatoes and leeks. Combine the lemon or lime juice, honey or agave nectar, and parsley. Stir into the soup pot, heat for a few minutes, adjust the seasonings, and serve. **Serves 4**

No-Cream of Mushroom Soup

If you have the time, it's worth the flavor to make your own mushroom soup rather than use the processed versions. Dried porcini mushrooms are sold at farmers' markets, but if you can't find them, look for other dried varieties like portobellos or chanterelles at natural food stores. The fresh cremini mushrooms add a nice texture to this creamy soup, which makes an excellent base for casseroles, other soups, and baked potato dishes.

½ cup dried porcini mushrooms

4 cups boiling water

1 tablespoon extra virgin olive oil or safflower oil

1 onion, finely chopped

2 to 4 cloves garlic, pressed or minced

1 tablespoon chopped bottled hot peppers or ¼ teaspoon crushed red pepper flakes

5 cremini mushrooms, sliced

2 tablespoons chopped fresh basil or 1 teaspoon dried

1 shelf-stable package silken tofu (soft or medium)

Salt

1 tablespoon balsamic vinegar

½ to 1 cup finely chopped parsley

1. Soak the porcini mushrooms in the hot water for 1 hour.

2. Heat a heavy soup pot or large saucepan over medium heat. Add the oil and onion, stir, and cook until the onion is soft. Add the garlic, peppers, and cremini mushrooms, stir, and cook until the mushrooms get soft. Blend in the basil.

3. Strain the mushroom water through cheesecloth. Stir 2 cups of the water into the mushrooms and onions. Cook for about 5 minutes. Cool slightly. Carefully puree the soup in a blender or food processor with the silken tofu and return to the pot or pan.

4. Add the porcini mushrooms and remaining mushroom water to thin. Stir in salt to taste and a tablespoon or more of the balsamic vinegar. Blend in the finely chopped parsley before serving. **Serves 6**

Cream of Celery and Autumn Root Soup

This creamy root soup takes the chill off of cool evenings. At farmers' markets in late summer and autumn, you can find celery, celeriac (or celery root), and rutabagas. If you're not going to use celeriac right away after peeling and cutting, plunge it into acidulated water (water with lemon juice or vinegar added) to avoid browning.

- **2 tablespoons extra virgin olive oil or safflower oil**
- **1 sweet onion, chopped**
- **3 cloves elephant garlic, or 6 cloves regular garlic, peeled and sliced**
- **1 fresh jalapeño, seeded and minced**
- **1 bunch celery, tops removed (save in the freezer for soup stock later), stalks cut into ½-inch pieces**
- **5 cups water**
- **1 cup peeled, chopped celeriac**
- **1 parsley root, sliced (optional)**
- **1 medium carrot, sliced**
- **1 medium rutabaga, diced**
- **2 medium red potatoes, diced**
- **2 cups chopped kale**
- **Salt**
- **3 tablespoons fresh lime juice**
- **½ cup sour cream or silken tofu**
- **½ cup chopped cilantro**

1. Heat a heavy soup pot over medium heat. Add the oil, onion, garlic, and jalapeño, stir to coat, cover, and sweat the onions until soft. Stir in the celery, continue to cook for a few minutes, then add the water. Bring to a boil, reduce the heat, and simmer until the celery is very tender, about 20 minutes. Allow to cool slightly.

2. Puree the soup in a blender, 2 cups at a time, until smooth and creamy.

3. Return the puree to the pot and add the celeriac, parsley root, carrot, rutabaga, potatoes, and kale. Bring to a boil, reduce the heat, and simmer until the vegetables are tender, about 20 minutes. Add salt to taste and remove from the heat.

4. Blend the lime juice into the sour cream or tofu and stir into the soup. Garnish with cilantro.

Serves 6

Wild Rice Soup with Sherry

This soup is perfect for special occasions, yet easy enough to make anytime. Onions, carrots, potatoes, and garlic make it an all-season soup. Freddy Guys in the Willamette Valley grows wild rice in addition to all their hazelnuts. This Northwest-grown black wild rice is as tasty as any you might order from Minnesota, where wild rice is traditionally hand-harvested by Native Americans.

1 head garlic

2 tablespoons extra virgin olive oil or safflower oil

1 large onion, chopped

1½ cups sliced mushrooms (cremini, portobello, porcini, or shiitake)

1 or 2 dry chipotle chile pods

1 or 2 potatoes, cut into very small chunks

1 carrot, diced (about 1 cup)

4 cups stock or water

½ cup dry wild rice

1 teaspoon chopped fresh rosemary

½ cup coconut milk

½ cup sherry

2 tablespoons fresh lemon juice

Salt

Parsley for garnish

¼ cup grated sharp Cheddar or Gouda cheese or feta (optional)

1. Preheat the oven to 350°F. Cut the top off of the head of garlic and lay the head on a piece of foil. Drizzle 1 tablespoon of the oil over the garlic head. Wrap it in foil and bake until very tender, about 45 minutes. Let the garlic cool before pressing it out into a small bowl.

2. While the garlic roasts, heat a heavy soup pot over medium heat. Add the remaining oil and the onion. Stir, cover, and sweat the onion until soft.

3. Add the mushrooms, stir, and continue to cook until the onions are lightly browned. Add the chile pods, potatoes, carrot, stock, wild rice, rosemary, coconut milk, and sherry. Bring to a boil, then reduce heat and simmer until the wild rice is done, about 55 minutes.

4. Remove from the heat and stir in the roasted garlic. Squeeze the lemon over the soup and mix in. Remove the chile pods. Season to taste with salt. Garnish with parsley and cheese if desired.
Serves 4 to 6

Borscht

This soup's origins may be Russian, but Northwest ingredients make it shine. I use fresh beets from Nash Huber's farm, celery from Willie Green's, and a potato from Olson Farms (famous for their 23 varieties of potatoes)—all found at the University District farmers' market. The baked potato gives this traditional Eastern European soup a creamy base. Lemon lends tangy tones. Lemons are a crop you might not associate with the Northwest, but some farmers bring Meyer lemons to Portland markets, and some Washington farmers sell yuzu, a Japanese citrus similar to lemons.

- 1 tablespoon extra virgin olive oil or safflower oil
- 1 large onion, chopped
- 5 cloves garlic, minced
- 2 stalks celery, chopped
- 1 or 2 carrots, diced
- 2 tablespoons tomato paste
- 5 cups water or vegetable stock (or half of each)
- 3 cups sliced beets, tops removed, not peeled
- ½ tablespoon chopped fresh dill or ½ teaspoon dried
- Salt and freshly ground pepper
- 1 medium baked potato, skin removed
- ¼ cup fresh lemon juice
- Zest from 1 lemon, finely chopped
- 1 to 2 tablespoons sugar
- Sour cream or plain yogurt (optional)
- Parsley sprigs

1. Heat a heavy soup pot over medium heat. Add the oil and onion, stir, cover, and sweat the onions until soft. Add the garlic, celery, and carrots, and cook for 5 minutes, stirring often. Add the tomato paste and mix well, continuing to cook for another minute or so.

2. Gradually add the water or stock, beets, and dill. Bring to a boil, reduce the heat, cover, and simmer for 20 minutes. Add salt and pepper to taste.

3. Puree 1 cup of the soup with the potato, lemon juice, and zest. Stir back into the soup pot along with sugar to taste. Adjust the seasonings. Serve with a dollop of sour cream or plain yogurt if desired. Garnish each serving with a parsley sprig. **Serves 4**

Smoky Corn Chowder

I always preferred corn to clam chowder as a child. Fresh corn is always the sweetest, so make this savory soup in the summer when corn is fresh. New potatoes are potatoes that have just been harvested. The skins are tender and the flesh is sweet.

- 2 tablespoons extra virgin olive oil or safflower oil
- 2 large sweet onions, chopped
- 2 cloves garlic, minced
- 1 red bell pepper, seeded and chopped
- 2 carrots, sliced
- 2 small zucchinis, sliced
- 3 medium new potatoes, cut into bite-size chunks
- 2 cups water
- 1 15-ounce can fire-roasted tomatoes
- Kernels from 3 ears of corn
- 4 or 5 dry chipotle chile pods, soaked in ½ cup hot water
- ¾ cup milk (dairy, soy, or rice)
- Salt
- ½ to 1 cup grated, aged Cheddar or Gouda cheese
- Croutons (optional)

1. Heat a heavy soup pot over medium heat. Add the oil, onions, garlic, and bell pepper. Stir and cook until the onions are lightly browned.

2. Add the carrots, zucchini, and potatoes, and stir to coat with the oil. Add the water, tomatoes, corn, and chile pods with their soaking water. Bring to a boil, reduce the heat, and simmer until all the vegetables are tender, about 20 minutes.

3. Add the milk and continue to cook on low for about 8 more minutes. Add salt to taste. Remove the chile pods and discard. Garnish with the cheese and with croutons if desired. **Serves 6**

Easy Creamy Turnip Greens Soup

I created this soup one afternoon when I was hungry and had two bunches of tender spring turnips with greens. I cooked the greens in a little water and then pureed them with a few ingredients to balance the flavors. The result was a little taste of heaven in an almost instant soup that I made week after week until spring turnips with greens were no longer on market tables. Other greens like kale, collards, or braising greens have a stronger flavor and take longer to cook, but you can still use them as long as you make sure they cook until tender. Hazelnut butter is my favorite local addition, but you could also add almond or cashew butter or a little cream. Serve this treasure with crusty artisan bread.

- 4 cups water
- 1 tablespoon fresh lemon juice or mild vinegar
- 8 to 10 cups turnip greens (3 or 4 bunches)
- 1 teaspoon honey or agave nectar
- 2 tablespoons hazelnut (or almond or cashew) butter
- Pinch of cayenne (optional)
- Salt

1 tablespoon rice flour (optional)

Plain yogurt (optional)

1. Heat a heavy soup pot over medium heat. Add the water, lemon juice or vinegar, and turnip greens. Bring to a boil, reduce the heat, and simmer until the greens are tender, a few minutes.

2. Puree all the greens and water in a blender, 1 cup at a time, adding the honey, nut butter, cayenne if desired, and salt to taste to the first batch.

3. Return the puree to the soup pot and heat gently for a few minutes. If the soup is too thin, add a tablespoon of rice flour and stir until thickened. Serve with a dollop of yogurt if desired. **Serves 4**

Curried Carrot Soup

In a CSA program newsletter from Nash's Organic Produce, a curried carrot soup recipe directed cooks to "use all your carrots." Intrigued by a recipe that offered no proportions, I sat down and determined my own ingredient portions. I added coconut milk for a smooth, creamy texture. I scrub but don't usually peel carrots unless they look very beat-up in the winter.

1 pound carrots, sliced into 1-inch lengths (3½ to 4 cups)

2 tablespoons extra virgin olive oil or safflower oil

½ teaspoon turmeric

½ teaspoon coriander

1 teaspoon mustard seeds

2 teaspoons minced ginger

1 5-ounce can coconut milk

4 cups water

Salt and freshly ground pepper

Cilantro sprigs

1. Preheat the oven to 350°F. Rub the carrots with a little oil and then with the minced ginger (reserving the ginger to sauté later.) Sprinkle the carrots with the turmeric and coriander, shake off the excess, and place them in a baking dish. Roast the carrots until fork-tender, 30 to 40 minutes.

2. While the carrots roast, heat a heavy skillet over medium heat. When the skillet is hot, add the remaining oil and the mustard seeds. As soon as the seeds begin to sizzle and pop, add the ginger. Cook and stir with your full attention so the ginger and seeds don't burn. When the ginger is golden, add the coconut milk and water, and simmer until the carrots have roasted.

3. Puree the roasted carrots in a blender, adding a little of the coconut milk mixture at a time. When the carrots are smooth, stir them into the remaining coconut milk mixture. Blend in the water and season to taste with salt and pepper. Garnish with cilantro sprigs. **Serves 4**

Garlic-Asparagus Soup

No matter how long asparagus lasts at the farmers' market in the spring, the season is always too short for me. Savor this soup like the transience of spring. Since local jalapeños aren't in season at the same time as asparagus, try a bottled variety of peppers like Mama Lil's, a longtime Washington favorite hot pepper, or (if you're in the area) the whole bottled jalapeños from the Gathering Together farm stand in Philomath, Oregon. Oats add thickening (and fiber) without the cream. While hazelnut butter (a local product) will work in this soup, the flavor competes with asparagus, the true diva of this show. Instead use a good organic almond or cashew butter for a creamy texture.

- 1 tablespoon extra virgin olive oil or safflower oil
- 1 medium onion, chopped
- 1 tablespoon chopped bottled hot peppers
- 4 cups water
- 2 pounds asparagus, washed, woody base discarded, and cut into 2-inch lengths, tips reserved
- 1 head garlic, cloves separated, peeled, and sliced
- ¼ cup quick-cooking oats
- ¼ cup almond or cashew butter
- 3 medium potatoes, such as Yellow Finn or Yukon Gold, cut into small chunks
- 1 medium carrot, sliced
- 3 cups sliced mushrooms, cremini or portobello
- ¼ cup white miso
- 2 to 4 tablespoons fresh lemon juice
- ½ teaspoon honey
- 1 small container of plain yogurt (dairy, goat, or soy) (optional)

1. Heat a heavy soup pot over medium heat. Add the oil, onions, and peppers, stir, cover, and sweat the onions until soft. Add the water, asparagus stems (reserve tips), garlic, oats, and 1 potato. Bring to a boil, reduce the heat, and simmer until the asparagus stems are very soft, about 15 minutes.

2. Puree all of the soup, 1 or 2 cups at a time, in a blender with the almond or cashew butter. Stir all but 1 cup of the soup back into the pot. Add the remaining potatoes along with the carrot, mushrooms, and asparagus tips. Simmer until all the vegetables are tender, about 15 minutes, stirring occasionally.

3. Blend the miso into the cup of reserved soup. Remove the soup pot from the heat and stir in the miso mixture, lemon juice, and honey. Top each serving with a dollop of yogurt if desired.

Serves 4

FOOD FOR THOUGHT: THE ASPARAGUS LIFE SPAN

Asparagus plants can live for 10 to 15 years. The size of the stalk indicates how old the plant is, and while young plants have thin stalks, they aren't necessarily more tender than thicker, more mature asparagus.

Cool and Spicy Fruit Soup

This cold fruit soup is a cool respite on Northwest summer days. If you love hot peppers, leave the jalapeño whole before pureeing. I like to use a locally made yogurt like Port Madison goat yogurt from Bainbridge Island in Washington, but the dairy-free version with silken tofu is also delicious.

- 2 cups of any one: pitted sliced plums, peaches, nectarines, or apricots (about 1½ pounds)
- 1 fresh jalapeño, seeded and minced
- ¼ cup fresh lemon or lime juice
- Zest of 1 lemon or lime, finely chopped
- 1 cup plain yogurt or silken tofu
- 4 cups peach or apricot juice
- 1 cup chopped fresh apricots, nectarines, or halved cherries
- ¼ cup chopped cilantro

1. Puree the fruit, jalapeño, lemon or lime juice and zest, and yogurt or silken tofu in a blender until smooth and creamy. Add the fruit juice and blend well.

2. Chill for 30 minutes or until ready to serve. Mix in the chopped fruit. Garnish with cilantro before serving. **Serves 6 to 8**

Hot Apple Soup

A sweet soup, served piping hot, is just the ticket for cool fall days. Make it for brunch or serve it after lunch or dinner and top it with a dollop of whipped cream.

- 3 sweet-tart apples, cored and sliced
- Juice of 1 lemon
- 2 cups apple cider
- 1 cup water
- ¼ cup maple syrup
- ½ teaspoon cardamom or cinnamon
- ¼ cup hazelnut butter
- Freshly grated nutmeg

Simmer apples in lemon juice, apple cider, water, and maple syrup with cardamom or cinnamon until tender, about 10 minutes. Mash apples; a potato masher will do the job. Stir hazelnut butter into soup, mixing well. Grate nutmeg over each serving of this sweet-tart soup. **Serves 4**

Sweet and Savory Yeast Breads

There's nothing like kneading bread dough for releasing tension. Pushing and folding in a rhythmic motion, you can sink into a meditative frame of mind. Setting the loaf to rise, shaping it, and finally baking it is one of the simple, sensual pleasures of life. When the aroma of freshly baked bread wafts throughout the house and the bread is finally sliced, top it with Northwest products like Rogue Creamery butter, Ayers Creek Farm loganberry preserves, or raspberry honey from Rockridge Orchards. For novice bakers, most of the recipes that follow are made with part unbleached white flour for easier handling. Once you have the techniques down and your confidence up, incorporate more whole-grain flour into the dough until you can successfully create whole-grain bread.

The basics: Yeast bread steps and tips

- Buy flour in small amounts or grind your own. Many home bakers recommend King Arthur's brand flour. The unbleached flour in bins at my local food co-op seems to work just as well for me. Store white flour for up to six months; use whole-grain flour within a few weeks or store it in the freezer for a few months.

- Never use more than 2 teaspoons yeast for a recipe. Don't use yeast that is over a year old because it is not as effective. Yeast is alive and is activated by warm water. Dissolve yeast by sprinkling it over warm water (105° to 115°F). Use a thermometer or a touch test with your finger. If the water is warm but not hot, it should be about right. Stir the yeast in or let it sink into the water.

- Add the sweetener right after you put the yeast in the water, or add it with the flour. Combining sugar with the water will make the yeast work faster. If you do this, watch it carefully. After the yeast begins to bubble up, add the flour and stir.

- Don't take the amount of flour in a recipe literally. For a more accurate measure and consistent bread quality, commercial bakers weigh flour to make bread. You can become more confident in bread making if you make small quantities (one loaf at a time) and pay attention to the texture of the dough when you add flour. I usually add 1 cup of flour to start with and stir well, then gradually add the rest of the flour as needed.

- For one loaf of bread, use about 2½ cups of flour (a little less if using whole wheat flour) to each cup of liquid in your recipe. Mix in the first cup and keep stirring until your arms begin to tire (about 150 strokes). Ingredients are always mixed in the same order in basic bread making.

- Kneading is tricky when you use all whole wheat flour. Because using all whole wheat flour makes the dough very sticky, it's easier to stir the dough with a wooden spoon. Don't add too much flour or the bread will have a dry texture. If you're new to bread making, use kamut flour instead of whole wheat. It's easier to work with.

- Stirring the dough develops gluten (a wheat protein) so bread can rise. Stir for as long as you can, about 200 strokes, and then poke and mash with a wooden spoon if using all whole wheat flour. Ultimately, you're aiming for a smooth and satiny texture. If you add too much flour (the most common mistake), the bread will be too dry.

- Kneading bread means turning the dough out onto a dry or lightly floured board and turning the far side toward you with a rhythmic, folding motion. Push the dough in a rolling motion each time you turn it. Oil your hands slightly to make kneading easier; you can add all the oil in this way. If the dough shows creases while you fold, stop adding flour; too much has already been added. Knead a few tablespoons of water into the dough if it becomes too dry. This takes patience and practice. Aim for a satiny smooth texture. Kneading and rising is often repeated in bread recipes for a lighter loaf.

- Oil a large clean bowl before placing the dough in it to rise. The dough will be easier to remove from an oiled bowl.

- Set the bowl with dough to rise in a warm place in your kitchen. Cover with a damp towel. The ideal temperature for rising is 80°F, but bread also rises below 70°F. At lower temperatures the first rise will take two to three hours. A slow rise infuses layers of flavors not present in bread that rises quickly.

- The dough should rise until nearly doubled in bulk. Use the poke test to determine whether the dough has finished rising. Poke a finger

into the dough. If the indentation fills in quickly, the dough needs more rising time. If the indentation remains, the dough has finished rising.

- Shape the dough into a loaf, roll it into sticks or rolls, or stretch and flatten it to make focaccia and let it rise again. It will double in bulk (unless you use all whole-grain flour, which doesn't quite double in size when proofed). A second rise takes about three-quarters as long as the first.

- Slashing or cutting the loaf before baking allows steam to escape. This isn't necessary when forming a loaf in a pan, but if you are making a peasant loaf on a baking sheet, it may tear at the base if you don't slash it.

- Bake bread until it is slightly browned on top and bottom. Most peasant loaves take 45 to 55 minutes, rolls about 25 minutes, and flatbread 15 to 20 minutes. If you're unsure whether the bread is done, remove it from the oven and the pan. Thump the bottom of the loaf with your fingers. It will sound hollow if it's done. If you aren't sure, return the loaf to the oven for another few minutes, remove, and thump again.
- Leave the bread on a cooling rack for 20 minutes after removing from the oven. Bread hot from the oven is doughy and doesn't slice well, so wait a few minutes before slicing it. One unbreakable bread rule is "Eat your mistakes while still warm."

More bread tips

- Rescue dough that has overrisen. If you forget about your rising dough and it collapses when you poke a finger into it, you've let it rise too long. Save it by simply gathering it up, kneading it again, and giving it one more rise. You should still have fairly good bread. If you don't do this, the loaf will have a texture like a brick when baked. A second rise takes about half to three-quarters as long as the first rise.
- Incorporate nuts, whole grains, or fruit into the dough. For example, you can knead in ½ cup of cooked whole grains. Nuts, seeds, sliced olives, and dried fruit are common additions that you can work in during the last kneading. You can also add fresh fruit if the moisture content isn't too high. Apples and pears are perfect for this. Dice the fruit into small pieces. As you knead it in, you will notice the dough becomes wet in places near the fruit. Incorporate a little more flour at this point, and your bread will turn out just fine.
- Mix in applesauce or another fruit puree for part of the liquid ingredients right after the yeast has been combined with liquid. Sweet ingredients like these give the loaf a slightly sweet taste. The bread stays fresh longer, too. Whatever your choice for the liquid measurement, make sure it's warm before activating the yeast in it.
- Stir in pureed vegetables such as squash, potato, and even roasted red peppers as a starting base for the liquid measurement. When you add pureed vegetables, the bread turns out moist and stays fresh longer.
- Freshly baked bread is meant to be savored now, not saved. That said, the classic *Laurel's Kitchen Bread Book* (2003) by Laurel Robertson says to store bread at cool room temperatures, loosely wrapped in a cloth or paper bag or stored in a breadbox. For longer than two days, slice the bread and place it in a plastic bag in the freezer. I never store freshly made bread beyond a month in the freezer.

Basic Bread

For this easy beginner's recipe, I usually like to use specialty flours like kamut from Bob's Red Mill or unbleached flour from Fairhaven Mills. Look for those flours in natural food stores. During the second kneading, you can add about ½ cup chopped toasted nuts, dried fruit, or olives to the loaf for variation. Experienced bread bakers can use all whole-grain flour in this or any other bread recipe.

- 1 cup warm water (about 105°F)
- 2 teaspoons yeast
- 1 tablespoon sweetener (honey, agave nectar, maple syrup, or sugar)
- ½ teaspoon salt
- 1 tablespoon melted butter or extra virgin olive oil
- 1¼ cups whole wheat, kamut, or spelt flour
- 1¼ cups unbleached white flour
- 2 tablespoons melted butter
- 1 tablespoon maple syrup

1. Sprinkle the yeast over the warm water in a large bowl. Let the yeast soften for about 5 minutes. Add the sweetener and let the mixture bubble up. Then mix in the salt and the butter or oil. Blend in the whole wheat, kamut, or spelt flour, stirring vigorously for about 150 strokes, scraping the sides of the bowl as you mix. Gradually add 1 cup of the unbleached flour. Keep mixing until the dough pulls away from the sides of the bowl. Turn out onto a lightly floured board. Oil your hands and knead until the dough feels smooth and elastic.

2. Place the kneaded dough in a large oiled bowl. Cover with a damp towel and allow to rise in a warm place until doubled in bulk, about an hour. While the bread rises, combine the melted butter with the maple syrup for topping. Set aside.

3. When the dough has risen, punch it down and scrape it out onto a lightly floured counter. Oil your hands and knead again, adding the rest of the flour if needed. Let the dough rest for 5 minutes before shaping into a loaf. Oil an 8-by-4-inch pan with oil or butter, and place the loaf in the pan. Cover loosely with a damp towel and let it rise a second time, about 1 hour.

4. Preheat the oven to 400°F. Brush the top of the loaf with the butter and maple syrup mixture. Bake for 10 minutes, then reduce the oven temperature to 325°F and bake for 45 minutes or until golden brown.

5. Remove from the oven and let the loaf sit for 5 minutes. Then run a knife around the edges of the pan and invert the loaf onto a cooling rack. Cool before slicing. Serve with farm fresh butter and jam. This loaf will keep for a few days stored in a plastic bag at room temperature. **Makes 1 loaf**

Squash Bread

You can enhance bread or even cinnamon rolls with baked squash, which adds moisture so the bread doesn't dry out the next day. You knead the squash into the dough and it imparts sweet tones that make kids sing for more. For variation, substitute baked yam or pumpkin in this recipe.

- **1 cup baked acorn or butternut squash (skins removed)**
- **1 cup hot water**
- **2 tablespoons maple syrup or molasses**
- **2 teaspoons yeast**
- **1 cup whole wheat, kamut, or spelt flour**
- **½ teaspoon salt**
- **1 tablespoon melted butter or extra virgin olive oil**
- **1½ cups unbleached white flour**

1. Puree the squash, hot water, and maple syrup or molasses together in a large bowl with a hand blender. Let the mixture cool to warm (about 105°F) before sprinkling the yeast over the top. Let the mixture sit until it becomes foamy on top from the yeast action, about 10 minutes.

2. Add all the whole wheat, kamut, or spelt flour to the squash-yeast mixture and stir vigorously for about 100 strokes, scraping the sides of the bowl often. Place in a large oiled bowl and cover with a damp towel. Let the dough rise in a warm place for about 1½ hours. You can also let it rise in a very cool room overnight (55° to 60°F).

3. Punch the dough down and then stir it again, blending in the salt and butter or oil. Add the unbleached flour ½ cup at a time, stirring well after each addition. The dough should begin pulling away from the sides of the bowl before you turn it out onto a lightly floured board. Oil your hands to prevent the dough from sticking as you knead the dough. Knead until smooth yet still slightly tacky. It is the tackiness of the dough that will give your bread a moist, soft texture.

4. Line a baking sheet with parchment paper. Alternatively, you can oil the baking sheet and dust it with cornmeal. Form the dough into a round peasant loaf and set it on the prepared baking sheet. Cover the dough with a damp towel and let rise again until almost doubled in bulk, 30 to 45 minutes. Remove the towel and press the dough with one finger. The dough will rebound very slowly from the indentation if the rising has finished.

5. Preheat the oven to 450°F. With a very sharp knife, make a diagonal cut about ½-inch deep across the top of the loaf. Bake for 10 minutes, then lower the temperature to 350° and bake for 35 minutes. Remove the loaf from the oven and thump it. It will sound hollow if it is done, dense if it is not done. Return it to the oven if it is not done and bake for a few more minutes.

6. For a rich dark crust, brush the top with melted butter for the last few minutes of baking. Cool before slicing. Spread with farm fresh butter and jam. This loaf will keep for a few days stored in a plastic bag at room temperature. **Makes 1 loaf**

Baked Bean Bread

Next time you have leftover baked beans (or even a can of baked beans will do) try making this savory bread recipe. Beans add moisture, and this bread stays moist and tender for a few days. Chopped toasted nuts add an interesting texture variation. Add ⅓ cup chopped hazelnuts or walnuts (two Northwest nuts) during the final kneading if you like.

- **1 cup baked beans (or baked bean stew)**
- **1 cup hot water**
- **1½ tablespoons molasses**
- **2 teaspoons yeast**
- **1 tablespoon butter or extra virgin olive oil**
- **½ teaspoon salt**
- **1 cup whole wheat, kamut, or spelt flour**
- **1½ cups unbleached white flour**
- **2 tablespoons butter**
- **1 tablespoon maple syrup**

1. Puree the beans, hot water, and molasses together in a large bowl with a hand blender until smooth and creamy. Let the mixture cool to warm (about 105°F) before sprinkling the yeast over the top. Let the mixture sit until it becomes foamy on top from the yeast action, about 10 minutes.

2. Add the butter or oil, the salt, and all the whole wheat, kamut, or spelt flour to the bean mixture and stir vigorously for about 100 strokes, scraping the sides of the bowl often. Add about ½ cup of the unbleached flour and stir again. Cover the bowl with a damp towel and put it in a warm place to rise until the dough has doubled in bulk, about an hour.

3. Punch the dough down and stir again, adding more flour about ⅓ cup at a time until the dough begins to pull away from the sides of the bowl. The dough will be slightly sticky to the touch. Turn the dough out onto a floured counter or board and knead until smooth, adding flour as needed.

4. Line a baking sheet with parchment paper. Alternatively, you can oil the baking sheet and dust it with cornmeal. Form the dough into a round peasant loaf and set it on the prepared baking sheet. Cover the dough with a damp towel and let rise again until almost doubled in bulk, 30 to 45 minutes. Remove the towel and press the dough with one finger. The dough will rebound very slowly from the indentation if the rising has finished.

5. Preheat the oven to 400°F. With a very sharp knife, make a diagonal cut about ½-inch deep across the top of the loaf. Combine the butter and maple syrup, blending until smooth and creamy, and brush on the top of the bread. Bake for 10 minutes, then lower the temperature to 350° and bake for 40 minutes. Remove the loaf from the oven and thump it. It will sound hollow if it is done, dense if it is not done. Return it to the oven if it is not done and bake for a few more minutes.

6. Cool before slicing. Spread with farm fresh butter and jam. This loaf will keep for a few days stored in a plastic bag at room temperature. **Makes 1 loaf**

Rosemary-Amaranth Flatbread with Roasted Red Peppers

I love these individual flatbreads because everyone gets their own to top. Try different toppings on each—sautéed or grilled zucchini, eggplant, onions, and mushrooms, for example—or simply bake all of them with grated cheese for the topping. A few Northwest farms grow amaranth, and you can too, if you order amaranth seeds from Wild Garden Seed at Gathering Together Farm. Otherwise, buy amaranth from the bulk grain section in natural food stores.

1 cup plus ¼ cup water

⅓ cup amaranth

1 teaspoon chopped fresh rosemary

2 teaspoons yeast

1 tablespoon honey

½ teaspoon salt

1 or 2 tablespoons extra virgin olive oil

1½ cups flour (unbleached, kamut, or both)

2 red bell peppers

½ cup sliced olives

½ cup grated aged cheese, your favorite variety

1. Combine 1 cup water with the amaranth and rosemary in a small saucepan. Bring to a boil, then reduce heat, cover, and simmer until the amaranth is soft, about 30 minutes.

2. Place the amaranth in a large bowl and add the remaining ¼ cup water. Mix well. Sprinkle the yeast over the top and gently fold the amaranth over the yeast. Make sure the yeast is blended in. Let the mixture sit until the yeast bubbles up.

3. Add the honey, salt, and oil. Blend thoroughly. Add ½ cup flour and stir vigorously, scraping the bowl often. Cover and set aside in a warm place for 25 to 30 minutes.

4. Blend in the remaining flour, ½ cup at a time, stirring after each addition. When the dough pulls away from the sides of the bowl, turn it out onto a floured board and knead 3 to 5 minutes. The dough should feel slightly sticky. Place the dough in a large oiled bowl, cover with a damp towel, and let it rise in a warm place until doubled in bulk, about an hour.

5. While the bread rises, place the peppers under the broiler and roast until the outside is charred and blackened. Remove and set in a saucepan, covering with a lid until cool. Peel the peppers and remove the seeds. Cut into strips and set aside.

6. When the dough has finished rising, punch it down. Turn it out onto a counter and knead about five turns. Set aside for 5 minutes. Preheat the oven to 425°F. Line a large baking sheet with parchment paper. Divide the dough into four portions and roll each into a log. Pat or roll into an oval shape about ¼ to ½ inch thick. The ovals should measure approximately 11 by 3 inches.

7. Place on a baking sheet and top each with the pepper strips, olives, and cheese. Bake for 15 to 17 minutes. Gently slide off the parchment paper to a cooling rack. These little flatbreads can be refrigerated and reheated in the microwave or oven later. **Makes 4 11-by-3-inch flatbreads**

Basic Focaccia

This popular bread is a great soup accompaniment. Add toppings to make focaccia pizza—a meal in itself.

- 1 cup warm water (about 105°F)
- 2 teaspoons yeast
- 1 tablespoon honey, agave nectar, or sugar
- ½ teaspoon salt
- 4 tablespoons extra virgin olive oil, divided equally in half
- 1¼ cups whole wheat, kamut, or spelt flour
- 1¼ cups unbleached white flour
- 3 or 4 cloves garlic, peeled and sliced
- ½ tablespoon chopped fresh rosemary

1. Sprinkle the yeast over the warm water in a large bowl. Let the yeast soften for about 5 minutes. Add the sweetener and let the mixture bubble up. Then mix in the salt and 2 tablespoons oil. Blend in the whole wheat, kamut, or spelt flour, stirring vigorously for about 150 strokes, scraping the sides of the bowl as you mix. Gradually add 1 cup of the unbleached flour. Keep mixing until the dough pulls away from the sides of the bowl. Turn out onto a lightly floured board. Oil your hands and knead until the dough feels smooth and elastic.

2. Place the kneaded dough in a large oiled bowl. Cover with a damp towel and allow to rise in a warm place until doubled in bulk, about an hour. While the bread rises, combine the remaining 2 tablespoons olive oil with the garlic for topping. Set aside.

3. When the dough has risen, punch it down and scrape it out onto a lightly floured counter.

Oil your hands and knead again, adding the rest of the flour if needed. Let the dough rest for 5 minutes before patting into a 14-inch circle.

4. Oil a pizza pan and sprinkle it with cornmeal. Place the circle of dough on the pan. Cover with a damp towel again and set aside to rise for about 45 minutes.

5. Preheat the oven to 400°F. When the dough has finished rising, remove the wrap. With the tips of your fingers, poke the surface of the dough until it is covered with indentations about ½ inch apart. Brush the garlic-infused oil over the surface of the focaccia. Sprinkle the rosemary over the top.

6. Bake until golden brown on top and bottom, about 20 minutes. Serve with olive oil for dipping. This bread is best eaten the same day.

Makes 1 14-inch focaccia

Focaccia Pizza

Pizza is fun any day and is a good way to encourage young children to eat more vegetables. You can try just about any Northwest vegetables on top.

1 14-inch focaccia made from Basic Focaccia recipe, above

½ cup pizza or marinara sauce

Approximately 1½ cups sautéed vegetables (try onions, peppers, eggplant, garlic, mushrooms, or summer squash)

Sliced tomatoes (optional)

½ cup shredded cheese, your favorite variety (optional)

Spread a thin layer of pizza or marinara sauce over the top of cooled focaccia. Add sautéed vegetables, along with sliced tomatoes and/or shredded cheese if desired. Place under the broiler or in a conventional oven until the topping is heated through—about 5 minutes. **Makes 1 14-inch focaccia pizza**

Approaching Ayers Creek Farm, southwest of Portland

Tito, the farm dog, making the rounds at Ayers Creek Farm, Gaston, Oregon

Growing Specialty Crops for Market

Some Northwest growers are naturally attracted to cutting-edge crops, and farmers' market shoppers love to sample new varieties of fruits and vegetables. Two Northwest farms with reputations for bringing quirky crops to chefs and urban markets are Rockridge Orchards in Washington and Ayers Creek Farm in Oregon.

Ayers Creek farmers Anthony and Carol Boutard are known at the Hillsdale farmers' market for growing unusual organic grains, beans, fruits, and vegetables with intriguing flavors. Stop at their booth in early summer, and Anthony and Carol are deep in conversation with customers about Ayers Creek fenugreek greens, red and black currants, and loganberries. As summer peaks, market conversations shift, and fragrant Charantais melons, sweet Chester blackberries, Arabian blue barley, pink currants, and dried fava beans fill the Boutards' market table. It doesn't take long to realize the Boutards are having a love affair with growing unique foods with great flavors, and they thoroughly enjoy offering their treasures to the community.

Anthony and Carol's 144-acre certified organic farm is about 30 miles southwest of Portland. Along tree-lined roads and up and down rolling hills, the drive from the city took me about an hour. Once I arrived in midsummer, the landscape wasn't filled with the tidy fields and high-density orchards I'd seen on other farms. The plum orchard sported a wild, scattered look, with trees so far apart they almost blended into the landscape like natives. Anthony told me the trees

were 18 feet apart, and I realized I carry a stereotypical orchard in my head with trees planted in neat rows and manicured weed-free spaces in between them. Anthony didn't seem so concerned about weeds scattered here and there, and the orchard displayed a healthy sustainable interplay bridging wild and cultivated.

Outside the Boutards' back door a lemon tree, heavy with bright yellow citrus, seemed unusual in the Northwest, and a crop of popcorn was just coming up in the fields. The Charantais melons, not something you would see in a grocery store, looked ripe, and Carol bent down, cradled one like a glass egg, and sniffed the stem. "Maybe next week," she said, and gently laid the melon down. Pampered crops are the secret to great flavors at this farm.

Anthony Boutard grew up with an appreciation of plants. His parents ran the Berkshire Botanical Garden in Stockbridge, Massachusetts, when he was young, and later Anthony worked with them, learning how to grow to plants. He and Carol met at the garden when she started working there, and they worked together preparing exhibits for flower shows.

"I watched Anthony win gold medals at the Boston Flower Show on a budget smaller than most people's coffee tabs," said Carol, who discovered gardening in her 20s when she lived on an old farm in New York. "I was fortunate to plant my first garden on top of a rich vein of composted manure," she told me.

Anthony was trained in forestry, and a conservation job initially drew the couple to Portland. Northwest agriculture seduced them after they got a 10-by-40-foot community garden plot. Carol taught classes through the Fulton Community Gardening Program. She told me that their 10-by-40-foot plot was "our best preparation for growing food in the Pacific Northwest."

The Boutards bought their farm in 1998, planted crops, built production, and in 2003 started selling produce at the Hillsdale farmers' market. One crop the Boutards became well known for is frikeh (free-keh), a green durum wheat that is threshed and burned while the grain is still young. These smoky, parched, immature grains are popular in many parts of the world, and Anthony recalled having seen frikeh a few years earlier at a popular deli. The Boutards researched the grain on the Web and finally located the right variety of wheat. They planted a crop and then combed the Web for recipes.

"It's not enough to toss something on a market table and expect people to buy and eat it," Anthony explained. Introducing chefs to a new ingredient can nudge them onto center stage. When their frikeh was ready to sell, they passed the intriguing grain to Chef Gregg Higgins at a wine event in Dundee, where he transformed the frikeh into a tabbouleh salad with lemon and mint. Other Portland chefs soon ordered frikeh for their own appetizers, salads, and pilafs. In 2007, the Boutards sold more than half a ton of the smokey grain to Hillsdale market shoppers and restaurants. However, in 2009 the Oregon Department of Agriculture adopted a broad definition of food processing that includes parching and drying, making frikeh a processed food, and notified the Boutards that they are prohibited from selling it because their operation is not licensed for processing. Anthony Boutard sent a "Farewell Frikeh" email to farm customers eulogizing the newest victim of what he called "Oregon's regulatory foolishness."

In addition to specialty grains like dry beans, the Boutards' winter greens provide local diversity through the cold months. Anthony told me that in the winter, greens have better flavor, and that our damp, cool, mild weather allows greens to flourish all winter here.

Another farm known for zesty salad greens in winter and other quirky crops is Rockridge Orchards in Enumclaw, a 100-acre farm 45 minutes southeast of Seattle. There, farmers Wade and Judy Bennett grow unusual fruits and vegetables and process orchard fruit and berries into cider, wine, and vinegar. They grow crops for wholesale, restaurants, and farmers' markets.

In the winter, shoppers at the University District, West Seattle, and Ballard farmers' markets look for Judy's sorrel, arugula, and pea vines, and a spicy salad mix with zippy mustard greens. In spring, summer, and fall, the Bellevue, Mercer Island, and Columbia City farmers' markets are added to their market lineup. Look for Judy or Wade behind Wade's award-winning apple cider and berry wine, with a story and various unusual types of produce to share.

With roots in the Northwest, Wade and Judy always had a garden, but they didn't became full-time farmers until 1982, when Wade left the movie business. The Bennetts' land was little more than a gravel pit when they bought it. "It might as well have been," Wade told me. "It's called Rockridge for that reason." Little by little they built up layers of compost, and now the farm's rich topsoil is three to four feet deep in places and supports apple, pear, Asian pear, plum, and fig orchards.

Row crops are planted in every available fertile space at Rockridge Orchards. Heirloom fruits like the Northwest native Belle Island grapes grow just outside the bamboo groves that boast 106 varieties of bamboo. Georgian fire garlic, sancho peppercorns, banana leaves, wasabi, and *gai lan* (Chinese broccoli) are just a few of their unusual crops. Their Asian pear orchard boasts 17 different kinds of pears, all with different flavors. And Wade and Judy are among the few Washington farmers cultivating figs. They grow many oddball crops like Bavarian horseradish, quince, and yuzu (a hearty Japanese citrus), for Seattle chefs who transform them into sweet and savory treats.

"It's not just a niche, it's a strategy," Wade explained. "We constantly have to adjust our business plan because food changes so quickly. We tried some things that we thought were cool but didn't work out—like sea berries, chokecherries, and persimmons."

Wade also grew, processed, and sold tea for a decade, but one spring he said he wasn't growing it anymore. "Production costs outstripped income," he said. It was too hard to compete with the price of Chinese tea. Now he grows a small amount for himself and a local restaurant. "Judy says I got out of tea too soon, so I may grow it again," he told me, leaving the door open for future possibilities.

One crop Wade and Judy haven't quit growing is bamboo. It is easy to grow, requires very little weeding, and is self-sustaining. They sell the plant starts to nurseries, large canes to furniture makers, and smaller canes to dahlia growers. Market shoppers and chefs snap up the tender young shoots in the spring. Multiple avenues for marketing crops is another strategy for this farm.

Wade never tires of introducing customers to his new and unusual crops. At the market, Wade stood behind his cider bottles, held up a humble brown shoot, and asked, "Have you ever had *takenoko*?" He paused, then continued, "Take a knife, hack them in two, brush the flat side with a little olive oil, and throw them on a hot grill. In a few minutes, take them off, pop the flesh out, and dip them in hoisin sauce. The flavor is a cross between asparagus and artichokes."

Who can resist a new market temptation? Before any new customers moved in, I reached for a few to add to my own grilling lineup.

Farmer Wade Bennett of Rockridge Orchards with his hard cider and sweet berry wine at the University District farmers' market

Starters and Side Dishes

Side dishes are one of the best ways to enjoy vegetables. Many traditional recipe books focus on one vegetable per dish, but a satisfying way to add more color and variety is to combine vegetables. Let parsnips enhance carrots, use celeriac to transform potatoes, and add fennel to brighten tomatoes. A wide variety of vegetables are represented in this section, but if you don't see your favorite produce, consider where it might be substituted for another ingredient. For example, chard can replace spinach, and leeks can fill in for onions. Any dish in this chapter can be altered in numerous ways. These recipes should be guides, not assignments.

But recipes aside, the beginning of any great dish is growing in your own garden or waiting for you at a farmers' market. At the Eugene farmers' market, I couldn't resist beets with their brilliant magenta root and bright green leaves from Horton Road Organics. Gentle steaming teases out their fresh earthy flavor. Add a little balsamic vinegar, but use only the best variety. Let your mind wander through flavor prospects each time you consider a vegetable.

As you dine from the local food basket, let the shift of the seasons steer your selection of side dishes. When the weather is mild and favorable, more variety is available, but through the winter, root vegetables and hearty greens become seasonal staples. Earthy Jerusalem artichokes, sweet carrots, and humble potatoes can be baked into savory gratins. Hearty Asian greens are easy to braise, and winter squashes with beets shine like jewels beside a casserole, pasta, or bean dish. In the spring, asparagus, artichokes, and pea vines revive our side dish variety, and in the summer the many vegetable opportunities make the farmers' market a treasure hunt for side dish candidates. Tiny 'Fairy Tale' eggplant from Gathering Together Farm and giant red and gold Italian peppers from Denison Farms were two great side dish prospects I found at the Wednesday Corvallis farmers' market in late summer.

I often glance through my own recipes and other recipe books before going to the market, and I let various side dish ideas inspire me as I shop. Bok Choy and Carrot Sauté from Jeff Miller at Willie Green's Organic Farm, Fava Bean Sauté from Denison Farms, and Suzi Fry's Quick Eggplant Parmesan from the Fry Family Farm are just a few of the farm-contributed side dish recipes you'll find here that might inspire your next trip to the market.

Japanese eggplant and potatoes for sale in the Fry Family Farm booth at the Ashland farmers' market

Extending the Seasons

A growing number of Northwest farmers have expanded their farming seasons by working through the winter. Continual multitasking, greenhouses, and year-round growing plans are the keys to their farming strategies. Two farms doing this are the Fry Family Farm in southern Oregon and Rent's Due Ranch in western Washington—both certified organic first-generation family farms.

Seeds for the Fry farm were sown decades ago when Steven Fry met his wife, Suzi, in Santa Cruz, California. "I used to plant flowers in his garden," Suzi told me. They got together and eventually moved north to Horse Creek, California, near the Klamath River with a group of "back to the land" types. "We had no electricity or running water and it was hard when we started a family," she added. So they moved north to Oregon, leased some land, and started farming.

In 1990, the Frys had one greenhouse and grew row crops on a few acres near Talent, about 10 minutes from Ashland. Their family and farm grew, and then unexpectedly the landlord decided to rent their farmland on a month-to-month basis. The Frys knew this arrangement wouldn't work, but suddenly, like magic, another piece of farmland was advertised for sale that same week. "Our land found us," said Suzi. Today, Steven and Suzi's five girls are grown, and the family farm is 65 acres with 10 greenhouses, a CSA program, and a cut-flower business that includes weekly flower shares for CSA program members who request them.

Suzi takes care of all the finances and coordinates the CSA program, farmers' market and retail sales, and florist deliveries, while Steven orchestrates field production and directs up to 20 workers during harvest season. Farm work doesn't always flow smoothly, and Steven often gets sidetracked fixing farm vehicles and machinery or repairing a water pipe someone backed over. Many skills are needed on the farm, and his years as an Army mechanic during the Vietnam War paid off with essential skills that help keep the farm going.

Since the farm has grown, one of Steven's biggest dilemmas is not getting to do as much actual farming anymore. "I'm the conductor of this orchestra now," he told me, standing on his tractor waving a wrench for the water pipe as he gazed over abundant fields of fennel, eggplant, melons, and corn. As their seasonal vegetable procession winds down in October with green beans, tomatoes, kale, and winter squash, the Frys deliver their last CSA boxes with the final flower bouquets—a mixture of safflower, dill, millet, hypericum, and spiraea blooms.

Taking only a week off at Christmas, Steven and Suzi are back in the greenhouses the first of January germinating seeds in a heating chamber and on warming tables. After the sprouted seeds are coddled in greenhouses till spring, the seedlings are transplanted to fields or prepped for plant sales where eager gardeners snap them up.

The Frys sell plant starts and cut flowers in early spring to the Ashland food co-op, local grocery stores, farmers' markets, and florists. They also offer bedding plants such as pansies, petunias, impatiens, and geraniums. They wrap up the plant-start season at the Master Gardener Spring Fair at the Jackson Country Fairgrounds near the end of April, and Suzi's beautifully arranged organic bouquets continue their colorful parade through the fall.

Organic flowers are now an essential part of their farm plan, and a few years ago, the Frys joined forces with Joan Thorndike, a local organic flower grower. Their goal was to provide a greater variety and better quality of flowers for CSA program customers, who can sign up to receive weekly flower deliveries. Organic blossoms from local growers like the Frys enrich farms and support native pollinators. Suzi also mentioned that most cut flowers sold in this country are imported (70 percent, according to the U.S. Department of Agriculture) and most come from Colombia and Ecuador, where they have been sprayed with toxic chemicals and grown under deplorable working conditions. This is one more reason to consider purchasing locally grown flowers.

Flowers and plant starts also launch the season at Rent's Due Ranch, a 45-acre organic farm in Stanwood, Washington, about an hour northwest of Seattle. Seventy thousand snow geese, bald eagles, and other migratory birds overwinter on the land while JoanE (E for Elizabeth) McIntyre and her husband, Michael Shriver, germinate seeds in greenhouses and then prep seedlings for spring sales.

JoanE and Michael grew up in Everett, just a half hour from Seattle. Neither one had farming roots, but Michael worked on farms and knew a lot about farming when he met JoanE. They started growing organic vegetables so their children would have good food, and it wasn't long before they generated a surplus. "I never really thought about farming as a career; it was all Michael," JoanE told me.

In 1980 they leased farmland on Fir Island, about three miles from where they are today. Their farm production grew there for 10 years, and they sold vegetables and berries at farmers' markets and to well-known Seattle chefs like Caprial Pence, Tom Douglas, and Kathy Casey. In the 1990s, PCC Natural Markets was also one of the farm's customers. Produce buyer Joe Hardiman was so impressed with the quality of their organic produce that PCC wooed Rent's Due Ranch away from their restaurant customers, and it became one of the first farms to supply PCC markets on a regular basis.

Then suddenly the pristine farmland they had been leasing was sold and carved up for a housing development. "That land was truly organic," said

Suzi Fry with Zeus, the Fry Family Farm dog

JoanE sadly. "Nothing had ever been there but a dairy farm, and now it's all houses." The insecurity of farming someone else's land is that the land can be snatched out from under the farmer. Luckily, they were able to locate and buy another piece of land a few miles away so they could continue farming.

Now three decades and four grown children later, Rent's Due Ranch has nine greenhouses. During harvest season, a semi truck drives up the narrow dirt driveway three times a week to transport Rent's Due vegetables to nine hungry Seattle PCC Natural Markets. And like at the Fry Family Farm, Rent's Due's seeds and flowers jump-start the season. Germinated in January, these plant starts are sold to nurseries, markets, and spring plant sales where they generate essential income, especially when spring rains delay their lettuce-planting schedule.

In late May or early June when rhubarb and asparagus appear at the University District farmers' market, JoanE arrives with trays of seedlings and flowers. She sets up heavy racks for tiny flowers and vegetable starts. Dressed in a denim jacket and vintage blouse, accented with a scarf and earrings that glitter, she works quickly, hoisting heavy trays and hanging fuchsias, smiling and making it look easy. Her blue eyes sparkle, and JoanE always shines as she chats about farming, food, or politics. Many market shoppers see JoanE as the first sign that spring has finally arrived.

At Rent's Due Ranch and the Fry Family Farm, a rainbow of vegetable and flower starts and hanging flowers lead the seasonal procession. Smiles spread across shoppers' faces at the farmers' market. Who can resist taking home a few plant starts for the promise of summer treasures?

JoanE McIntyre of Rent's Due Ranch at the University District farmers' market

FOOD FOR THOUGHT: BRINGING BEETS TO MARKET

At Nash Huber's farm in Sequim, Washington, farmworkers harvest beets by machine using a root digger—a tractor with an excavator attachment. The root digger pulls beets from the ground, removes the tops, and sends the roots up a conveyer belt that dumps them into bins on a truck driving alongside the tractor. It is a coordinated movement with two vehicles, and when the bins are filled, beets are transported to the packing shed and prepped for sale or put into storage for winter. Farm market workers bring a variety of beets (Chiogga, Detroit, cylinder, and golden) to the market year-round.

Locally Based Dips and Spreads

Vegetables, beans, and herbs that grow in the Northwest provide the ingredients to create salsas, dips, and spreads. A number of different kinds of dried beans have made appearances at Northwest farmers' markets. Make hummus with locally grown garbanzo beans or black bean salsa with black beans from the local market. Be creative and adapt your favorite dip recipes to include our Northwest bounty.

Tom's Fresh Tomatillo-Tomato Salsa

My husband, Tom, is the salsa maker at our house. Every salsa he makes is a little different. This recipe is one I wrote down after we both decided we liked that day's version. Some farms like Gathering Together Farm in Oregon and Billy's Gardens in Tonasket, Washington, make and sell their own fresh salsa at farmers' markets.

4 medium tomatillos, husked and chopped

½ cup minced sweet onion

1 medium tomato, chopped

1 cup peeled and diced cucumber

½ cup green salsa

½ cup chopped cilantro

¼ cup fresh lemon juice

Honey

Salt

Place the tomatillos, onion, tomato, cucumber, salsa, cilantro, and lemon juice in a blender, salsa maker, or food processor and briefly puree. Drizzle in honey and add salt to taste. Serve with chips. **Makes about 2 cups**

Easy Black Bean Dip

This black bean spread is so easy to make that you may get addicted to the recipe. Use your favorite salsa and farmstead cheese. Look for all the recipe ingredients at Northwest farmers' markets. Although I usually soak and cook black beans, you can get Northwest canned beans packed by the Salem-based Truitt Brothers in Oregon natural food stores.

1¾ cups cooked, drained black beans

¼ cup hot salsa

1 medium red onion, finely chopped

3 cloves garlic, pressed

Water, as needed, to thin

¼ cup chopped cilantro (optional)

⅓ cup sharp Cheddar cheese

1. Place the black beans and salsa in a blender or food processor and mix until creamy.

2. Stir in the onion and garlic, and thin to the desired consistency with water. Add the cilantro if desired and the cheese. Heat in a heavy skillet, stirring until the cheese melts. **Makes 2 cups**

Favamole

Fava beans are one of the specialty crops at Denison Farms in Corvallis. They grow a number of varieties, and their sweet favas inspired this unique version of guacamole. Look for favas at a farmers' market where you live. Remove the favas from the pods before blanching. There is no need to double-peel these beans if they are grown properly.

1½ cups fava beans, blanched

1 fresh jalapeño, minced

1 small avocado, peeled and pit removed

1 small sweet onion, diced

2 heaping tablespoons green salsa

2 tablespoons fresh lime juice

1 teaspoon honey

½ teaspoon salt

1 small tomato, finely chopped

2 tablespoons chopped cilantro

1. Place the fava beans and the jalapeño in a blender and puree.

2. Scrape the mixture into a bowl and mash the avocado in. Stir in the onion, salsa, lime juice, honey, and salt. Mix well. Gently fold in the tomato and cilantro. **Makes about 1¼ cups**

Baba Ghanouj

I can never get enough eggplant during summer months, and this Middle Eastern spread, adapted from a Fry Family Farm CSA newsletter, is one of my favorite ways to enjoy this vegetable. Lemon juice and zest add a zing to the flavor. Make it ahead and serve it with vegetables or crackers.

2 1-pound eggplants, halved lengthwise

2 to 4 tablespoons extra virgin olive oil

¼ cup tahini

¼ cup fresh lemon juice

Zest of 1 lemon, finely chopped

1 to 4 cloves garlic, minced

Salt and freshly ground pepper

Paprika

1. Preheat the oven to 375°F. Oil a baking sheet. Place the eggplant cut side down on the sheet. Roast until the eggplant is very soft, about 45 minutes. Cool slightly. Scoop out the pulp and allow to drain in a strainer for ½ hour.

2. Transfer the pulp to a blender or food processor. Add the oil, tahini, lemon juice, zest, and garlic and process until smooth. Season with salt and pepper to taste. Sprinkle with paprika before serving. **Makes about 1¾ cups**

Carrot Hummus

I first sampled carrot hummus at a farm lunch served at Nash's farm in Sequim, Washington. I was so impressed with the carrot version of this spread created by farm Chef Ankur Shah that I went home and made my own version.

- 1 cup cooked, drained garbanzos
- 1 cup sliced carrots, steamed
- ¼ cup tahini
- ¼ cup fresh lemon juice
- Zest of 1 lemon, finely chopped
- 1 to 3 teaspoons honey or agave nectar
- 2 to 4 cloves garlic, minced or pressed
- Pinch of ground cumin
- Pinch of cayenne (optional)
- Salt
- Chopped cilantro

1. Place the garbanzos, carrots, tahini, lemon juice, zest, 1 teaspoon honey or agave nectar, and garlic in a blender or food processor and puree until smooth.

2. Mix in the cumin and cayenne and add salt to taste. Add more honey if desired. Garnish with cilantro. **Makes 2 cups**

Winter Squash–Hazelnut Spread

This recipe is a great way to use winter squash. Kabocha, buttercup, and Hubbard squash are all good in this recipe. You can also substitute yams for the winter squash. Hazelnut butter is also a Northwest product; most of our nation's hazelnuts or filberts come from Oregon, where they have been grown for more than 100 years. Six hundred and fifty Oregon farm families cultivate these Northwest treasures.

- 2 cups baked, peeled, and mashed winter squash
- 2 tablespoons hazelnut butter
- 1½ tablespoons honey
- ¼ teaspoon salt
- 1 tablespoon red currants or fresh lemon juice
- 3 tablespoons finely chopped hazelnuts

1. Blend the squash, hazelnut butter, honey, and salt together with a hand blender until smooth and creamy.

2. Add the currants or drizzle with the lemon juice and stir in the hazelnuts. Spread on soft flour or crisp corn tortillas. **Makes 2 cups**

Spicy Seasonal Green Dip

When you have an overabundance of kale or collards from your garden or CSA box, this is the perfect recipe. If you have curly kale, blanch it before sautéing it or the dip may taste bitter. Use this dip as a spread for crisp corn or soft flour tortillas, serve it with chips, or offer it as a side dish. If fresh local hot peppers aren't available, use bottled peppers or a dash of cayenne.

2 tablespoons extra virgin olive oil

1 cup finely chopped shallots or onions

3 to 4 cloves garlic, minced or pressed

1 fresh jalapeño, seeded and finely chopped

6 cups chopped Tuscan (black) or Russian kale or collards

½ cup apple juice or cider

2 tablespoons fresh lemon juice or 1 tablespoon apple cider vinegar

2 tablespoons hazelnut or almond butter

Pinch of salt

Finely chopped hazelnuts, toasted (optional)

1. Heat a heavy skillet over medium heat. Add the oil, shallots or onions, garlic, and jalapeño. Stir and cook until the onions are soft and the garlic is lightly browned.

2. Mix in the greens, stir to coat with the oil, and add the apple juice or cider. Cover and cook until the greens are very soft, 20 to 25 minutes. Check every once in a while to make sure there is enough water. Add only a very small amount if needed.

3. Place the greens, lemon juice, hazelnut butter, and salt in a blender and puree until smooth and creamy. You can sprinkle with finely chopped hazelnuts for presentation if desired. **Makes about 1½ cups**

Harvesting greens at Whistling Duck Farm in Grants Pass, Oregon

The recipes in this section use a wide range of vegetables, and many of them can be made using vegetables other than those specified. For example, if you don't like squash, consider using sweet potatoes or yams, or if you want to make lemon-garlic sauce but don't have asparagus to put it on, try it on zucchini or eggplant slices. These recipes offer multiple opportunities to sample our Northwest harvest.

Asparagus with Mushrooms and Rhubarb

Rhubarb, asparagus, and morel mushrooms make this dish pure spring. I often get mushrooms from Donna Weston, a forager who calls her business "Wild Things" and sells her foraged mushrooms, nettles, and berries at the University District farmers' market. Donna was born into a foraging family in Washington and remembers picking alpine strawberries and mushrooms as a child. This recipe is adapted from one of Donna's. She uses morels but other kinds of mushrooms can also be used.

2 tablespoons extra virgin olive oil

1 tablespoon butter

1 pound asparagus, tough ends snapped off, tops left whole

½ pound morels, washed, trimmed, and halved

2 cups finely diced rhubarb

2 tablespoons honey

¼ teaspoon salt

Freshly ground pepper

1. Heat a heavy skillet over medium heat. Add the olive oil and butter. When the butter melts, stir in the asparagus and mushrooms and cook for 2 minutes.

2. Stir in the rhubarb and cook for 3 more minutes. The rhubarb will break down and create enough moisture so the asparagus and mushrooms don't burn.

3. Remove from the heat and stir in the honey, salt, and pepper to taste. Let this dish sit 5 minutes before serving. **Makes 4 servings**

Roasted Asparagus with Lemon-Garlic Sauce

Roasted asparagus absorbs the flavors of lemon and garlic in this recipe, and the tender spears practically melt in your mouth. When purchasing, select medium or large asparagus stalks. As for garlic, look for bulbs at Northwest markets or buy them in natural food stores for this spring recipe.

- 1 head garlic
- 2 tablespoons extra virgin olive oil, divided
- ¼ cup fresh lemon juice
- 1 tablespoon finely chopped lemon zest
- 1 tablespoon minced bottled hot peppers
- 1 teaspoon honey or agave nectar
- ½ teaspoon salt
- 2 pounds asparagus

1. Preheat the oven to 350°F. Cut the top off of the head of garlic and lay the head on a piece of foil. Drizzle 1 tablespoon of the olive oil over the garlic head. Wrap it in foil and bake until very tender, about 45 minutes. Let the garlic cool.

2. Press the roasted garlic out into a small bowl. Blend the garlic with the lemon juice and zest, hot peppers, honey or agave nectar, and salt.

3. Snap off the tough base of the asparagus stalks and lay the stalks in a shallow baking dish. Drizzle 1 tablespoon of the olive oil over the asparagus. Place the asparagus in the oven for about 5 minutes, then stir to coat each stalk with oil. Spoon half of the lemon-garlic sauce over the asparagus. Return to the oven for 20 to 25 minutes, stirring occasionally. When the asparagus is fork-tender, remove from the oven. Drizzle the remainder of the sauce over the asparagus. Serve warm or let cool and serve with a spring salad.
Serves 4 to 6

Farm Fresh Green Beans

Green beans are at their best when cooked simply. At Winter Green Farm in Noti, Oregon, farmer Jabrila Via makes a similar easy green bean recipe. She says her secret is to cook the beans just until they turn bright green. Another secret is to buy fresh, firm beans at the market, and when cooking, add a little olive oil so the butter doesn't accidentally brown.

- 1 pound green beans, ends removed and cut into 1-inch pieces (approximately 4 cups)
- 1 teaspoon extra virgin olive oil
- 3 tablespoons butter
- Salt and freshly ground pepper
- Fresh lemon juice

1. Heat a heavy skillet over medium heat. Add the olive oil and spread around the skillet, then add the butter.

2. When the butter has melted, add the green beans and stir constantly until they turn bright green.

3. Remove from the heat and sprinkle with salt and pepper to taste. Squeeze lemon juice over the beans before serving. **Serves 4**

Green Beans with Mushrooms

Mushrooms enhance green beans in this easy recipe adapted from one of forager Donna Weston's. I use porcini for this dish, but you can use another variety of mushroom if you want. If you don't have access to a forager's treasures at your farmers' market, check the natural food store.

4 cups trimmed and cut green beans, in 1-inch lengths

½ cup sliced mushrooms

¼ cup finely chopped onion

1 teaspoon extra virgin olive oil

2 tablespoons butter

2 tablespoons chopped fresh basil

Freshly ground pepper

½ cup Parmesan cheese (optional)

1. Steam the green beans in a saucepan until fork-tender. Drain and set aside.

2. In a skillet over medium-high heat, fry the mushrooms without oil until they begin to squeak and then lose their moisture. Stir them constantly so they don't burn. Reduce the heat to medium and add the onion, oil, and butter, and stir and cook until tender.

3. Stir in the drained green beans until each one is coated with butter and cook until warm. Sprinkle with pepper and Parmesan cheese if desired. **Serves 6**

Easy Shell Beans

Fresh shell beans, once hard to find at Northwest farmers' market, are becoming more available. Alm Hill Gardens in Everson, Washington, near the Canadian border, sells fresh organic shell beans at the Bellingham farmers' market and at various Seattle markets. Ayers Creek Farm in Gaston, Oregon, sells organic Vermont cranberry, cannellini, and flageolet beans at the Hillsdale farmers' market. Fresh shell beans don't keep as long as dried beans, so use them within a few days or freeze them.

1 cup fresh or soaked dried shell beans

½ strip kombu (optional)

2 cups water

1 tablespoon extra virgin olive oil

1 large onion, chopped, or 1 cup chopped shallots

1 fresh jalapeño, chopped

2 cloves garlic, pressed

1 red, yellow, or green bell pepper, seeded and chopped (optional)

Salt and freshly ground pepper

1. Place the beans and the optional kombu (a sea vegetable that helps insure digestibility) in a medium saucepan with the water and bring to a boil over high heat. Reduce the heat and simmer until the beans are soft, an hour or more.

2. Heat a heavy skillet over medium heat. Add the olive oil, onion, and jalapeño. Stir and cook until the onion and pepper are soft. Add the garlic and bell pepper. Continue cooking until the pepper becomes soft. Stir in the cooked beans. Season with salt and pepper to taste. **Serves 4**

Orange-Beet Puree

Buying beets is a produce bonus because you get two vegetables in one—the greens and the roots. You can find beets throughout Oregon and Washington; any kind will do in this dish. This sweet puree goes well with savory casseroles and lightly steamed beet greens. This is a great side dish for a summer picnic or supporting character for a Thanksgiving dinner.

> 6 medium beets, sliced ¼ inch thick
>
> Juice and finely chopped zest of 1 orange
>
> ½ tablespoon fresh lemon juice
>
> ¼ cup raisins or currants
>
> 2 to 4 tablespoons chopped walnuts, toasted

1. Steam the beets in a saucepan until tender, about 20 minutes.

2. Puree the orange juice and zest, lemon juice, and cooked beets in a blender or food processor until smooth. Stir in the currants or raisins and garnish with walnuts. **Serves 4**

Roasted Rosemary Beets with Horseradish Sauce

I knew only canned beets as a child, but now fresh beets appear on my regular market shopping list. When beets are roasted, the sugar in them caramelizes, making them even sweeter. Horseradish sauce adds the perfect flavor to balance the sweet, earthy taste. If you don't care for tofu or can't eat soy, make the sauce with ½ cup plain yogurt and omit the lemon juice.

> 6 medium-large beets
>
> 2 tablespoons extra virgin olive oil
>
> ½ to 1 teaspoon dried rosemary, crushed
>
> Salt and freshly ground pepper
>
> ½ cup soft silken tofu or plain yogurt
>
> 2 tablespoons lemon juice
>
> 1 teaspoon finely chopped lemon zest
>
> ½ tablespoon Dijon mustard
>
> 1 teaspoon prepared horseradish
>
> 1 teaspoon sugar or honey
>
> 1 teaspoon extra virgin olive oil

1. Preheat the oven to 350°F. Cut the beets into small cubes and combine with the olive oil and rosemary in a baking pan, blending well. Season with salt and pepper to taste. Bake until fork-tender, 35 to 45 minutes, stirring occasionally.

2. While the beets roast, prepare the horseradish sauce. Blend the tofu (or yogurt), lemon juice (if using tofu), zest, horseradish, sugar or honey, and olive oil in a blender or with a hand blender until smooth and creamy.

3. When the beets are tender, serve with a dollop of sauce on top. **Serves 6**

Spicy Sesame Beets and Greens with Rice

I made this recipe using jasmine rice for years until I stopped at the San Francisco Ferry Plaza farmers' market and bought rice from an organic rice farmer (Massa Organics). I loved this rice so much I now order it from their Web site. Visiting farmers' markets when you travel outside the Northwest is a great way to make sweet and savory food connections with farmers who sell foods that grow outside our region. Look for beet greens and beets at any Northwest farmers' market.

- 1 bunch of beets, roots and greens, separated and washed
- 1¾ cups water
- 1 cup rice (your favorite variety), rinsed
- Pinch of salt
- ½ tablespoon extra virgin olive oil
- 1 large onion, diced, or 1 cup chopped shallots
- 5 cloves garlic, pressed
- ¼ cup water
- 2 tablespoons fresh lemon juice
- ½ tablespoon tamari
- Freshly ground pepper
- 3 tablespoons chopped hazelnuts, toasted

1. Cut the beets into ¼-inch slices and the leaves on the diagonal in about 1-inch lengths. Set aside.

2. Bring the water to a boil in a medium saucepan over high heat. Add the rice and salt and bring to a second boil. Reduce the heat, cover, and cook on low until the rice is done and the water has been absorbed, about 45 minutes. Add more water or cook longer uncovered if necessary. Remove from the heat and fluff the rice with a fork.

3. About 15 minutes before the rice is done, heat a heavy skillet over medium heat. Add the oil and onion. Stir, reduce the heat, cover, and cook until the onions are soft. Add the garlic, stir, and continue to cook for another minute. Add the sliced beets and ¼ cup water. Stir, cover, and cook until the beets are tender, 5 to 7 minutes.

4. When the beets are nearly done, add the greens and cook until wilted, 2 to 3 minutes. Blend in the lemon juice and tamari. Season with pepper to taste. Serve over rice and top with toasted hazelnuts. **Serves 4**

Nash Huber's carrots and beets at the University District market

Bok Choy and Carrot Sauté

This recipe is adapted from one created by Jeff Miller at Willie Green's Organic Farm in Monroe, Washington. Visit the farmers' market near you and check out farm booths for baby carrots and bok choy. Nash's Organic Produce in Sequim, Washington, Springwater Farm in St. Helens, Oregon, and Mad Creek Mushrooms in Gates, Oregon, grow and sell organic shiitake mushrooms.

- **1 teaspoon extra virgin olive oil**
- **2 tablespoons butter**
- **1 or 2 cloves garlic, minced**
- **2 shiitake mushrooms, sliced ¼ inch thick**
- **2 bunches baby bok choy, halved and rinsed**
- **1 bunch baby carrots, left whole or halved**
- **Salt and freshly ground pepper**
- **Fresh lemon juice (optional)**

1. Heat a heavy skillet over medium-high heat. Add the oil, butter, garlic, and mushrooms and cook, stirring constantly, until the mushrooms begin to soften.

2. Add the bok choy and carrots. Stir and cook over medium heat until the carrots and bok choy are tender, adding a little broth or water if necessary. Season with salt and pepper to taste and add a squeeze of lemon juice if desired. **Serves 4**

Broccoli and Lemon-Saffron Rice

For this dish, you can use broccoli sold at farmers' markets in the summer or try the chartreuse Romanesco cauliflower with ornate conical florets in the fall.

- **1¾ cups water**
- **1 cup rice (your favorite variety)**
- **2 pinches saffron threads**
- **1 tablespoon finely chopped lemon zest**
- **¼ cup fresh lemon juice, divided**
- **½ tablespoon honey**
- **½ teaspoon salt**
- **Pinch of cayenne**
- **4 cups broccoli florets, blanched**
- **½ cup thinly sliced green onions**
- **Red or pink currants (optional)**
- **½ cup chopped hazelnuts, toasted (optional)**

1. Bring the water to a boil in a saucepan over high heat and add the rice, saffron, lemon zest, 2 tablespoons lemon juice, honey, salt, and cayenne. Stir once, bring to a second boil, then reduce the heat, cover, and simmer until the rice is done and all the water has been absorbed, about 45 minutes.

2. Remove the rice from the heat and let it sit 5 minutes. Then fluff with a fork and stir in the remaining lemon juice and the blanched broccoli. Stir in the green onions and garnish with currants and hazelnuts if desired. **Serves 6 to 8**

Brussels Sprouts and Caramelized Onions

I first tasted fresh Brussels sprouts pulled from the stalk in a CSA box from Willie Green's one fall. I fell in love with the sweet, fresh flavor, and I'm sure other people would, too, if they tasted fresh Northwest-grown Brussels sprouts. Brussels sprouts become sweeter as the temperature dips, so I wait until after the first frost to buy them. I sometimes sprinkle raspberry vinegar over the cooked sprouts for an exotic flavor.

1 tablespoon extra virgin olive oil

1 large onion, sliced, or 1 cup diced shallot

1 pound Brussels sprouts, halved

2 cloves garlic, pressed

¼ cup stock or water

Salt and cayenne

1. Heat a heavy skillet over medium heat. Add the oil and onion or shallot, stir, cover, reduce the heat, and sweat the onion until soft. Remove the lid and continue to cook the onions until caramelized. Add the garlic, stir, and cook for 1 minute.

2. Add the Brussels sprouts and stir to coat with oil and garlic. Add the stock or water, cover, and cook until the sprouts are bright green. Sample the sprouts for desired tenderness at 4 minutes. Season with salt and cayenne to taste. **Serves 4**

TIPS ON BLANCHING VEGETABLES

Before blanching vegetables like broccoli or green beans, cut the vegetables into ½- to 1-inch pieces. For tomatoes and peaches, cut an X on the bottom so the skins will peel off easily. Plunge the produce into boiling water, trying not to disturb the boil. How long to blanch is determined by the size, type, and degree of ripeness of the produce.

To prepare broccoli, peel large or tough stems and cut into 1-inch lengths. The tops cook more quickly, so blanch the stems for a minute or so before adding the tops. Blanch for 1 more minute.

Broccoli from Nash's Organic Produce at the University District farmers' market

Lemon Brussels Sprouts

Lemon enhances so many vegetables that I can't resist squeezing a little over anything new. If you want to eat only locally grown fruits and vegetables, some Northwest gardeners and farmers grow and sell Meyer lemons. Look for some at the Saturday Portland farmers' market, or if you want to plant a lemon tree of your own, check nurseries like Raintree in Morton, Washington.

1 pound Brussels sprouts, cut in half

2 tablespoons butter

¼ cup fresh lemon juice

1 teaspoon honey or agave nectar

Salt and freshly ground pepper

1. Steam the Brussels sprouts in a saucepan until tender, about 5 minutes. Remove from the heat and set aside.

2. While the Brussels sprouts cook, combine the butter, lemon juice, and honey or agave nectar. Toss with the Brussels sprouts in a serving bowl. Season with salt and pepper to taste.

Serves 4

Burdock, Carrots, and Leeks

Burdock is an Asian specialty vegetable with a reputation for its detoxifying and health-giving properties. This humble brown root is one of the specialty crops grown at Winter Green Farm in Noti and Whistling Duck Farm in Grants Pass, both in Oregon. Leeks add a bit of sweetness to this recipe. They are easier to wash after they have been sliced. The carrots also sweeten the earthy burdock.

2 cups water

½ teaspoon salt

2 tablespoons rice vinegar

2 medium burdock roots (½ to ¾ pound), peeled and grated

1 tablespoon extra virgin olive oil

1 tablespoon butter (optional)

1 medium leek, white part only, sliced thin and washed thoroughly

1 cup grated carrots

¼ cup sake or white wine

1 teaspoon honey

Generous pinch of nutmeg

Salt and freshly ground pepper

Finely chopped curly parsley

1. Combine the water, salt, and vinegar in a bowl and add the grated burdock root.

2. Heat a heavy skillet over medium heat. Add the oil, butter if desired, and leek. Stir and cook until softened, about 5 minutes.

3. Drain the burdock and add to the skillet along with the grated carrots. Cook for about

3 minutes, then add the wine and honey. Cook until the burdock is tender but still has some bite and texture to it. Add more water if necessary. Season with nutmeg, add salt and pepper to taste, and sprinkle with parsley. **Serves 4**

Braised Cabbage with Honey-Mustard Sauce

When I was young, I feasted on steamed cabbage with mustard mixed with honey and a little butter. In the Northwest you can find cabbage through much of the winter at year-round farmers' markets like Hillsdale in Portland and Ballard in Seattle.

- **2 tablespoons extra virgin olive oil**
- **4 cloves garlic, minced**
- **1 tablespoon chopped bottled hot peppers (optional)**
- **4 cups shredded green cabbage (any variety)**
- **¼ cup water**
- **¼ cup Dijon mustard**
- **¼ cup honey**
- **Salt and freshly ground pepper**

1. Heat a heavy skillet over medium heat. Add the oil, garlic, and peppers if desired. Stir and cook for about 1 minute. Add the cabbage and stir, then add the water, cover, reduce the heat, and cook until the cabbage is soft, about 5 minutes.

2. While the cabbage cooks, blend the mustard and honey together. Blend with the cabbage in a serving bowl and season with salt and pepper to taste. **Serves 4**

Red Cabbage with Apples and Red Wine Vinegar

Red cabbage adds color and pairs beautifully with sweet-tart apples like the organic Prairie Spy apples from Grouse Mountain Farm in Chelan, Washington. Some Northwest farmers like Nash Huber in Sequim, Washington, sell green cabbage and red cabbage.

- **1 medium tart or sweet-tart apple, peeled and cored**
- **2 tablespoons fresh lemon juice**
- **2 tablespoons extra virgin olive oil**
- **1 large onion, chopped**
- **1 fresh jalapeño, seeded and minced (optional)**
- **2 cloves garlic, pressed**
- **3 cups finely shredded red cabbage**
- **¼ cup red wine vinegar**
- **¼ cup sugar (brown or white)**
- **¼ cup water**
- **Salt and freshly ground pepper**

1. Grate the apple, toss it with lemon juice, and set aside.

2. Heat a heavy skillet over medium heat. Add the oil, onion, and jalapeño. Stir, reduce the heat, cover, and sweat the onion and pepper until soft. Add the garlic, stir, and cook for a few more minutes. Add the shredded apple, cabbage, vinegar, sugar, and water.

3. Cover and cook on medium-low heat until the cabbage is soft, about 10 to 15 minutes. Season with salt and pepper to taste. **Serves 6**

Carrots with Fennel and Hazelnuts

Carrots are a sweet, popular vegetable that pairs well with fennel, and this simple recipe can easily impress company. Toast fennel seeds in a skillet over medium heat until fragrant, and then use a spice grinder or mortar and pestle to crush the toasted seeds. (You can toast more fennel seeds than you need and store them in a jar in the pantry for a few months to use in soups and with vegetables.)

  2 cups thinly sliced carrots

  ¼ cup water

  1 teaspoon toasted, ground fennel seeds

  2 tablespoons maple syrup

  1 tablespoon cold water

  1 tablespoon arrowroot powder

  Salt and freshly ground pepper

  2 tablespoons chopped hazelnuts or walnuts, toasted

1. Steam or blanch the carrots in a saucepan until tender-crisp. Drain, reserving ¼ cup water. Add the water back to the pan.

2. Combine the ground fennel, maple syrup, cold water, and arrowroot. Mix in with the carrots and water. Gently heat, stirring until the mixture thickens and the carrots are fork-tender. Season with salt and pepper to taste and garnish with nuts. **Serves 4**

Sweet and Sour Carrots with Parsnips

Sweet and succulent, carrots and earthy-flavored parsnips can team up in recipes, and both are available through the winter. This recipe makes a refreshing sweet-tart side dish that goes well with many entrees.

  3½ cups sliced carrots

  1 to 2 tablespoons extra virgin olive oil or butter

  ½ cup finely chopped red onion

  1 cup diced parsnips

  2 tablespoons red wine vinegar

  2 tablespoons maple syrup

  Salt and freshly ground pepper

1. Steam the carrots in a saucepan until tender-crisp. Remove from the heat and set aside.

2. Heat a heavy skillet over medium heat. Add the oil, red onion, and parsnips. Stir and cook until the onion and parsnips are soft and slightly browned.

3. Add the red wine vinegar and maple syrup, and stir to coat the vegetables. Mix in the carrots and cook until they are heated through. Season with salt and pepper to taste. **Serves 4**

Simple Corn-on-the-Cob

Cook corn as soon as possible after picking or the taste becomes bland rather than sweet. You can combine spices like chili powder and chipotle chile powder with the butter for a spicy corn flavor. Or try blending a little balsamic vinegar and mayonnaise together and brush on for a more exotic taste.

- 4 ears corn
- 2 tablespoons butter
- Salt and freshly ground pepper

Steam the corn in a large pan for 4 to 7 minutes, depending on size and age. Brush with butter and season with salt and pepper to taste. **Serves 4**

Japanese eggplant and potatoes for sale in the Fry Family Farm booth at the Ashland farmers' market

Suzi Fry's Quick Eggplant Parmesan

At the Fry Family Farm near Grants Pass, Oregon, Suzi and Steven Fry grow lots of tomatoes, eggplant, and peppers to sell at the farmers' market in the summer. They cultivate the more familiar elongated or pear-shaped variety as well as Japanese eggplants, which are thin and tapered. Suzi always includes eggplant recipes on her Web site for CSA program members in the summer. This is an adaptation of Suzi's favorite recipe.

- ¼ cup extra virgin olive oil
- 1 large eggplant or 2 Japanese eggplants, sliced ¼ inch thick
- 2 eggs, beaten
- 1½ cups Italian bread crumbs
- 2 cups tomato or pasta sauce
- Mozzarella cheese, grated
- Parmesan cheese
- Chopped basil leaves

1. Preheat the oven to 350°F. Heat the oil in a heavy skillet over medium heat.

2. Dip the eggplant slices into the egg and then the breadcrumbs. Fry in the hot oil. You may need to add more oil since the eggplant really absorbs it. Cook all the breaded eggplant slices until tender and golden.

3. Place the eggplant in a baking dish and cover with the tomato sauce. Top with grated mozzarella and Parmesan cheese. Bake until the cheese is browned, about 15 minutes. Sprinkle with the basil leaves. **Serves 4**

Fava Bean Sauté

This recipe comes from Elizabeth Kerle at Denison Farms in Corvallis, who says you can also just blanch and serve favas plain for a healthy, satisfying snack. In this recipe, blanching makes a little more work, but the rewards are worth the extra labor.

> 2 pounds fava beans
>
> 1 tablespoon extra virgin olive oil
>
> ½ sweet onion, diced
>
> 1 clove garlic, minced
>
> 1 bunch chard or other greens, washed, rolled, and sliced thin
>
> 1 teaspoon tamari

1. To blanch the favas, remove the beans from the shell, drop them into a large pot of boiling water, and boil for 30 seconds. Drain and cover the favas with cold water. Set aside.

2. Heat a heavy skillet over medium heat. Add the oil, onion, and garlic. Sauté until soft.

3. Add the fava beans, chard, and tamari to the skillet. Stir and cook until tender, adding a small amount of water if necessary. **Serves 4 to 6**

Roasted Fennel

In this easy recipe adapted from one online at the Fry Family Farm Web site, fennel gets a sweet tang from balsamic vinegar that helps it caramelize as it roasts. I like to use Fini balsamic vinegar, but you can use your own favorite brand. Sprinkle with a little parsley and serve this as a delicious side dish.

> 2 fennel bulbs, crowns cut off, bulbs sliced ⅛ inch thick
>
> 1 to 2 tablespoons extra virgin olive oil
>
> 1 tablespoon balsamic vinegar
>
> Salt and freshly ground pepper

1. Preheat the oven to 400°F. Place the fennel slices in a baking dish and drizzle with the oil and balsamic vinegar. Stir to coat. Season with salt and pepper to taste.

2. Roast until the fennel begins to caramelize or brown, 15 to 20 minutes. **Serves 4**

Kia Armstrong picking fava beans at Nash's organic farm in Sequim, Washington

Lemon-Glazed Jerusalem Artichokes

The lemon juice, butter, and sugar in this recipe help tame the strong earthy tones of Jerusalem artichokes, which you can find in the fall and winter at Northwest farmers' markets.

1 pound Jerusalem artichokes, thinly sliced (about 3 cups)

¼ cup fresh lemon juice, divided

½ teaspoon extra virgin olive oil

2 tablespoons butter

Pinch of cayenne

1 tablespoon finely chopped lemon zest

½ tablespoon sugar

Salt

1. Plunge the artichokes into water with 2 tablespoons lemon juice. Heat the oil, butter, and cayenne in a skillet over medium heat. Drain the artichokes and add them to the skillet. Stir and cook until they are soft and begin to brown.

2. Combine the remaining lemon juice with the lemon zest and sugar. Mix in with the artichokes and continue to cook for another few minutes. Season with salt to taste. **Serves 4**

Kale Chips

This recipe is dedicated to my good friend and longtime fellow market shopper Sam Fain, who passed away much too young in 2009. Sam and his wife, Patty, shopped at the University District farmers' market and cultivated many relationships with the farmers there. This recipe is one of Sam's favorites, and Patty says it can make anyone a kale convert. Use Tuscan, not curly, kale for this recipe. Use an oil spray or gently rub olive or safflower oil on the leaves with your hands, taking care not to add too much oil. These chips can quickly go from crisp to burned, so pay attention, especially during the last few minutes of roasting. Enjoy them while still warm, as they don't save very well.

1 bunch Tuscan (black) kale

Olive or safflower oil

Salt or dehydrated garlic

1. Preheat the oven to 400°F. Rinse the kale and pat dry. Strip the kale leaves from the stems with a knife or your hand and tear the leaves into bite-size pieces.

2. Lay the kale flat on baking sheets and don't overlap any pieces. Spray with oil.

3. Place in the oven for 4 minutes, then remove, stir the chips, and return to the oven. Each chip should be separate so all can get crisp.

4. When the edges begin to brown, test for crispness before transferring to a serving platter. Sprinkle with salt or dehydrated garlic. **Serves 2 to 4**

Braised Kale with Leeks and Apples

Many people are unfamiliar with braising, an easy cooking technique that uses a small amount of liquid in a covered pan. First, sauté onions or vegetables with a little oil. Then stir in not more than a half cup of liquid and cover a few minutes or until the vegetables are tender. You can use any kind of liquid for braising. For this recipe, I use Rockridge Orchards sweet apple cider. You can substitute hard cider or white wine for variety. (If you choose the curly kale, be sure to blanch it briefly before sautéing or it will be bitter.)

- 1 to 2 tablespoons extra virgin olive oil
- 2 leeks, white part only, sliced thin and washed thoroughly
- 2 cloves garlic, minced or pressed
- Dash of bottled hot sauce
- 1 bunch kale (Tuscan, curly, or Russian)
- ¼ cup apple cider
- 1 small sweet-tart apple, cored and diced
- ½ teaspoon salt
- 2 tablespoons fresh lemon juice (optional)

1. Heat a heavy skillet over medium heat. Add the oil and leeks, stir, cover, reduce the heat, and cook until the onions are soft. Remove the lid and continue to cook until slightly browned. Stir in the garlic and hot sauce. Cook for a few minutes.

2. Strip the kale leaves from the stems with a knife or your hand. Roll and thinly slice. Add to the skillet and stir in the cider and apples. Cover and braise until the kale and apples are tender. Season with the salt and add lemon juice if desired. **Serves 4**

Gingered Kohlrabi

Kohlrabi is a member of the turnip family, and it's been around for a long time though not many people are familiar with it. Fresh kohlrabi can be found year-round, and this recipe is simply perfect when you also find fresh ginger at the farmers' market in late summer and fall. If it isn't fall, or you can't find ginger at the market, check the produce section of the grocery store. You can also add a cup of grated carrots to this recipe for color and sweetness.

- ½ teaspoon extra virgin olive oil
- 1 to 2 tablespoons butter
- 1½ pounds kohlrabi, peeled and diced
- 1 teaspoon minced ginger
- 2 teaspoons honey or agave nectar
- 1 tablespoon fresh lemon juice or rice vinegar
- Salt and freshly ground pepper

1. Heat a heavy skillet over medium heat. Add the oil, butter, and kohlrabi. Stir and cook until tender, about 5 minutes.

2. While the kohlrabi cooks, blend the ginger with the honey or agave nectar and the lemon juice or rice vinegar. Add to the cooked kohlrabi and stir to coat. Season with salt and pepper to taste. **Serves 4**

Wine-Braised Okra with Rice

Use the first okra of the season for this recipe. Okra and tomatoes were meant to be together, and tiny new okra has a fantastic sweet taste with very little of the sticky, slippery texture of more mature okra.

- 1 tablespoon extra virgin olive oil
- 2 tablespoons butter
- ½ cup finely chopped shallots or sweet onions
- 1 tablespoon chopped bottled hot peppers
- 1 pound whole baby okra, rinsed
- ½ cup red wine (Merlot is a good choice)
- 2 medium tomatoes, blanched, peeled, and chopped
- 1 teaspoon maple syrup
- Salt
- 2½ cups cooked rice (your favorite kind)
- ½ cup grated aged cheese

1. Heat a heavy skillet over medium heat. Add the oil, butter, shallots or onions, and peppers. Stir and cook until the shallots or onions are soft.

2. Add the okra, stir, and cook for a minute or so before blending in the wine, tomatoes, and maple syrup. Cover and cook until the okra is tender, about 10 minutes. Add salt to taste. Mix in the cooked rice and sprinkle with the cheese. **Serves 4**

Heirloom tomatoes from Denison Farms at the Corvallis Wednesday farmers' market

Curried Parsnips

Looking like off-white carrots, parsnips are an earthy-sweet, nutty-tasting fall and winter crop. Like Brussels sprouts and kale, they become sweeter the colder it gets outside. You don't really need to peel the parsnips here, but it makes them look nicer when cooking for dinner guests. You can also use carrots, sweet potatoes, or delicata squash for part of the parsnips in this recipe. If you use squash, cut it into ½-inch slices.

1 pound parsnips, peeled, cut into 2-inch matchsticks

1 to 2 tablespoons extra virgin olive oil

2 teaspoons curry powder

⅛ teaspoon cayenne

½ teaspoon salt

1. Preheat the oven to 350°F. Place the parsnips in a shallow baking dish and toss with the oil and curry powder, making sure the curry powder is well distributed. Sprinkle with the cayenne.

2. Bake until the parsnips are soft and browned, about 45 minutes. Sprinkle with the salt, stir, and serve. **Serves 4**

Parsnip and Roasted Garlic Puree

Try this easy parsnip puree instead of mashed potatoes for a change of pace. When you puree parsnips, there is no need to peel them first. If you like foods hot and spicy, add some chopped pickled jalapeño or hot bottled peppers.

2 heads garlic

2 tablespoons extra virgin olive oil, divided

2 pounds parsnips, sliced ½ inch thick

⅛ cup light cream or soy milk

½ cup chopped chives or green onions

½ to 1 tablespoon maple syrup

1 to 2 tablespoons fresh lemon juice

Salt and freshly ground pepper

1. Preheat the oven to 350°F. Cut the tops off of the heads of garlic and lay the heads on a piece of foil. Drizzle 1 tablespoon oil over the garlic heads. Wrap them in foil and bake until very tender, about 45 minutes. Let the garlic cool and press it out into a small bowl.

2. Steam the parsnips in a saucepan until very soft. Mash with the remaining oil, garlic, cream or soy milk, chives or green onions, maple syrup, and lemon juice. Continue to mash until smooth and creamy. Add more lemon juice if desired. Season with salt and pepper to taste. **Serves 6**

Pepper-Feta Kale

Cheryl Harrison of the Skagit Valley Co-op shared this recipe that's absolutely perfect when red and yellow bell peppers appear at markets in the fall. Denison Farms in Corvallis sells the biggest and sweetest red and yellow peppers I've ever tasted. At some markets, farmers grill peppers to sell; using already-grilled peppers cuts cooking time for this dish. I have also found fresh feta cheese at the Ballard and the University District markets in Seattle.

- 3 large red bell peppers
- 1 to 2 tablespoons extra virgin olive oil
- 1 red onion, chopped
- 6 cloves garlic, minced
- 2 small yellow or orange bell peppers, diced
- 1 teaspoon minced fresh rosemary
- 8 cups chopped Tuscan (black) or Russian kale
- ¾ cup or more crumbled fresh feta

1. Grill the red peppers on a grill or under a broiler until the skin becomes blistered and turns black. Place the peppers in a paper bag until cool, peel the skins off, seed, cut into bite-size pieces, and set aside.

2. Heat a heavy skillet over medium heat. Add the oil, onion, garlic, yellow or orange peppers, and rosemary, and sauté until the peppers begin to soften. Add the kale and cover. Stir occasionally. When the kale is tender, place in a serving dish with the red peppers, sprinkle with the feta cheese, and gently blend. **Serves 4 to 6**

Mashed Potatoes with Celeriac and Parsley

Mashed potatoes are pure comfort food. There are many varieties of potatoes at farmers' markets, so take your pick for this recipe. You don't need anything expensive or fancy—I prefer the basic organic red or white potatoes like those from Rent's Due Ranch in Stanwood, Washington. Rent's Due Ranch also sells great-tasting curly parsley and celeriac that pairs perfectly with potatoes. Peel the knobby celeriac root carefully with a paring knife.

- 1 pound celeriac, peeled and cut into medium dice
- 1 pound potatoes, peeled and cut into medium dice
- 4 cloves garlic, peeled
- ¼ cup butter
- 1 teaspoon vinegar
- 2 to 4 tablespoons cream
- Salt and freshly ground pepper
- ¼ cup crumbled blue cheese
- ¼ cup chopped curly parsley

1. Steam the celeriac, potatoes, and garlic cloves until tender, about 15 minutes.

2. Mash the vegetables with the butter, vinegar, and 2 tablespoons cream. Add more cream if desired. Season with salt and pepper to taste. Blend in the blue cheese and parsley. **Serves 4 to 6**

Potato and Jerusalem Artichoke Gratin with Porcini Mushrooms

This earthy Jerusalem artichoke gratin is enhanced with potatoes and mushrooms. Look for Jerusalem artichokes in the fall, though some farmers continue to harvest them through spring. Check foragers' booths for dried porcini mushrooms; if you can't find them at the market, try specialty or natural food stores. Some farmers process and sell dehydrated garlic at markets.

1 cup dried porcini mushrooms

1½ cups boiling water

2 tablespoons extra virgin olive oil

2 pounds Jerusalem artichokes, scrubbed and sliced ¼ inch thick

½ teaspoon salt

½ teaspoon dehydrated garlic

1 sprig fresh rosemary

2 tablespoons rice vinegar

2 tablespoons arrowroot powder

1½ pound potatoes, thinly sliced

1 large carrot, thinly sliced

1½ cup aged cheese (Cheddar or Gouda)

¼ cup crumbled Gorgonzola cheese (optional)

Freshly ground pepper

1. Pour the boiling water over the mushrooms in a bowl and set aside for 30 minutes.

2. Heat a heavy skillet over medium heat. Add the oil and when it's hot, add the Jerusalem artichokes, stir, and cook until browned.

3. Preheat the oven to 350°F. Drain the mushrooms and then combine with the salt, garlic, and rosemary. In a separate small bowl, combine the vinegar and arrowroot, then stir into the mushrooms. Add the whole mixture to the Jerusalem artichokes and cook for a few minutes.

4. Place half the Jerusalem artichokes in a 1 ½-quart casserole dish. Layer with the potatoes, carrot, and 1 cup of the aged cheese. Top with the remaining Jerusalem artichokes. Cover and bake until the carrots and potatoes are tender, about 45 minutes.

5. Sprinkle the remaining cheese over the top and place the gratin under the broiler until the top is brown and crispy. Garnish with Gorgonzola cheese if desired and serve with crusty artisan bread. **Serves 4**

Romanesco with Northwest Berry Vinegar

Romanesco is classified as a cauliflower and wears a broccoli label, but no matter what you call it, this vegetable is sweet and delicious. This recipe uses berry vinegar; you can purchase it from the store but farmers and vendors make and sell it at some Northwest markets. In Washington, Rent's Due Ranch sells raspberry vinegar with a sprig of rosemary added, and Rockridge Orchards makes berry-apple vinegar, fermented naturally on the farm. Both are sold at the University District farmers' market.

 1½ pounds Romanesco (1 average head), cut into bite-size pieces

 2 tablespoons butter

 ¼ cup finely chopped shallot or onion

 2 tablespoons raspberry vinegar

 Salt and freshly ground pepper

1. Blanch the pieces of Romanesco in a large pot of boiling water until fork-tender, just a few minutes. Remove from the heat, drain, and rinse with cold water to stop the cooking process.

2. Heat the butter in a heavy skillet over medium heat. Add the shallot or onion and cook until soft and lightly browned. Stir in the raspberry vinegar. Then blend in the Romanesco and add salt and freshly ground pepper to taste. **Serves 4**

Roasted Rutabaga Puree with Red Currants

Rutabagas can easily replace potatoes and are much more nutritious. In this recipe I use red currants, fresh frozen from summer's harvest, and they sparkle like jewels. This specialty crop can sometimes be found next to berries at farm booths in the summer. If you don't have red currants, try dried sour cherries or cranberries that you've rehydrated by pouring boiling water over them and allowing them to soak until they plump up, about an hour.

 ½ teaspoon extra virgin olive oil

 2 tablespoons butter, melted

 2 tablespoons maple syrup

 2 pounds rutabagas, peeled and sliced ¼ inch thick

 ¼ cup milk (dairy or soy)

 Salt and freshly ground pepper

 1 or 2 tablespoons red currants, fresh or frozen

1. Preheat the oven to 350°F. Combine the oil, butter, and maple syrup in a small bowl.

2. Lay the rutabaga slices flat on a baking sheet. Use a pastry brush to baste with the oil mixture. Bake until lightly browned, about 45 minutes, turning halfway through. Baste frequently using all of the basting liquid.

3. Remove from the oven, season with salt and freshly ground pepper to taste, and let cool for about 10 minutes. Place in a mixing bowl and mash with the milk until smooth and creamy.

4. Place in a small casserole dish, season with salt and pepper to taste, and blend in the currants. Return to the oven and bake for another 10 minutes. **Serves 4**

Curried Rutabaga

I invented this dish after I enjoyed a curried turnip side dish at an Indian restaurant. The lemon juice adds an acidic tang, but mild rice vinegar also works in this dish. Garam masala is a sweet curry blend that you can find in natural food stores and ethnic markets.

1 pound rutabagas, cut into chunks (about 4 cups)

1 teaspoon garam masala

1 tablespoon sugar

Pinch of cayenne

2 tablespoons lemon juice or rice vinegar

2 to 3 tablespoons butter

Salt

Steam the rutabaga until very tender, about 10 minutes. Puree it with the remaining ingredients. **Serves 4**

FOOD FOR THOUGHT: HOW RUTABAGAS AND TURNIPS DIFFER

Rutabagas and turnips are often thrown into the same category. To a novice vegetable shopper, the two can easily be confused because they are usually right next to each other in the produce department. Turnips have a light skin that is purple and white. Inside, the flesh is white. The taste is sharp and radishlike. Rutabagas are sweeter than turnips. They have a purple skin that fades into yellow. Although you can get turnips in the spring and summer, the bigger turnips and rutabagas are late fall crops in the Northwest and help fill out farm market tables in the winter.

Winter Squash and Potatoes with Porcini Mushrooms

Sweet winter squash signals the return of fall at Northwest farmers' markets. Market tables are laden with this fall treasure, and I often buy so many that I eat squash for breakfast, lunch, and dinner. As for dried porcini mushrooms—some markets have foragers who dehydrate them, but if you can't find these dried treasures at the market, check natural food and specialty stores. Dried mushroom medleys composed of chanterelles, morels, and other wild mushrooms will also work. This dish can also pass as an entrée when paired with a salad, steamed vegetables, or braised greens and cornbread.

¾ cup boiling water

1 ounce dried porcini mushrooms

½ teaspoon extra virgin olive oil

2 tablespoons butter

1 onion, thinly sliced

2 stalks celery, diced

2 cloves garlic, minced or pressed

1 tablespoon chopped bottled hot peppers (optional)

½ cup red wine (Merlot is a good choice)

½ teaspoon salt

2 cups sliced delicata squash

2 cups thinly sliced potatoes (any red, yellow, or white variety except russet)

1½ cups shredded Cheddar or Gouda cheese

1. Preheat the oven to 350°F. Pour the boiling water over the mushrooms and let them soften

for at least 30 minutes, then drain and save the liquid for soup stock.

2. Heat a heavy skillet over medium heat. Add the oil, butter, onion, and celery. Stir and cook until soft. Add the garlic and hot peppers if desired and cook for a few more minutes. Stir in the softened mushrooms with their liquid and the red wine and continue to stir. Mix in the salt.

3. Layer the onion mixture, squash, potatoes, and cheese in a 1½ quart casserole dish, ending with the cheese. Cover and bake 1 hour. Remove the cover and continue baking for ½ hour.
Serves 4 to 6

Braised Turnips, Squash, and Seasonal Greens

This recipe boasts ingredients that can be found at just about any farmers' market from southern Oregon to northern Washington. Turnips sweeten when sautéed until lightly browned. Winter squash adds more sweetness, and raspberry vinegar delivers a tangy flavor. If you have red currants frozen from summer's harvest, toss in a few at the last moment and stir until heated, for a colorful presentation. If you don't have any currants, try dried sour cherries or cranberries.

- ½ teaspoon extra virgin olive oil
- 2 tablespoons butter or ghee (clarified butter)
- 1 onion, chopped
- 3 or 4 cloves garlic, minced
- 1 chopped fresh jalapeño, seeded and minced
- 4 medium turnips, thinly sliced
- 1 cup winter squash, cut into bite-size pieces
- 4 cups braising greens or finely cut kale or collards
- ⅓ cup water
- 2 tablespoons red currants (optional)
- Raspberry vinegar
- ¼ cup finely chopped parsley (optional)

1. Heat a heavy skillet over medium heat. Add the oil, butter, onion, garlic, and jalapeño. Stir, reduce the heat, cover, and sweat the onions until soft.

2. Add the turnips and squash to the skillet. Stir to coat, then blend in the greens, stir, and add the water. Cover and cook on medium-low until the turnips and squash are very tender and the greens are soft, about 15 minutes.

3. Stir in the red currants if desired. Remove from the heat and sprinkle with vinegar and parsley if desired. **Serves 4 to 6**

Mashed Turnips with Crispy Shallots

Memories of my grandmother's creamy mashed potatoes inspired this comforting side dish. I sometimes make this a base for a main dish and top it with braised greens and crumbled Gorgonzola cheese.

½ teaspoon extra virgin olive oil

1 tablespoon butter

5 or 6 medium shallots, peeled and sliced into ¼-inch rings

1 pound turnips, roughly chopped

1 pound red potatoes, peeled and roughly chopped

¼ cup cream

1 teaspoon lemon juice or mild vinegar

1 to 2 tablespoons butter

Salt and freshly ground pepper

1. Heat a heavy skillet over medium heat. Add the oil, butter, and shallot rings. Stir and cook until the shallots are crisp but not burned. Set aside.

2. While the shallots cook, steam the turnips and potatoes in a saucepan until tender.

3. Combine the cream and lemon juice or vinegar in a large bowl. Add the cooked turnips and potatoes and mash with the cream mixture. Blend in the butter.

4. Season with salt and pepper to taste. Top with the crispy shallots. **Serves 4**

Gingered Yams

Though yams and sweet potatoes are normally associated with southern cooking and they have a long growing season, some varieties can be grown in the Northwest. Denison Farms at the Corvallis farmers' market and Ayers Creek Farm at the Hillsdale farmers' market in Oregon grow and sell yams. If you don't have or don't like yams, use winter squash. Mair Farm-Taki in Yakima, Washington, sells fresh ginger at the University District market in Seattle during late summer and early fall.

2½ cups baked yams, skins removed

2 tablespoons orange juice

2 tablespoons cream or soy milk

1 teaspoon grated fresh ginger

¼ teaspoon salt

¼ cup finely chopped walnuts, toasted

Freshly ground pepper

1. Perheat the oven to 350°F. Blend the yams, orange juice, cream or soy milk, ginger, and salt in a mixing bowl. Place in a small oiled casserole dish.

2. Bake for 30 minutes. Alternatively, you can heat the yam mixture gently in a small pan on the stovetop. Top with the walnuts and season with freshly ground pepper to taste. **Serves 4**

Grilled Zucchini with Lemon-Garlic Butter

What do you do with a bumper crop of zucchini? This recipe was adapted from a Fry Family Farm CSA newsletter. Use any variety of summer squash for this recipe.

8 medium zucchini (about 8 inches long),
  ends removed and cut in half lengthwise

½ cup melted butter

2 tablespoons fresh lemon juice

1 tablespoon finely chopped lemon zest

½ teaspoon freshly ground pepper

1 teaspoon garlic powder

1 teaspoon oregano

Pinch of salt

¼ cup grated Parmesan cheese (optional)

1. Preheat a grill. Score the zucchini halves with a sharp knife, making diagonal cuts about ¼ inch deep at 1-inch intervals all the way down.

2. Combine the butter with the lemon juice, zest, pepper, garlic powder, oregano, and salt. Brush the zucchini halves with the mixture, then grill them until the sides become charred, 10 to 12 minutes.

3. Sprinkle the zucchini with the Parmesan cheese if desired, close the lid of the barbecue, and heat until the cheese softens, about 1 minute. **Serves 6 to 8**

Zucchini Marinara

I invented this dish when I was in high school and Dad's tiny garden produced a lot of zucchini. One day I combined Dad's summer squash with Mom's pasta sauce, added some croutons and cheese, and called it dinner. Add additional vegetables (eggplant, peppers, mushrooms) and use less zucchini, if you like.

8 cups sliced zucchini (about 10 small
  zucchini)

1 tablespoon olive oil

3 cups pasta sauce (or 1 24-ounce jar
  tomato or pasta sauce)

¼ cup chopped fresh basil

2 cups croutons

2 cups Parmesan cheese

1. Heat a 10-inch heavy skillet over medium heat. Add zucchini and olive oil. Cook and stir until zucchini softens—10 to 15 minutes. While zucchini cooks, preheat oven to 350° F.

2. Add pasta sauce and basil to zucchini and transfer to a 9-by-13-inch baking dish. Top with croutons and sprinkle Parmesan cheese evenly over the surface. Bake for 15 minutes or until cheese melts and sauce is bubbling. **Serves 6**

Farming Dreams

One of the few professions still passed down in families, farming is changing in the Northwest. Many successful farms that sell at markets today started with just a dream and no family bundle of land to be passed down from one generation to the next. Tom Denison of Denison Farms and Vince Alionis of Whistling Duck Farm are two farmers who followed childhood dreams, discovered emerging opportunities, and cultivated their passions to grow food.

Tom Denison's family moved to Corvallis when he was in grade school, and Tom remembers earning 2½ cents a pound picking pole beans for the local cannery. When Tom was a teenager, he decided he wanted to be a farmer. So after high school he went to the agriculture school at Cornell University in New York, where his father had earned his PhD. After two years of school and apprenticing with a New York farmer, Tom decided the best place to learn about farming was the farm. So in 1978, he returned home to Oregon, leased some land, planted crops to sell, and saved money to buy his dream.

He grew a lot of different crops; some of his all-stars of the '80s were melons, zucchini, cucumbers, tomatoes, and peppers. He sold vegetables and fruit at farmers' markets, the Corvallis food co-op, and a family-owned grocery store. Business was slower then because the retail spotlight on locally grown foods was focused on seasonal fruit that already had a clear Northwest identification—pears, apples, and berries.

In 1990, Tom bought the farm he'd dreamed about—20 acres on a hill overlooking the Jackson-Frazier Wetland in Corvallis. One of the first things he did was plant a small cherry orchard with a hundred trees. A few years later, Tom hired Pablo Herrera, a skilled farmer who now manages 10 full-time farmworkers and day–to-day essential farm tasks, while Tom puts his farm plans into action. And in 1995, Tom and Elizabeth Kerle married, and now Elizabeth handles the farm's finances, coordinates their CSA program, and writes weekly newsletters to go in the vegetable boxes.

In the winter, Tom pours over seed catalogs and searches the Internet for the best varieties of vegetables and fruit for the area. He plants his favorite varieties from past years, and when he wants to try something new, he selects 8 to 10 seed varieties and grows test trials. He discovers which varieties work best and rotates these into his farm plan. "He's done that with tomatoes, raspberries, and cherries," Elizabeth told me.

Tom's fava beans were grown in test trials and have became a Denison farm specialty. "If the fava plants are small in the fall after they're planted, they can overwinter," Tom said. "If they're too tall, the plants can freeze," he explained. Market shoppers and restaurant diners enjoy these tasty beans every spring. Tom says he is always trying to find ways to extend their farm season and increase their bottom line. Crops that remain in the ground through winter are a plus to jump-start spring sales.

To increase production, Tom installed a number

of passive solar greenhouses. His beans thrive inside these giant hoop tunnels, and in midsummer they nearly reach the top. He grows a variety—Blue Lake poles, green and yellow Romanos, and shell or dried beans as well as favas. Combine the vibrant beans inside and those staked outside, and it looks like these abundant crops could sustain the entire city of Corvallis.

Healthy, seasonal, and locally focused—that's the Denison farm. In the 1990s, Tom and Elizabeth made a conscious decision to focus on local markets. Tom told me that the local food tides shifted in Corvallis after the publication of *Animal, Vegetable, Miracle* by Barbara Kingsolver in 2007. This book plus the notion of the 100-mile diet, born from the book *Plenty* by Alisa Smith and J. B. Mackinnon, also published in 2007, nudged mainstream shoppers into local food awareness. One of the benefits of the "buy local" slogan is that the Denisons receive more calls about their growing CSA program. "We never turn anyone away," said Elizabeth.

Small farm success demands long hours, and one challenge Tom and Elizabeth struggle with is juggling farm and family. With an average of 14-hour workdays in the summer, the Denisons are grateful for precious time spent with their two sons. One of their favorite memories is when one son picked sour pie cherries and Elizabeth baked a pie. "Life is simpler close to home," Tom told me with a twinkle in his eye.

Vince Alionis of Whistling Duck Farm just south of Grants Pass mentions this same family and farmwork challenge. He and Mary, his wife, ran a CSA program for nine years on their certified organic farm, but after the birth of their second child, they found the demands of their CSA too cumbersome and they stopped, at least for a while. They were also in the middle of building their straw-bale house and had little time to coordinate and pack CSA boxes. Farm life is filled with never-ending tasks along the road to the rewards.

When I asked him how he got into agriculture, Vince said he'd always thought about farming. Originally from New York, he remembered that his grandfather's garden sparked his passion for growing food. As a young adult, Vince farmed for a while in New York and then moved to Texas, where he got a community garden project going and learned more about farming. Later, he moved to northern California to farm with Mary, but they never developed a connection to the land there, so they moved to Oregon's Willamette Valley.

Tom Denison and Elizabeth Kerle in the greenhouse with their vibrant pole beans

When the gray days proved to be too gray, they moved south to Trail, northeast of Grants Pass at 1900 feet, where they started a farm and a family in 1992. It was colder and growing conditions were different, but they farmed there for nine years, selling their produce at markets, the Ashland food co-op, and restaurants. In 2003 they relocated Whistling Duck Farm to just south of Grants Pass, to a lower elevation on 22 acres in the Applegate Valley.

Out in the fields at his farm, wearing a conical straw hat and a gray t-shirt and sweatpants as he tended his crops, Vince told me that growing conditions in southern Oregon have more in common with northern California than with the Willamette Valley. He talked about the Northwest soils—silty loams, clay loams, colluvial and alluvial soils. "The soil patterns are like a jigsaw puzzle here," he said. A farmer also has to know geology, and Vince's farming experiences from New York to Texas to California and Oregon have given him a wider geological picture of farmland.

"We're a mixed crop multi-succession farm," Vince explained, meaning they grow hundreds of different crops in succession. At the Ashland food co-op and markets they're known for their

Sign welcoming customers to the Whistling Duck farm store near Grants Pass, Oregon

fantastic greens, cruciferous vegetables, and berries. Vince said they always grow enough pumpkins in the fall for kids. At the farm, their store is a pay-as-you-go bare-bones affair where you select your fresh vegetables or eggs and drop your money in a locked box, but business is steady with cars pulling in and people leaving with vegetables.

It's all hands-on farming at Whistling Duck, where they cultivate eight acres and have three greenhouses and one propagation house. They also have about 20 hives of bees on their property, borrowed from their neighbor each summer, to boost their berry harvest. Napa cabbage, broccoli, leeks, celeriac, celery, carrots, and tomatoes are just a few of their annual crops, enjoyed by the locals in southern Oregon.

These treasures from the earth all make an appearance at farmers' markets, so when you stop at the Ashland farmers' market, stop and say hello to Vince, whose farm dreams feed the community.

Savory Vegetarian Entrées

Vegetarian main dishes ventured out of the closet in the 1970s with *Diet for a Small Planet* by Francis Moore Lappé and *The Moosewood Cookbook* by Molly Katzen. During the 1980s and '90s, meat-free main dishes lost much of their fat, and the emphasis shifted from cheese and soy to fresh vegetables.

Easy-to-make is the key, and one has only to look at fresh hot foods sold at the farmers' market to see just how easily local produce is incorporated into entrées. At the Ballard farmers' market in Seattle, Patty Pan Grill market vendor Devra Gartenstein sautés seasonal vegetables and folds them into savory quesadillas. When you start with great ingredients, savory vegetarian entrées are a snap. Tortillas, pizza, pasta, and polenta are great canvases for vegetables year-round. Consider unpretentious rustic casseroles with root vegetables in the winter. Make a stir-fry, or fire up the grill and make some kabobs in the summer.

When making a vegetarian main dish, think simple and start with a member of the onion family—shallots, leeks, or sweet, red, or yellow onions. You can use spice blends such as Thai curry paste or fresh roasted Indian spice blends, but you don't have to rely on these because vegetables grown in fertile soil and harvested when ripe don't need many supporting actors to be stars. Add some olive oil and a little butter to a hot skillet, chop and sauté the onions, and then add something sweet like carrots, or earthy like morels, or hot like jalapeños. Add a little minced garlic and a few pinches of herbs like basil, thyme, or coriander. Rely on grains and beans for protein, and then add vegetables, nuts, or a sprinkling of cheese if you want.

Follow the recipes in this section as they are written or scan them for ideas and branch out, changing grains, beans, or vegetables. The recipe world is continually shifting, and though some recipes simply can't be improved upon, for the most part recipes evolve to fit our desires, pantries, and lifestyles.

Shopping at the farmers' market is a great excuse for purchasing impulsively. You can bring a list, but then you may find that green beans don't look promising while beets and carrots are perfect. Open up to new possibilities for combining

Organic new potatoes and cauliflower at the University District market, grown by Michaele Blakely of Growing Things Farm in Carnation, Washington, just east of Seattle

vegetables. Strike up conversations as you peruse farm offerings, because some of the best dinner ideas are exchanged while waiting in market lines.

Think dinner at the market and you'll hear basil and tomatoes calling out for eggplant or summer squash for a tasty sauté served with rice or pasta. You'll understand that fire-roasted peppers, corn, salsa, and black beans were simply meant to be together. When you shop locally every week, imagine vegetable and herb pairings as you reach for squash, parsnips, or potatoes, and vegetarian main dishes will become easier to concoct.

Healing the Earth and Feeding the Community

Winter Green Farm in Noti, Oregon, is a familiar vendor at five farmers' markets—four in Portland and one in Bend. Many regular customers return week after week to the farm's booth for vibrant vegetables and delectable berries, but some shoppers may not realize that this 150-acre certified organic farm is a collaborative venture. The farm is owned and run by three families who use biodynamic farming techniques to enhance their harvest. In addition to growing tasty vegetables and juicy berries, these farmers share a driving passion to give back to the community that sustains them.

A unique Northwest farm, Winter Green Farm was started in 1980 by Jack Gray and Mary Jo Wade. Four years later, Wali and Jabrila Via joined Jack and Mary Jo on the farm, and in 1990 they started a CSA program and began offering weekly farm shares of fresh vegetables. Winter Green Farm also raises cattle and hay and wholesales burdock (a bittersweet root that tastes slightly like artichoke hearts). They also process four and a half acres of basil into pesto and pesto base in their processing kitchen. In 2008, longtime farm market managers Chris and Shannon Overbaugh became the third family co-owners of Winter Green Farm.

To produce abundant crops, the farm is abuzz with activity during the planting and harvest seasons. While all the owners are on the farm's management team, each owner has multiple specializations and chores in this year-round farming operation. Jack is in charge of the cattle, hay, and irrigation, and he is the farm's project manager. Jack also looks after farm machinery, and with Wali, manages the wholesale crops, basil, and pesto processing. Wali takes care of the labor and the biodynamic applications, and he's also in charge of the compost. Jabrila manages the propagation greenhouses and the CSA program and together with Chris calculates how much acreage is needed for the community food program, which includes the CSA and farmers' markets since these crops are grown together. In addition to field crops, Chris manages the farmers' markets, cultivation, and the production greenhouse program. Mary Jo takes care of the farm's finances with help from Wali and Jack. Shannon is a full-time mom to two young children and also works a few days each week on the farm and sells produce at the Bend farmers' market.

Farming with co-owners isn't really different from other farming operations where farmers rely on paid workers for many of these chores. Everyone has a job to do to produce the food we see at markets. When asked about co-ownership, Jabrila told me, "I wouldn't have it any other way, because you're tied to the farm when you farm by yourself. It's hard to take a vacation. Having other owners allows us the flexibility to get away if we want." She also said that like other Northwest farmers, they couldn't do any of this without their farm crew. "They're a wonderful group of people

FOOD FOR THOUGHT: AT THE MERCY OF WEATHER

Even if a farmer does everything right, when it comes to weather, it's a roll of the dice. One year Rockridge Orchards in Enumclaw, Washington, experienced a late spring freeze and a few days later a hailstorm finished off much of what was left of the spring crops planted by farmers Wade and Judy Bennett. Another year, winter winds swept across the Enumclaw plateau at more than 70 miles an hour, ripped two greenhouses from their cement foundations, and blew them end over end down a hillside. Frost, hailstorms, floods, or drought—to us these are passing weather conditions, but for a farmer they are the risks faced when bringing food to market.

Multipurpose silos and barns above a hay field at Winter Green Farm in Noti, Oregon.
Photo courtesy of Winter Green Farm.

dedicated to working closely with the earth and growing and harvesting quality produce."

Winter Green Farm also reaches out to other farms. Jabrila told me that there isn't a farmer around that she couldn't call for advice about what to grow. "We sometimes combine orders with other farmers," she said. "We order things like seed potatoes and divide them up." She said that other growers are also great resources when the farm has problems with anything from insects to fixing farm equipment.

When it comes to farming, biodynamic techniques help improve the quality of their produce.

Farmworkers transplanting seedlings to the field at Winter Green Farm. Photo courtesy of Winter Green Farm.

Biodynamic agriculture dates back to the 1920s and Rudolph Steiner's lectures about farming in Germany. The soil and the farm are treated as a living organism, and the soil is nurtured to preserve it for the generations to come. Biodynamic techniques feed the billions of organisms in the soil and improve the humus content. Also essential to this farm plan is a crop planting system ruled by planetary movements that determine ideal time frames for planting each crop. "It's all about keeping the earth healthy," Jabrila explained.

Wild spaces, wetlands, and forests are also part of this farm's biodynamic landscape. These wild areas provide homes for natural predators and pollinators that help boost the farm's annual abundance. "Poodle Creek runs through the farm, and along the banks native trees and shrubs and wildflowers lure a variety of beneficial insects," Jabrila told me. "The hawks and owls help control the rodent populations, and sparrows and swallows keep insect populations under control."

To share its abundance, the farm strives to include a wider economic range of families in its local food program. It offers low-income subsidies to those who otherwise couldn't afford nourishing food. "Everyone deserves to eat nutritious food," said Jabrila.

Winter Green Farm is generous with subsidies because of community donations. Eight dollars from every CSA subscriber's fee is designated for the farm's low-income fund, and CSA subscribers often donate additional money. Other community members contribute to this fund in various ways, dropping money in a donation jar at farm events or giving through a program started by John Pitney in Eugene called "That's My Farmer," which introduces farmers to the community through churches and in the process helps raise awareness about local farm subsidy programs. Jabrila told me, "Giving creates a wonderful feeling in those who can afford to help as they reach out to help community members in need."

In addition to donating to the subsidy fund, Winter Green Farm CSA members also contribute weekly produce boxes to Food for Lane County, which delivers the boxes to Womenspace, a transitional women's shelter in Eugene. And like many Northwest farms, Winter Green Farm delivers produce left over from farmers' market sales to food banks. These gifts of essential fresh food mean a lot to low-income people and add a rainbow of hope to their lives. For those who want to donate more, the Winter Green Farm Web site (www.wintergreenfarm.com) makes it possible to donate any amount of money toward farm fresh produce for the financial assistance program.

Another thing that's rewarding for the farmers at Winter Green Farm is that their CSA program brings families to the farm. "Our CSA is very family oriented," Jabrila told me. Members are welcomed to the farm with the spring open house potluck during which they can get to know their farmers, explore "their" farm, and trade life stories over good food. Depending on the season, they may be invited to events like garlic-braiding parties. And at the annual fall harvest celebration, children enjoy a hayride to a pumpkin patch where they can select their own pumpkin, and everyone enjoys the fresh cider that farmer Wali Via presses.

At Winter Green Farm, a string of long days of farm work combined with healthy farming techniques adds up to enough food to feed the community. Its community outreach generates a contagious good feeling. This organic farm not only sustains itself but also gives back.

Creative Casseroles

Twice a year at Nash Huber's farm on the Olympic Peninsula, a potluck and barn dance are held for the community. Cars are ushered into the dirt lot in front of the barn and a $10 charge, which goes to the local farm-to-school program, is collected. Long picnic tables are filled with salads, dips, side dishes, casseroles, and desserts. Gazing down the table at the variety of simple, home-cooked entrées using Northwest vegetables brings to mind other potluck suppers where good times and stories are shared, and favorite dishes and recipes are exchanged. Try a few of these recipes, then go forth and share these or your own versions with others. That's what creative casseroles are all about.

Rice, Roasted Red Pepper, and Snap Bean Casserole

We have many cool summer days in the Northwest, so making a summer casserole isn't as crazy as someone in Arizona might think. Red bell pepper, carrots, and green beans are the essence of summer. At some markets, farmers grill peppers and sell them. These already grilled peppers save time and impart a seductive smoky flavor. You can make the soup stock according to the basic recipe in "Seasonal Soups and Homemade Breads" or use one of the convenient cartons of organic vegetarian stock available in natural food stores.

2 red bell peppers

1 cup vegetarian stock

2 teaspoons arrowroot powder

3 cloves garlic, pressed

1½ cups carrots cut into 1-inch matchsticks

4 cups fresh green snap beans (about 1 pound), tips removed and cut into 1-inch lengths

2½ cups cooked brown rice

½ cup sliced jalapeño-stuffed green olives

½ cup finely chopped parsley

Salt

1. Place the bell peppers in a shallow pan, prick them with a fork, and broil until their skins turn black and blister. Using long tongs, turn them every 5 minutes until all sides are blackened. Put the peppers in a paper bag, close, and let cool for about 15 minutes. Peel, seed, and slice into thin strips.

2. Combine the stock and arrowroot in a saucepan and mix well. Add the garlic, carrots, and green beans. Bring to a boil, and then simmer until the carrots and beans are cooked and the mixture thickens, about 7 minutes.

3. Combine the brown rice and olives in a medium bowl. Place half in the bottom of a casserole dish, spoon half of the bean and carrot mixture over the top, and add a layer of grilled pepper strips. Repeat the layers.

4. Cover and bake for 20 minutes. Garnish with parsley and season with salt to taste. **Serves 6**

Shepherd's Pie

Meat lovers will never miss the meat in this market-inspired vegetarian shepherd's pie. The recipe incorporates fresh favas or shell beans, cultivated by a number of Northwest farmers. I start thinking about this dish whenever I make mashed potatoes, and I always mash more potatoes than I need so I can use them in dishes like this later in the week. For more heat, leave some jalapeño seeds in the mix.

¼ cup salsa

2 cups mashed potatoes

1 to 2 tablespoons ghee (clarified butter)

1 small onion, chopped

1 fresh jalapeño, seeded and minced

1 red, green, or yellow bell pepper, seeded and chopped

1 cup diced carrots

Kernels from 1 ear of corn

1 cup cooked beans (fava or light-colored shell beans)

3 to 4 cups mixed seasonal vegetables (winter squash, zucchini, cauliflower, celery, turnips, parsnips, carrots, or peas) cut into small chunks

1 cup water, divided

1 tablespoon arrowroot powder

Salt

½ cup shredded sharp cheese

1. Preheat the oven to 350°F. Blend the salsa into the mashed potatoes in a medium bowl and set aside.

2. Heat a heavy ovenproof skillet over medium heat. Add the ghee, onion, and jalapeño. Stir and cook until the onions are soft and lightly browned. Add the bell pepper, mix well, and cook for 5 minutes. Add the carrots, corn, beans, and mixed vegetables. Stir, then blend in ¾ cup water. Cover and simmer for about 10 minutes.

3. While the vegetables cook, combine the remaining ¼ cup water with the arrowroot in a small bowl and then blend with the vegetables. Cook and stir until the sauce begins to thicken, about 5 minutes. Remove from the heat.

4. Gently spread the mashed potatoes over the vegetables. Season with salt to taste and sprinkle with the cheese. Bake until bubbly and slightly browned, about 30 minutes. **Serves 4 to 6**

TIPS ON PUTTING CASSEROLES TOGETHER

- Cook beans or grains ahead of time. See "Northwest Beans and Grains" in the back of the book for detailed cooking instructions.
- Cut vegetables into small pieces so they cook faster.
- Sauté onions and steam or blanch vegetables before combining.
- Have plenty of ingredient options on hand such as sauerkraut, salsa, artichokes, pickled vegetables, tomato sauce, olives, and baby corn.
- Use just a few ingredients, rather than adding everything you have on hand.
- Imagine how the flavors will blend together before adding things.
- Add foods with different textures and flavors— for example, chopped apples, sun-dried tomatoes, finely chopped celery, reconstituted dried mushrooms, or toasted nuts.
- Make your casserole ahead and refrigerate it to bake later. If it's cold from the refrigerator when you put it in the oven, add 15 to 20 minutes to your cooking time.

Rum-Spiked Baked Beans and Yams

These hearty beans with yams will keep you warm on cold winter evenings. More farmers are bringing Northwest-grown yams to the markets. At the Hillsdale, Oregon, farmers' market, Ayers Creek Farm sells a variety of yams. Look for yams at a market in your neighborhood; if you can't find them, you can use squash instead. White beans are traditional for baked beans, but you can use pintos or cranberry beans if you have them. I like these beans best with brown sugar, but you can use a light-colored honey. (Darker, more flavorful honey competes with the molasses flavor.)

½ cup ketchup

1 tablespoon Dijon mustard

¼ cup brown sugar, honey, or agave nectar

¼ cup molasses

½ cup dark rum

½ cup water

2 tablespoons ghee (clarified butter)

2 large onions, sliced into rings

Pinch of cayenne

2 cloves garlic, pressed

1 large yam, diced

2½ cups white or pinto beans, cooked

Salt

1. Preheat the oven to 350°F. Combine the ketchup, mustard, brown sugar or honey or agave nectar, molasses, rum, and water in a saucepan and simmer for 10 minutes.

2. Heat a heavy skillet over medium heat. Add the ghee, onions, and cayenne. Stir, cover, and sweat the onions until soft. Add the garlic, stir, and cook until the onions are lightly browned.

3. Combine the sauce and the onions and garlic with the yam and beans in a 2½-quart casserole and mix well. Cover and bake for 1 hour. Season with salt to taste. **Serves 4**

FOOD FOR THOUGHT: THE BAKED BEAN TRADITION

The tradition of baked beans involves long, slow cooking so the beans soak up lots of flavor as they become tender. According to Jaqueline Williams in *Wagon Wheel Kitchens*, emigrants traveling by wagon over the Oregon Trail set bean crocks in Dutch ovens in the coals to cook. Crock-Pots are used by many cooks today. You can also place covered baked beans in the oven for an hour or so, until the flavors are absorbed. If you want a smoky flavor, add three or four chipotle chili pods; remove the pods before serving.

Cranberry Beans, Squash, and Corn

Molasses and mustard combine with orange juice to lend a sweet tang to this delicious baked bean casserole. This recipe originally called for black-eyed peas, but I discovered that locally sourced cranberry beans work just as well. Try another variety if you want; most dried beans are interchangeable in recipes. So is squash. If you have another type of squash or yams, substitute 2 cups of either one, peeled and cut into bite-size pieces. Some farmers bring dried tomatoes to market, and you can use these or buy bottled sun-dried tomatoes for this recipe.

- **1 cup dried cranberry beans, cooked**
- **½ cup orange juice**
- **¼ cup water**
- **¼ cup chopped sun-dried tomatoes (bottled or dried)**
- **1 medium delicata squash, halved, seeded, and sliced ½ inch thick**
- **¼ cup unsulphered molasses (not blackstrap—the flavor is too overpowering)**
- **½ tablespoon Dijon mustard**
- **½ teaspoon salt**
- **1 fresh jalapeño, seeded and minced**
- **1 cup fresh corn, cut off the cob**
- **1 red onion, diced**
- **1 cup crushed red or blue tortilla chips**

1. Preheat the oven to 350°F. If using dried tomatoes, combine the orange juice and water with the tomatoes in a small bowl and allow them to rehydrate for 20 to 30 minutes. Steam the squash slices in a saucepan until fork-tender, about 10 minutes. Let cool while the tomatoes rehydrate.

2. Combine the orange juice mixture with the molasses, mustard, salt, and jalapeño in a blender and puree until smooth and creamy. If using bottled sun-dried tomatoes, add them now. Combine the mixture with the cooked beans, squash, corn, and onion in a large bowl and mix well.

3. Place the bean mixture in a 2-quart casserole dish and press it down with the back of a spoon. Cover and bake until the casserole is bubbling, about 30 minutes. Top with the crushed tortilla chips. **Serves 6**

Eggplant and Red Pepper Lasagna

In midsummer when eggplant is in season, I try as many eggplant recipes as I can, but there are always favorites I repeat year after year and this is one. In this dish the combination of eggplant, pasta sauce, and merlot makes a perfect vegetarian lasagna. Check farmers' markets or farm stores in your area for locally grown and processed pasta sauce; for instance, Winter Green Farm of Noti, Oregon, sells an excellent bottled tomato sauce at Portland farmers' markets and Gathering Together Farm in Philomath offers an equally tasty pasta sauce in their farm store. You can easily create a dairy-free dish by using silken tofu blended with a little lemon juice and olive oil, instead of ricotta cheese. Blend the tofu with a shredded vegan cheese or simply substitute 3 to 4 cups of hummus for the blended filling. In autumn try lightly steamed Romanesco cauliflower, fennel, carrots, and delicata squash instead of eggplant, peppers, and zucchini.

- 1 large eggplant (local summer varieties are the best)
- 2 large red bell peppers
- 2 cups ricotta
- 3 cups Parmesan cheese (or a dry hard local cheese or vegan Parmesan cheese substitute)
- ½ cup chopped fresh basil, or 1½ teaspoons dried
- 2 cups torn spinach or thinly shredded and chopped kale
- ¼ to ½ teaspoon crushed red pepper flakes
- 2 tablespoons extra virgin olive oil or safflower oil
- 1 large onion, chopped
- 1 green, red, or yellow bell pepper, chopped
- 3 cups sliced mushrooms (porcini, cremini, or portobello)
- 1 pound summer squash such as zucchini, sliced
- 1 25-ounce jar pasta sauce
- ¾ cup dry red wine (like Merlot)
- ½ cup sliced olives, your favorite variety (optional)
- 8 to 10 lasagna noodles

1. Place the eggplant and bell peppers in a shallow pan, prick them with a fork, and broil until their skins turn black and blister. Using long tongs, turn them every 5 minutes until all sides are blackened. The eggplant will take longer than the peppers to roast. Put the blackened vegetables in a paper bag, close, and let cool for about 15 minutes. Peel, seed, and slice into thin strips. Reserve the juice from the eggplant for the sauce.

2. Preheat the oven to 350°F. Combine the ricotta, 1 cup Parmesan, basil, spinach, and pepper flakes in a large bowl and set aside.

3. Heat a heavy skillet over medium heat. Add the oil, onion, and bell pepper. Stir, cover, reduce the heat, and sweat for 5 minutes. Add the mushrooms and squash and cook for 10 minutes. Blend in the pasta sauce, wine, reserved eggplant juice, and olives if desired. Continue to cook until the mushrooms are tender, about 25 minutes.

4. Ladle ⅓ of the sauce into a 9-by-13-inch baking dish. Place the dry noodles on top (use about four noodles or enough to cover the surface).

Spread half of the filling over the noodles. Lay half the strips of eggplant and peppers over this layer. Repeat—noodles, filling, and eggplant. Pour the remaining sauce over the top. Cover securely with a glass lid or foil. Bake for 1 hour.

5. Sprinkle with the remaining 2 cups Parmesan cheese. **Serves 6**

Erbazzone

This is a savory combination of pie and calzone adapted from a popular recipe from the Swan Cafe at the Community Food Co-op in Bellingham, Washington. The defining ingredient here is the Parmesan cheese; without it the Erbazzone has no character. The crust is pizzalike and requires a food processor or electric mixer for blending or it will be seriously tough. (If you substituted cold butter and cut it into the flour with a pastry blender, the dough would be tender and pastrylike.)

4 tablespoons extra virgin olive oil, divided

1 clove garlic, pressed

2½ cups flour (unbleached white)

¼ teaspoon salt

¾ cup water

3 cups diced yellow onions or leeks

2 tablespoons minced garlic

8 cups shredded Swiss chard or spinach

3 cups shredded Parmesan cheese

2 eggs, beaten

1. Preheat the oven to 350°F. Oil a 10-inch cake pan. Mix 1 tablespoon oil with the pressed garlic in a small bowl and set aside to brush on the top crust.

2. Combine the flour and salt in the bowl of a food processor and use the processor or an electric mixer to cut in 1½ tablespoons oil. Turn into a mixing bowl and stir in the water to make a smooth dough. The dough should be stiff enough to touch without being too sticky; if it's not, add a little more flour. Cover, set aside, and let rest.

3. Heat a heavy skillet over medium heat. Add 1½ tablespoons oil and the onions and minced garlic, stir, and cook until browned, about 10 minutes. Add the chard and cook until wilted. Remove from the heat and stir in the Parmesan cheese first and then the eggs. Let the mixture cool, because a warm filling can make the bottom crust soggy and tough. While the filling cools, prepare the crust.

4. Divide the dough into thirds and knead two of the thirds together on a lightly floured board, adding more flour if necessary. Starting from the center of the dough, roll outward into a large circle, lifting the dough frequently so it doesn't stick to the cutting board. Add a little more flour if the dough sticks.

5. Place the rolling pin on one side of the dough and carefully roll the dough loosely over the pin, then unroll the circle of dough over the prepared cake pan and press it down. Pinch together any uneven sides.

6. Fill the pan with the cooled chard mixture. Roll out the remaining dough into a circular top crust. Follow the same procedure with the rolling pin and unroll this dough on top of the chard mixture, crimping the two crusts together.

7. Brush the garlic-oil mixture over the top crust. Bake for 40 minutes. Allow to cool slightly before cutting. **Serves 5**

Fire-Roasted Tomato Bread Pudding

This rustic savory pudding is pure comfort food. My grandmother made a humble stovetop version during the 1930s and called it simply "bread and tomatoes." Call it what you want, it's an excellent excuse to indulge in mushrooms, artisan bread, and farmstead cheese. Many Northwest farmers' markets have artisan bread makers, and of course onions, garlic, fresh herbs, and farmstead cheese are usually available. At the Hillsdale market, I buy mushrooms from Springwater Farm of St. Helens, Oregon. Portobello mushrooms are also available in grocery stores if you don't find a mushroom vendor at your market.

1 tablespoon ghee (clarified butter)

1 large onion, diced

3 cloves garlic, minced or pressed

1 portobello mushroom, stem and gills removed, sliced and cut into bite-size pieces

Dash of hot sauce

4 heaping cups cubed artisan bread

1 28-ounce can diced fire-roasted tomatoes

1 teaspoon sugar

¼ cup chopped fresh basil, or 1 teaspoon dried

1 tablespoon fresh marjoram, or ½ teaspoon dried

½ teaspoon salt

1 cup grated extra-sharp Cheddar or Gouda (optional)

1. Preheat the oven to 350°F. Heat a heavy skillet over medium heat. Add the ghee, onion, garlic, mushroom, and hot sauce. Stir, reduce the heat, cover, and cook until the onion and mushroom are soft.

2. Combine the bread, tomatoes, sugar, basil, marjoram, and salt in a large mixing bowl and mix well. Stir in the onion and mushroom.

3. Place the mixture in a 2-quart casserole dish and press it down with the back of a spoon until very compact. Let the casserole sit for at least ½ hour before baking. The bread will absorb the tomato sauce.

4. Top with cheese if desired and bake for 30 minutes or until lightly browned around the edges. **Serves 4**

Wild Rice with Cranberries and Mushrooms

I originally created this dish for a Thanksgiving family gathering, where it quickly disappeared. My idea was to tuck typical stuffing seasonings into a grain base baked with vegetables. Look for Northwest-grown wild rice and hazelnuts from Freddy Guys in Monmouth, Oregon, at farmers' markets. Some farmers sell cranberries and foragers sell chanterelles in the fall, but if you can't find these at the market, try a natural food store.

1¾ cups vegetarian stock or water

1 cup wild rice

2 tablespoons ghee (clarified butter)

1 large red onion, finely chopped

1½ cups finely chopped celery

1 cup diced carrots

2 cloves garlic, pressed

1 teaspoon dried sage

¼ teaspoon dried marjoram

½ teaspoon freshly ground black pepper

Salt

1 cup fresh cranberries

2 cups chanterelle mushrooms, cleaned and sliced

1 cup cream or soy milk

½ cup finely chopped parsley

½ cup chopped hazelnuts, toasted

1. Preheat the oven to 350°F. Bring the stock or water to a boil in a medium saucepan. Add the rice, cover, reduce the heat, and simmer until the rice is done and all the liquid has been absorbed, about 1 hour.

2. Heat a heavy saucepan over medium heat. Add the ghee and onion, stir, and cook until the onion is soft. Add the celery, carrots, garlic, sage, and marjoram. Cover and cook on low until the vegetables are soft. Add the pepper and season to taste with salt. Stir in the cranberries and cook until soft, 7 to 10 minutes, adding a little water if necessary. Stir in the mushrooms, blend in the cream or soy milk, and heat for a few minutes.

3. Remove from the heat and puree 1 cup of the mixture in a blender. Set aside.

4. Combine the rice with the vegetables in a 2½-quart casserole dish. Pour the pureed vegetables over all, cover, and bake for 25 to 30 minutes. Sprinkle with parsley and hazelnuts.
Serves 6

Cranberries for sale from Rainier Mountain Cranberries at the University District farmers' market in Seattle

Savory Whole Grains and Legumes

Local grains and beans are great raw materials for filling main dishes, and an increasing number of Northwest farmers are growing grains and legumes. At Nash's Organic Produce in Sequim, Washington, the farm crew cultivates wheat, rye, and triticale, and Ayers Creek Farm has gained a reputation at the Hillsdale farmers' market in Oregon for its specialty grains and beans. Willie Green's Organic Farm in Monroe, Washington, sells light green flageolet and white cannellini beans, and Stoney Plains Organic Farm in Tenino cultivates organic pinto, black, and white beans. Each year, it seems like another row crop farmer brings one or two varieties of dried beans to market. When shopping locally, start with beans and grains—the foundation of vegetarian entrées.

Easy Spanish Quinoa

This is a simple way to use up a leftover ear of cooked corn. Some Northwest farms like Tanni Creek Farm, a small biodynamic farm on Bainbridge Island, Washington, grow quinoa, a high-protein grain. I sometimes add a can of rinsed, drained red beans to this recipe near the end of cooking, or I sprinkle a cup of grated farmstead Cheddar or Gouda cheese over the top before serving.

1 14-ounce can diced tomatoes with liquid

¾ cup water

1 cup quinoa, rinsed

1 teaspoon chili powder

Pinch of cayenne

3 cloves garlic, minced

Kernels from 1 ear of corn

¼ cup sliced green onions (optional)

¼ cup chopped cilantro (optional)

Salt and freshly ground pepper

½ cup chopped walnuts or hazelnuts, lightly toasted

1. Bring the tomatoes and water to a boil in a medium saucepan. Add the quinoa, chili powder, cayenne, and garlic. Cover, reduce the heat, and simmer for 15 minutes. Remove from the heat.

2. Stir in the corn along with the green onions and cilantro if desired. Season with salt and pepper to taste. Sprinkle with the nuts. **Serves 4**

TIP ON THE BEST COOKING VESSELS FOR ACIDIC INGREDIENTS

When cooking with acidic ingredients like tomatoes, use a pan made of a nonreactive metal like stainless steel. Tomato-based sauces, vinegar, and citrus juices pull metals like iron and aluminum into the food, adding a distinct, undesirable metallic flavor.

Quinoa, Corn, and Caramelized Walnuts

I like to make this dish when I have fresh walnuts, like the sweet, shelled Oregon walnuts I get whenever I shop at the Saturday Portland farmers' market. In the fall, at the University District farmers' market in Seattle, I buy walnuts from Grouse Mountain Farm in Chelan. You can crack Grouse Mountain walnuts with your hand, and inside is a sweet nut with a smooth flavor.

1 cup quinoa

1¾ cups water

1 cup corn, fresh off the cob or frozen

Pinch of cayenne

½ cup walnuts

1 tablespoon melted butter or ghee
   (clarified butter)

1 tablespoon brown sugar or maple syrup

Salt

1. Soak the quinoa in the water in a covered bowl overnight.

2. Bring the soaking water, quinoa, corn, and cayenne to a boil in a medium saucepan over high heat. Reduce the heat and simmer until the quinoa is done and all the water has been absorbed, about 15 minutes.

3. While the quinoa cooks, heat a skillet over medium heat. Add the walnuts, stir, and toast until lightly browned. Stir in the oil and brown sugar or maple syrup. Make sure all the nuts are coated. Let the nuts dry out a bit.

4. When the quinoa is done, mix in the walnuts. Season with salt to taste. **Serves 4**

Fresh Shell Beans with Fennel, Raspberry Vinegar, and Hazelnut Oil

This is adapted from a simple bean recipe from Ayers Creek Farm in Gaston, Oregon. Carrot and fennel add sweetness, and raspberry vinegar lends tangy tones. I have also used balsamic vinegar for an exotic flavor. If you can't find hazelnut oil at your market, use extra virgin olive oil. Serve this dish with rice and braised greens.

1 onion, diced

1 carrot, diced

1 bulb fennel, diced, or 2 cups diced celery

4 cups water, divided

1 bay leaf

2 cups fresh shell beans, rinsed

Salt and freshly ground pepper

1 to 2 tablespoons raspberry vinegar

Hazelnut oil (optional)

Fennel greens, chopped

1. Simmer the onion, carrot, fennel, 3 cups water, and bay leaf in a 2-quart saucepan over low heat until the vegetables have softened, about 25 minutes.

2. Add the beans and up to 1 cup water, as needed, to cover the beans. Simmer until the beans are moist and tender all the way through, 15 to 30 minutes. Remove from the heat.

3. Season with salt and pepper to taste. Blend in the raspberry vinegar, drizzle with a little hazelnut oil if desired, and sprinkle with some fennel greens. **Serves 4 to 6**

Wild Rice and Hazelnut Pilaf

Sage, carrots, celery, hazelnuts—this recipe has the essential earmarks of fall. Whenever I shop at the Saturday Portland farmers' market, I stop at the Freddy Guys booth, where I buy wild rice and hazelnuts. This dish also has the sweet tart tones of cranberries. Even though Northwest farmers grow lots of them, it's hard to find died cranberries at Seattle markets, so I often substitute tart pie cherries that I dry during the summer when cherries are plentiful at the markets.

1¾ cups vegetarian stock or water

1 tablespoon fresh sage, or ½ teaspoon dried

1 tablespoon fresh marjoram, or ¼ teaspoon dried

½ teaspoon fresh thyme, or ¼ teaspoon dried

¼ teaspoon crushed red pepper flakes

1 cup wild rice, rinsed

1 tablespoon extra virgin olive oil or safflower oil

1 onion, finely chopped

1 or 2 stalks celery, chopped

1 medium-size carrot, diced

4 cloves garlic, minced or pressed

Salt

½ cup chopped hazelnuts, lightly toasted

½ cup dried cranberries or sour cherries (optional)

1 tablespoon hazelnut oil

½ cup finely chopped parsley

1. Bring the stock, sage, marjoram, thyme, and red pepper flakes to a boil in a medium saucepan. Add the wild rice, reduce the heat, cover, and simmer until the sides of the rice burst open to reveal a soft gray interior, about 55 minutes. Remove from the heat and let sit for 5 minutes before fluffing with a fork.

2. While the rice cooks, heat a heavy skillet over medium heat. Add the oil, onion, celery, and carrot. Stir, reduce the heat, cover, and cook until the vegetables are very soft, about 10 minutes. Add the garlic, stir, and cook until the onion is lightly browned.

3. Combine the wild rice and vegetables in a serving bowl. Season with salt to taste and blend in the hazelnuts, cherries or cranberries if desired, and parsley. **Serves 4**

Squash, Cranberries, and Barley

Tart fresh cranberries and sweet squash pair up in this dish with a spicy flavor. Look for hull-less barley in natural food stores, or if you live near Portland, look for the Arabian Blue naked (hull-less) barley sold by Ayers Creek Farm at the Hillsdale market. This barley must be soaked overnight, then rinsed and cooked with enough fresh water to cover, until done, about an hour.

- 2 tablespoons ghee (clarified butter)
- 1 large onion, chopped
- 1 or 2 fresh jalapeños, seeded and minced (add seeds for more heat)
- ¼ cup apple juice
- ⅓ cup currants
- 1 cup fresh cranberries
- 1 pound butternut or delicata squash, cut into bite-size pieces (about 2 cups)
- ½ teaspoon salt
- 2 cups cooked naked (hull-less) barley
- 1 cup finely chopped celery
- ½ cup chopped walnuts or pecans, lightly toasted

1. Heat a heavy skillet over medium heat. Add the ghee, onion, and jalapeño. Stir, cover, and cook until the onions are soft, about 5 minutes. Remove the lid and cook on low, stirring occasionally, until the onions are lightly browned.

2. Add the apple juice, currants, cranberries, and squash. Cover and cook until the squash and cranberries are tender, about 15 minutes. Stir in the salt and barley and continue to cook until heated through. Transfer to a serving bowl and mix in the celery and walnuts. **Serves 4**

TIP ON WASHING PRODUCE

Farm fresh produce harvested next to the soil like lettuce or cranberries in bogs should always be washed. Bogs and fields are sometimes visited by wildlife like moose and deer, and unwashed produce from the ground may harbor unsavory organisms that tax digestive systems. It's better to be cautious and wash fresh produce before enjoying it.

Sweet Dumpling winter squash at BelleWood Acres, Lynden, Washington

Smoky Beans with Rice and Collards

Smoky beans, coleslaw, and cornbread are perfect comfort foods for cool fall evenings. I use local cranberry beans for this recipe, but don't be fooled by the beans' name, because they don't look like and aren't related to cranberries. These beans are white with pink speckles, and they usually arrive at farmers' markets in August or September. They team up with rice in this dish for a super protein profile. Add collards and a leek and you've got a great fall entrée. If you can't find cranberry beans, try any other light-colored bean. For a quick meal, prepare this dish in a pressure cooker, using half the amount of water.

2 tablespoons ghee (clarified butter)

1 large leek, thinly sliced and rinsed well

3 or 4 cloves garlic, pressed or minced

¼ to ½ teaspoon chipotle chili powder or 1 whole chipotle chili in adobo sauce

1 bay leaf

3 cups water, or 2 cups water and 1 cup stock

1 cup cranberry beans, soaked and drained

1 bunch collards, removed from stems, rolled, and cut into fine strips

1 cup cooked brown or white rice

½ teaspoon salt

¼ cup fresh lemon juice

1. Heat a heavy soup pot or a pressure cooker over medium heat. Add the ghee and leek. Stir, cook for a few minutes, and then stir in the garlic and chipotle chili powder. If using a pressure cooker, remove from the heat.

2. Add the bay leaf, water, and beans. Pressure cook for 15 minutes, or cook on the stovetop until the beans are tender, about 1 hour.

3. Add the collards, rice, and salt and continue to cook until the collards are soft. Just before serving, remove the bay leaf and blend in the lemon juice. **Serves 4**

TIP ON COOKING AND USING COLLARDS

In the South, collards are sometimes cooked all night long with pork fat until they are a soft mass. Thankfully, the Northwest doesn't have that tradition! An alternative is to simmer or braise collards with stock, apple juice, or dry white wine for 10 minutes. The collards will be tender and have a good texture, and they will retain more vitamins than the southern version. Drizzle with lemon or raspberry vinegar blended with a little agave nectar and salt. Collards contain about the same amount of calcium as milk. Stir them into soups, stews, and casseroles.

TIP ON PREPARING LAVENDER VINEGAR

To make lavender vinegar, simmer about 3 cups of vinegar for a few minutes. (I like to use rice vinegar because it is less acidic than wine vinegar.) Pour the vinegar into a quart jar over ½ cup rinsed and dried lavender buds or herbs. Cover and let steep for 2 weeks. Turn the jar upside down once in a while to distribute the flavors.

Red Lentils with Greens and Lavender

Red lentils are the quickest-cooking legumes. For this recipe, I use any kind of kale I have on hand; if I don't have kale, I'll use collards, chard, or even spinach. But if you add spinach, add it at the end of cooking and let it cook until just wilted. Look for culinary lavender at a farmers' market in July and let it dry so you can use it all year. Or you can make lavender vinegar and use that instead of adding lavender and vinegar separately. If you visit the annual Lavender Festival in the Sequim-Dungeness Valley in July, you might find a farm-made lavender vinegar.

- 1 tablespoon extra virgin olive oil or safflower oil
- 1 small onion, diced
- 1 fresh jalapeño, minced
- 1 teaspoon culinary lavender
- 1 cup diced carrots
- 1 medium to small potato, cut into small chunks
- 1 pear (Anjou or Bosc) or 1 sweet-tart unpeeled apple, cored and cut into small pieces
- 2 to 3 cloves garlic, minced
- ½ cup finely chopped kale, collards, chard, or spinach
- ½ cup red lentils
- 1½ cups water
- Salt
- ¼ teaspoon crushed red pepper flakes
- Rice vinegar
- 1 cup croutons

1. Heat a heavy skillet over medium heat. Add the oil, onion, jalapeño, lavender, and carrots. Stir and cook until the onions are soft.

2. Blend in the potato and pear or apple, then cover and cook for 5 minutes. Stir in the garlic, kale, lentils, and water. Bring to a boil, then reduce the heat and simmer until the lentils are soft, about 25 minutes.

3. Season with salt to taste. Add the pepper flakes, drizzle with a little vinegar, stir in, and then sprinkle the croutons on top. **Serves 4**

Northwest pumpkins pile up at natural food stores, farmers' markets, and farm stands in October. Photo by Sheila and Brad Zahnow.

Black Bean Fiesta Pizza

I use a frozen cornmeal crust from the refrigerated case in natural food stores for this recipe, but any good-quality frozen pizza crust will do. Gathering Together Farm in Philomath, Oregon, and Billy's Gardens in Tonasket, Washington, make great fresh salsa and sell it at Portland and Seattle markets. You can also find good locally sourced salsas in natural food stores.

- 1 tablespoon extra virgin olive oil or safflower oil
- 1 large yellow onion, cut in half and thinly sliced
- 2 fresh jalapeños, seeded and minced
- 2 to 3 cloves garlic, pressed

Fresh local vegetables for sale in the farm store at BelleWood Acres

- 1 cup cooked black beans
- 2 to 4 tablespoons fresh salsa
- ½ cup corn kernels fresh off the cob
- Salt
- 1 cup grated sharp or smoky Cheddar or Gouda cheese
- 1 9-inch frozen pizza crust, thawed
- ¼ cup chopped cilantro

1. Preheat the oven according to the directions for the crust.

2. Heat a heavy skillet over medium heat. Add the oil, onion, jalapeños, and garlic. Stir, cover, reduce the heat, and sweat the onions until they begin to brown. Blend in the beans, stir, and cook for another minute. Stir in 2 tablespoons of the salsa and the corn. Season with salt to taste. Spread the mixture over the crust and sprinkle with the cheese.

3. Bake according to the crust directions. Sprinkle with cilantro and add more salsa if desired. **Serves 4**

Stovetop Pasta and Toppings

Pasta is something anyone can cook. You need a large pot—one that holds at least 4 quarts of water. Bring this water to a boil. Any Italian cook will tell you to add salt to the water, plenty of it, but a teaspoon is all you really need. When the water comes to a rolling boil, add the pasta and give it a stir so it moves with the water. Bring it back to a boil and keep it boiling until the pasta is done. It's helpful to fish some pasta out to sample for doneness starting at about 5 minutes. Pasta is done when it is al dente or slightly chewy. Cooking pasta isn't an exact science, and the time specified on the package is just an estimate; it takes only minutes to overcook, so be alert. Drain and serve it with sauce or toss it with a little cheese and your favorite vegetables. Garnish with parsley, basil, or freshly grated cheese.

Ribbons with Sweet Onions, Zucchini, and Spinach

Zucchini and sweet onions make this summer pasta a delight. In the spring, sweet onions are small and zucchinis are mere babies. At Growing Things Farm in Carnation, Washington, farmer Michaele Blakely separates her summer squash into babies and toddlers, depending on how large they are, but by midsummer they're big but still sweet. Try grilling the onions and zucchini for this recipe. Cut the vegetables into larger pieces to grill and then roughly chop them after grilling.

2 tablespoons extra virgin olive oil or safflower oil

2 sweet onions, diced

1 fresh jalapeño, seeded and minced

3 or 4 cloves garlic, pressed

1 medium zucchini, sliced ½ inch thick

½ cup marinated sun-dried tomatoes, chopped

1 tablespoon each: chopped fresh basil and marjoram (or 1 teaspoon dried)

2 cups baby spinach

½ teaspoon salt

2 cups ribbon noodles

Freshly grated Romano or Parmesan cheese

1. Heat a heavy skillet over medium heat. Add the oil, onions, jalapeño, and garlic. Stir, cover, reduce the heat, and sweat the onions until soft.

2. Add the zucchini, sun-dried tomatoes, basil, marjoram, and spinach. Cover and cook until the zucchini and spinach are done, about 15 minutes. Stir in the salt.

3. While the vegetables cook, cook the pasta in a large pot of boiling salted water until al dente. Drain and combine with the vegetables in a serving bowl. Garnish with cheese. **Serves 4**

Orzo with Shallots, Kale, and Walnuts

I used to make this dish with spinach and pine nuts (often sourced from China), but I discovered Northwest kale and walnuts have more character in this dish. I like to make this pasta in the fall when my favorite walnuts are harvested from Grouse Mountain Farm in Chelan, Washington, and sold at the University District market in Seattle. You can use locally processed apple cider (for example, from BelleWood Acres at the Bellingham markets or from Rockridge Orchards at Seattle markets) instead of Riesling wine to add a touch of sweetness to this recipe.

> 1½ tablespoons extra virgin olive oil or safflower oil
>
> 1 cup diced shallots
>
> ⅛ teaspoon cayenne
>
> ½ cup Riesling or apple cider
>
> 2 cups water
>
> ½ teaspoon salt
>
> 1½ cups orzo pasta
>
> 2 cups finely chopped fresh kale
>
> ½ cup chopped walnuts, lightly toasted

1. Heat a heavy skillet over medium heat. Add the oil, shallots, and cayenne. Stir and cook until the shallots are soft and slightly browned. Add the Riesling or apple cider and stir. Add the water and salt and bring to a boil.

2. Add the orzo pasta. Reduce the heat to medium and cook until the liquid has been absorbed by the pasta, about 13 minutes. Stir in the kale and cook until wilted. Blend in the walnuts. **Serves 4**

Fava Pesto with Pasta

Fava beans make a great pesto, and this recipe can quickly convert people who love pesto but aren't sure about fava beans. Fresh favas are a specialty crop at Denison Farms in Corvallis, Oregon, and their tender sweet beans can be found at the Corvallis Wednesday market. Elizabeth Kerle of Denison Farms contributed this recipe and says to weigh the favas before removing the pods, so be sure to check their weight at the market. She uses Kasseri cheese in this recipe but says Romano is also good.

> 2 pounds fava beans, removed from pods
>
> 1 bunch basil, roughly chopped
>
> 1 clove garlic, pressed
>
> ½ cup extra virgin olive oil
>
> ¼ cup fresh lemon juice
>
> 1 teaspoon tamari
>
> 1 12-ounce package pasta (your favorite variety)
>
> ½ cup grated sharp cheese

1. Steam the favas for 5 minutes. Combine with the basil, garlic, and oil in a food processor and process until finely chopped. Add the lemon juice, tamari, and fava beans and continue to process until coarsely chopped.

2. Cook the pasta in a large pot of boiling salted water until al dente. Drain.

3. Mix the fava pesto with the pasta in a serving bowl and sprinkle with the cheese. **Serves 6**

Fettuccine with Roasted Red Pepper Sauce

This decadent-tasting sauce depends on gathering the sweetest peppers. At the Corvallis, Oregon, farmers' market, the giant supersweet gold and red bell peppers from Denison Farms are perfect. At the Ashland farmers' market, Fry Family Farm sells equally sweet peppers. Try red peppers for the sauce and yellow for garnish. For a vegan version of this dish, use ½ cup silken tofu blended with 1 teaspoon lemon juice to replace the yogurt. Top this dairy-free version with finely chopped toasted walnuts.

½ tablespoon extra virgin olive oil or safflower oil

1 large onion, chopped

2 red bell peppers

½ cup plain yogurt

2 cloves garlic, pressed

½ tablespoon minced hot peppers

Salt

12-ounce package fettuccine

Shredded Parmesan cheese or toasted finely chopped walnuts

1. Heat a heavy skillet over medium heat. Add the oil and onion, stir, reduce heat, cover, and sweat the onions until soft.

2. While the onion cooks, place the bell peppers in a shallow pan, prick them with a fork, and broil until their skins turn black and blister. Using long tongs, turn them every 5 minutes until all sides are blackened. Put the peppers in a paper bag, close, and let cool for about 15 minutes. Peel and seed.

3. Combine the yogurt, garlic, and hot peppers in a blender. Add the red peppers to the yogurt mixture and blend until smooth and creamy. Add salt to taste.

4. Cook the fettuccine in a large pot of boiling salted water until al dente. Drain and serve with the sauce, sprinkled with cheese or walnuts.
Serves 4

FOOD FOR THOUGHT: HOT AND SWEET PEPPERS

Peppers are divided into two categories—hot and sweet. Hot peppers are used as a spice, and sweet peppers are considered vegetables. A bright red color indicates ripeness, but there are also chocolate, orange, and yellow peppers. And what about green peppers? These are immature red peppers and always arrive first to announce that red peppers are just around the corner. Northwest peppers come into season in mid to late summer through early autumn. Some farmers, like Billy Alstot of Billy's Gardens in Tonasket, Washington, bring big roasters to Northwest markets and roast their organic peppers to sell.

Zucchini Cream Sauce and Pasta

The idea for this recipe came from Stacy DuCharme, whose boyfriend, Bob, won an award for the best home garden in Washington in 2008. Bob grew up cultivating vegetables every summer. After touring Bob and Stacy's picturesque garden, I noticed a zucchini as big as a baseball bat on the kitchen counter, and that's when Stacy told me how she uses up big zucchinis. She discovered a zucchini cream sauce recipe in an old Italian cookbook. She says this is a little like macaroni and cheese, and I say it's a grand idea for using that big zucchini that often only feeds the compost pile. Add a handful of fresh basil for color.

- 4 cups washed and roughly chopped zucchini
- 1 12-ounce package pasta (your favorite variety)
- ¾ cup Parmesan cheese
- ½ teaspoon nutmeg
- Pinch of freshly ground black pepper
- ½ cup roughly chopped fresh basil
- ½ to 1 cup toasted bread crumbs

1. Add the zucchini to a large pot of boiling salted water and reduce the heat. When the zucchini is very tender, drain and save the water. Using the back of a spoon, press as much water as you can from the zucchini.

2. Pour the zucchini cooking water into a pot, add enough water to cook the pasta, and bring it to a boil. Add the pasta and cook until al dente.

3. While the pasta cooks, place the zucchini in a food processor with the cheese, nutmeg, and pepper. Process until very smooth.

4. Toss the pasta with the zucchini sauce and basil in a serving bowl. Top with bread crumbs. **Serves 6**

Mushroom Cream Sauce

Mushroom forager, friend, and veterinary acupuncturist Richard Panzer donated the recipe for this excellent sauce that can be made with morels in the spring or chanterelles in the fall. He says you can also use portobellos if you want, any time of year. This sauce is great on pasta, rice, polenta, or potatoes, or just enjoy it over toast.

- 1 teaspoon extra virgin olive oil or safflower oil
- 3 tablespoons butter
- 3 cloves garlic, minced
- 1 shallot, diced
- 2 pounds mushrooms, roughly chopped
- 1 cup cream (half and half is fine)
- Salt and freshly ground black pepper
- Crushed red pepper flakes

1. Heat a heavy skillet over medium heat. Add the oil and butter. When the butter has melted, add the garlic and shallot and cook until soft.

2. Add the mushrooms and sprinkle with salt. Stir and sauté until well cooked.

3. Add enough cream to cover the mushrooms halfway (add more if necessary). Stir and cook until thickened.

4. Season with salt, pepper, and pepper flakes to taste. **Serves 4**

Hot and Savory Sandwiches

More people are opting for easy fixes at home these days instead of eating fast food, and sandwiches are casual dining at its finest. These entrées are put together quickly with a few slices of whole-grain or artisan bread, some filling and condiment options, and your imagination. Vegetarian sandwiches can include just about anything—pickled beets, sliced cucumbers, grilled asparagus or zucchini, or sautéed mushrooms and leeks, to name just a few creative ingredients.

Roasted Onion and Elephant Garlic Sandwiches with Spinach

Many farmers' markets sell sweet onions in the summer. It's hard to resist adding them to sandwiches. This sandwich is perfect in late summer or early fall, and you can create variations by adding sliced zucchini, roasted red peppers, sun-dried tomatoes, or whatever else strikes your fancy at the market.

4 medium sweet onions, peeled

½ tablespoon extra virgin olive oil, divided

1 head elephant garlic, cloves separated, peeled, and sliced in half lengthwise

2 ounces soft goat cheese

2 tablespoons fresh salsa

Spinach leaves, rinsed and dried

Mayonnaise, aioli, or mustard

4 slices whole-grain bread

1. Preheat the oven to 350°F. Place the peeled onions in a baking dish and brush with ¼ teaspoon oil. Toss the garlic with the rest of the oil and add to the baking dish.

2. Bake until the onions are fork-tender and the garlic is very soft, about 45 minutes. Remove from the oven. Slice the onions in half and mash the garlic with a fork.

3. Spread one side of the bread with goat cheese. Flatten the onions and place them on the goat cheese, spread with garlic, and add a spoonful of salsa. Top with spinach leaves and spread the other slice of bread with a thin layer of mayonnaise, aioli, or mustard before putting the sandwich together. **Makes 2 sandwiches**

Grilled Eggplant, Caramelized Onion, and Tomato Sandwiches

Even meat lovers go for these grilled eggplant sandwiches with caramelized onions. Any type of eggplant will do here, as long as it's locally grown. Imported eggplant purchased from grocery stores in winter is tasteless and tough compared to sweet Northwest varieties.

- 2 tablespoons extra virgin olive oil
- 1 clove garlic, pressed
- 1 onion, sliced ½ inch thick
- 4 slices of medium to large eggplant, ½ inch thick
- 4 thin slices of cheese
- Tomato slices
- Salsa, aioli, or mayonnaise
- Arugula leaves
- 4 French or whole-grain rolls

1. Prepare the grill. Combine the oil and garlic in a small bowl and brush over the onion and eggplant slices. Grill until the vegetables are fairly soft. Lay the vegetables on the bottom half of the roll.

2. Lay the cheese, tomato slices, and arugula leaves over the vegetables. Spread the top roll with salsa, aioli, or mayonnaise. **Makes 4 sandwiches**

Chipotle Sloppy Joes

This vegetarian version of my favorite childhood sandwich features Northwest Walla Walla or sweet onions, bell peppers, tempeh, and chipotle chile powder. Tempeh is a fermented soy product that can be found in the refrigerated section at natural food stores.

- 1 tablespoon extra virgin olive oil or safflower oil
- 1 large Walla Walla or sweet onion, chopped
- ½ each: red and green bell pepper, coarsely chopped
- 4 cloves garlic, pressed
- 2 teaspoons chili powder
- ¼ to ½ teaspoon chipotle chile powder
- 4 ounces tempeh, crumbled
- 1 8-ounce can tomato sauce
- 1 tablespoon apple cider vinegar
- 1 tablespoon molasses
- Pinch of salt
- 2 burger buns

1. Heat a heavy skillet over medium heat. Add the oil, onion, and peppers. Stir, reduce the heat, cover, and cook until the onions are soft. Add the garlic, chili powder, chipotle chile powder, and tempeh. Stir and cook for 5 minutes.

2. Blend in the tomato sauce, vinegar, molasses, and salt. Cover and cook until the tempeh is heated thoroughly, 15 to 20 minutes. Add more salt if necessary. Serve on the buns. **Makes 2 sandwiches**

Roasted Asparagus with Hummus, Spinach, and Tomatoes in Pita Bread

Some people prefer skinny and some like fat asparagus. I use a medium to large size for this recipe. You can use canned, drained, and rinsed garbanzos and skip the bean-cooking step, or better yet, use freshly made hummus from the food co-op or farmers' market and skip most of step 2. As our seasons change, try other vegetables like roasted red pepper, grilled eggplant, or beet slices with this hummus sauce. To make thinner hummus, add a little more water.

> 1½ pounds fresh asparagus, base twisted off and discarded, tips removed and cut into 3-inch lengths
>
> 1 to 2 tablespoons extra virgin olive oil
>
> ¼ cup lemon juice, divided
>
> 1 teaspoon honey or agave nectar
>
> 2 to 3 cloves garlic, pressed
>
> Pinch of cayenne
>
> 1 cup cooked garbanzos
>
> 4 to 5 cloves garlic, pressed
>
> ½ cup water
>
> ¼ cup raw tahini
>
> ¼ teaspoon salt
>
> 2 tablespoons chopped cilantro
>
> Freshly ground pepper
>
> 4 rounds of whole-wheat pita bread
>
> 2 cups washed and torn spinach
>
> 1 large tomato, finely chopped

1. Preheat the oven to 350°F. Place the asparagus in a shallow baking dish. Combine the oil, 2 tablespoons lemon juice, honey or agave nectar, garlic, and cayenne in a small bowl. Pour over the asparagus and toss, then roast the asparagus until tender, about 25 minutes.

2. While the asparagus roasts, combine the garbanzos, garlic, water, tahini, and salt in a small saucepan, bring to a simmer, and cook for a few minutes. Mash together and add the remaining 2 tablespoons lemon juice, cilantro, and pepper to taste.

3. Distribute the asparagus spears evenly among the rounds of pita bread. Top with the hummus sauce, spinach, and tomato. **Makes 4 pita sandwiches**

Fresh corn from the last harvest on a Washington farm near Marysville destined for development. Photo by Sheila and Brad Zahnow.

Black Bean Tostadas

A tostada is an open-faced bean sandwich on a crisp tortilla, and it's easy to find local ingredients for this recipe. This recipe calls for cooked black beans and rice, so cook more on the weekends when you have time and make this later in the week. Look for black beans at the markets or use two cans of drained, rinsed Truitt Brothers black beans, processed in Salem, Oregon, and available in Northwest natural food stores and co-ops. You can roast the garlic and broil the pepper ahead of time.

2 heads garlic

2 tablespoons extra virgin olive oil or safflower oil, divided

1 large red bell pepper

12 corn tortillas

4 cups cooked black beans

1½ cups cooked brown rice

¼ cup water

1 teaspoon coriander

¼ teaspoon cayenne

½ teaspoon salt

1 cup sliced green onions

1 cup finely chopped tomato

1 large avocado, cut into thin slices (optional)

1. Preheat the oven to 350°F. Cut the tops off of the heads of garlic and lay the heads on a piece of foil. Drizzle 1 tablespoon oil over the garlic heads. Wrap them in foil and bake until very tender, about 45 minutes. Let the garlic cool. Press the roasted garlic out into a small bowl.

2. While the garlic roasts, place the bell pepper in a shallow pan, prick it with a fork, and broil until the skin turns black and blisters. Using long tongs, turn it every 5 minutes until all sides are blackened. Put the pepper in a paper bag, close, and let cool for about 15 minutes. Peel, seed, and slice into thin strips.

3. Lay the tortillas flat on a baking sheet and lightly brush with the remaining oil. Bake until crisp, 8 to 10 minutes.

4. Place the beans, rice, water, coriander, cayenne, and salt in a saucepan. Mash together and heat on low for 10 minutes. Add water as needed to keep the mixture from sticking to the pan. The mixture should be very thick. Mash in the roasted garlic and green onions.

5. Spread the bean mixture on the crisp tortillas. Top with the chopped tomato, strips of roasted red pepper, and avocado if desired.

Makes 12 tostadas

Chipotle, Bean, and Potato Tostadas

Potatoes, chiles, and beans thrive in the Northwest and can be found at most farmers' markets. For quick preparation, simmer the cranberry beans the night before or use a pressure cooker.

- 1½ cups finely grated carrots
- ½ cup finely chopped red or green bell pepper
- 2 tablespoons lime juice
- 1 cup cranberry beans, soaked overnight
- 3 cups water, approximately
- 2 to 3 tablespoons extra virgin olive oil or safflower oil, divided
- 1 large onion, chopped
- 2 white or red potatoes (not russets), cut into small chunks
- 1 clove elephant garlic, peeled and sliced (or use 4 cloves regular garlic, minced)
- ½ teaspoon chipotle chile powder
- ½ cup chopped cilantro (optional)
- ½ teaspoon salt
- 8 to 10 corn tortillas

1. Combine the carrots, bell pepper, and lime juice in a small bowl. Mix well and set aside until the tostada filling is ready.

2. Drain and rinse the beans, then combine with the water in a medium saucepan. Bring to a boil, reduce the heat, and simmer partially covered until the beans are very tender, about an hour.

3. When the beans are done, drain and mash them with a potato masher until they make a thick paste. Alternatively, you can cook the beans in a pressure cooker using only 1 cup water and 1 tablespoon olive oil for 10 minutes.

4. While the beans cook, heat a heavy skillet over medium heat. Add 1 tablespoon oil and the onion. Stir, reduce heat, cover, and sweat the onion until soft. Add the potatoes, garlic, and chipotle chili powder. Mix well, cover, and cook until the potatoes are soft, stirring occasionally. You may have to add a little water to keep the potatoes from sticking.

5. When the vegetables and beans are done, blend them together without mashing the potatoes. Mix in the cilantro and salt; keep on low heat until the tortillas bake.

6. Preheat the oven to 350°F. Lay the tortillas flat on a baking sheet. Lightly brush one side of each tortilla with oil. Bake until the tortillas are crisp, about 10 minutes. Spread about ⅓ cup filling on each tortilla. Top with the carrot-pepper mixture. **Makes 8 to 10 tostadas**

Roasted Chile, Squash, and Potato Tacos with Goat Cheese

A friend once served sweet potato tacos for breakfast and I've been in love with the idea of vegetable tacos ever since. Enjoy these any time of day and substitute sweet potatoes if a farmer at your market grows them. I like to use Port Madison Farm goat cheese from Bainbridge Island for this recipe, but you can use your own favorite soft cheese—goat, sheep, or cow. Northwest farmers sell fresh Anaheim chiles in late summer and fall at markets, and if you can buy these chiles already roasted, you can skip the first two steps of this recipe.

- **4 fresh Anaheim chile peppers, green or red (about 5 inches long)**
- **4 tablespoons melted butter or ghee (clarified butter)**
- **1 tablespoon maple syrup**
- **1 medium delicata squash (1 pound), cut in half lengthwise, seeded, and cut into ½-inch slices**
- **3 medium potatoes cut into bite-size chunks**
- **8 corn tortillas**
- **2 ounces goat cheese, crumbled**
- **1½ cups chopped arugula or baby spinach**
- **Fresh salsa**

1. Place the peppers in a shallow pan, prick them with a fork, and broil until the skin turns black and blisters. Using long tongs, turn them every 5 minutes until all sides are blackened. Put the peppers in a paper bag, close, and let cool for about 15 minutes. Peel, seed, and slice into thin strips.

2. Preheat the oven to 350°F. Combine 2 tablespoons butter or ghee and the maple syrup. Pour the mixture over the squash slices and potatoes in a baking pan and stir to coat. Bake until the squash and potatoes are soft and slightly browned, about 30 minutes. Remove from the oven.

3. Lay the corn tortillas flat on a baking sheet. Lightly brush both sides of the tortillas with the remaining butter. Place in the oven until the tortillas are warm and soft, about 5 minutes.

4. Remove from the oven and place the warm roasted squash, potatoes, and pepper strips on half of each tortilla. Sprinkle the cheese and arugula and a spoonful of salsa over the squash and peppers. Fold the tortillas over and enjoy. **Makes 8 tacos**

Northwest Farm Memories

Sales at the University District farmers' market in Seattle don't start until the bell rings, but many shoppers have no idea that a farmer's story resonates behind this bell as it clangs. A close look at it reveals the words "Donated in memory of Bob Meyer" engraved on the side, and market manager and founder Chris Curtis thinks about Bob every time it rings. This is the story of farmer Bob and Stoney Plains Organic Farm.

Bob Meyer's journey to farming started long before he bought his first patch of land. Originally from St. Paul, Minnesota, Bob was a solid man, a union director whose voice boomed with authority and whose longtime dream was to be a farmer. He and his wife, Patricia, rented four community garden plots at a historical mansion in St. Paul, and as they gardened, Bob's farming dream germinated. The Meyers started out using only organic techniques because they wanted good food for their seven children. Bob learned as much as he could as he farmed those garden plots and dreamed about the day he'd have a farm of his own.

In 1977, Bob's job took him to Washington state. He and Patricia lived on a small farm in Lacey, near Olympia, while Bob searched for a bigger piece of land. They bought an old strawberry farm in Tenino a little farther south. It was just 10 acres, and the soil was embedded with so many rocks that Bob christened it "Stoney Plains." Even today after years of pulling rocks out of the soil, Patricia says the field workers still harvest mountains of rocks for a few weeks every year in the spring before planting begins.

Patricia ran the farm in the late 1970s, and Bob farmed whenever he could squeeze in extra hours after work. They didn't have any machinery at first, so Bob bought an old rototiller and carried in produce on a handcart. Bob started selling their farm's produce at the Olympia farmers' market in 1978, just three years after the market opened. His sons Terry and Tom say they helped their dad sell at that market when they were just 10 years old. It wasn't long before Bob became president of the Olympia Farmers' Market Association, where he served for years.

Patricia told me, "Bob was born with the gift of gab." He could talk to anyone at the market. He knew a lot and answered anyone's farm questions. He rattled off produce information like he was born with it, telling customers things like the fact that if fava beans are grown correctly and picked fresh, they don't need to be peeled twice. Bob said the secret to his sweet corn was keeping the freshly picked ears on ice and selling them that day, and he wasn't a bit surprised when people said his was the sweetest corn at the market. Bob was generous with information, sharing his farm tips and "secrets" with anyone.

In the 1980s Stoney Plains generated so much organic produce that Bob got together with four other Washington farmers (one was Nash Huber in Sequim) and started a wholesale co-op that they called "Farmers' Own." Soon they invited five farmers from eastern Washington to join them. They rented a warehouse and hired workers. Each farmer brought his farm's produce to the warehouse for distribution.

Jerry Pipitone at Pipitone Farms, one of the eastern Washington farmers, recalled that their co-op moved millions of dollars worth of produce and one of their biggest customers was the Associated Grocers. Eventually these farmers realized it was difficult moving organic produce wholesale through mainstream grocery stores because the price was higher than that of conventionally grown fruits and vegetables. They sold their co-op business to Charlie's Produce, a Seattle distributor, and the farmers got back to farming.

In 1993, the University District farmers' market opened, and Bob was one of the first farm vendors. Chris Curtis recalled that Bob was enthusiastic about the market's success from the beginning, and she told me that Bob loved interacting with customers and always had helpful advice for other farmers. Later he sold at "Organic Wednesdays" at Pike Place Market and at the Lake City and Columbia City markets. The Meyers saved every extra dollar from produce sales to buy land and equipment.

They grew their farm, and finally in the mid-1990s Bob "retired" to his dream job. He got up at the crack of dawn every day to tend his fields and ride his tractor. "Bob was always learning new things about farming," said Patricia. When daylight faded, Bob picked up farming books and read, learning all he could. Patricia told me, "He tried out things and grew test trials of crops for the Department of Agriculture and later he shared his knowledge with other farmers."

No one ever imagined Stoney Plains without Bob, but in 2002 he died suddenly as a result of complications from gall bladder surgery. The family was stunned. "What will we do with the farm?" Patricia asked.

Everyone wanted to keep the farm going, but they were shocked when Bob's youngest son, Patrick, volunteered to run the farm. Patricia never dreamed any of her children would be interested in farming careers. They had all worked on the farm when they were young but then moved on to other jobs. Young Patrick said that farm work took him away from sports, and he left home at an early age but later returned to work with his dad on the farm and at markets for a few years. No one thought 26-year-old Patrick wanted to farm for a living.

Patricia agreed to let Patrick take over their 45-acre organic farm while she managed the finances. She took over selling at the Columbia City and Olympia markets; a memorial bench for Bob stands outside the covered Olympia market. The first season transitioned smoothly, and many longtime customers stopped by to give condolences and share stories about Bob.

Stepping in to take over a productive 45-acre organic farm is no small task, but Patrick grew up absorbing a lot of farm knowledge, and his work ethic matched Bob's. "He's a carbon copy of his dad," Patricia told me. "Patrick always wants to grow crops more efficiently and to learn more."

At the market, tall, blond Patrick, now in his early 30s, shares secrets about the crops he grows, and when asked about Stoney Plains' specialty crops he says, "We grow 150 crops, you can take your pick." His blue eyes light up as he explains why his carrots are the sweetest at the market. "Just try them," he says. Somewhere Bob must be gazing down smiling.

Another thing that would please Bob is the scholarship fund that was set up in his name for agriculture students by the Friends of the Olympia Farmers' Market (a group that raises money for the market). Stoney Plains Farm also donates 1 percent of the proceeds from CSA subscriptions to the fund, which awards a one-year scholarship to an agriculture student. With this money the Friends of the Olympia Farmers' Market are able to give one or two scholarships each year. Patricia says it's gratifying helping others carry on Bob's passion.

Some Northwest farmers leave this world with such a big heart, community members and fellow farmers sing praises for them long after they're gone. The farming world that Bob Meyer loved also loved him. "He did a lot for other farmers," Wade Bennett of Rockridge Orchards told me.

Bells were donated in Bob's name to each of the markets where he sold produce, and a market worker walks around the market ringing the bell when sales begin. Those who knew Bob stop and listen and remember that tall, burly guy in the blue apron that said "Stoney Plains Organic Farm."

Tops of cornstalks on farmland slated for development in Snohomish County, Washington. Photo by Sheila and Brad Zahnow.

Fresh Fruit Desserts

Whether you crave a buttery apple crisp or an old-fashioned berry ice cream, nothing trumps local fruit for the best flavors and the simplest ways to please the palate. Take the peach, for example. At the most basic level, it's a transportable dessert—just wrap and carry it. But remember to pack it carefully because tree-ripened peaches are fragile and bruise with the slightest touch. Fruit grower Katsumi Taki at Mair Farm-Taki in Washington says even driving can jar fresh juicy peaches and create bruises. When you take a bite, get out your napkin to wipe the sticky juice from your chin. Or take a more civilized approach—peel and slice your peach into a bowl, then sprinkle with a bit of sugar to draw the juices out. For a special dessert, let the peach slices marinate in a little local raspberry wine like that produced by farmer Wade Bennett at Rockridge Orchards in Washington. Just assemble a few simple ingredients—that's how easy dessert is when you use fresh local options.

The variety of Northwest fruit available at farmers' markets is growing. Each season, a few new fruits appear at markets. One year, golden raspberries were sold by a few farmers, and a few years later, these berries became market regulars at a number of farmers' markets. Another year, berry farmers at markets posted signs for Waldo or Chester blackberries, heirloom varieties with exceptional flavors. And more recently, mulberries, pawpaws, pink currants, and elephant heart plums have lured market shoppers to sample fruits off the beaten track.

The Northwest fruit procession begins with strawberries in the spring. Drive out to the country in spring and summer to discover the farms that post "U-pick" signs near their berry fields. By midsummer, market baskets are filled with cherries, raspberries, blueberries, and peaches. Later, lines form for nectarines, plums, figs, and melons. Just as these tasty treats move off the tables, blackberries, apples, pears, Asian pears, and huckleberries take their places.

When using ripe fruit from your garden or the farmers' market, add flavorings sparingly. Let fresh fruit be the star of the show. In the spring and summer, try berries with cream; in midsummer save a few peaches or nectarines to grill. In the fall, try sliced apples and pears drizzled with lavender honey, and in the winter, drizzle pears and

Country farm market sign near Medford, Oregon

figs with orange juice and add a dollop of yogurt or a dusting of finely chopped hazelnuts. Even when you cook local fruit, don't detract from it by adding too much sugar or too many spices or herbs.

This section is filled with ideas inspired by Northwest fruit grown on sustainable farms like Pennington Farms near Grants Pass, Oregon, and Grouse Mountain Farm in Chelan, Washington. Markets draw fruit lovers in the summer, so go early. And no matter which dessert you choose, let fresh local fruit be part of the winning recipe.

Challenges and Rewards in Northwest Orchards

When summer tree fruit ripens, markets fill with fruit lovers milling around tables laden with cherries, figs, peaches, and nectarines. Fruit growers pamper these delicate fruits from bloom to market, dodging seasonal storms, insects, disease, and wildlife to bring us the fruits of their harvests. Four Northwest farmers shared stories with me about the challenges and rewards of growing the tastiest tree fruit in the Northwest.

In Wapato, Washington, 160 miles east of Seattle, Katsumi Taki of Mair Farm-Taki grows organic sweet and sour cherries, apricots, peaches, nectarines, and many varieties of plums. He chauffeurs these sweet treats over the Cascades to the Saturday University District market spring through fall.

The son of a Buddhist minister, Katsumi earned a degree in agriculture and fish biology in Japan. Later, Katsumi converted to Christianity and began growing organic food, first at an orphanage in Japan and then in New Guinea, where he helped others learn how to grow food. Through the influence of a college professor, Katsumi and his family moved to just south of Yakima in eastern Washington in 1990. Katsumi worked on a farm and helped the frail, elderly owner, Rose Mair, until she passed away.

When Mair Farm was put up for sale, Katsumi turned to his relatives in Japan, who helped him buy it in 1993. Katsumi left the name Mair Farm to honor the Mairs, who had no children. He kept half of this 36.5-acre farm uncultivated for wildlife habitat and worked hard restoring orchards that had been in disrepair for many years.

Katsumi told me that some of the cherry trees are more than 50 years old, and they still produce great-tasting cherries. He said weather, weeds, and insects challenge him, but he added, "Cherries are easy compared to apples that get coddling moths." Katsumi watches weather forecasts for spring frosts, which damage delicate stone fruit blossoms. If frost is predicted, he turns on sprinklers that save cherry blooms by encasing them in ice. (Apple, orange, and cranberry growers also use this technique that saves fruit from frostbite.) Later, when the ripe stone fruit is picked, it must be cushioned to avoid bruising. "The road over the mountains is not always so smooth," said

Katsumi, referring to his two-hour drive to the market.

In the early days at his farm, Katsumi nearly lost everything when floods damaged his crops and reduced his income below the level needed to renew his green card. Church members wrote letters, and Senator Patty Murray stepped in to help him keep his green card and continue farming. These days Katsumi is carving out another niche at the market—specialty Asian vegetables like unique greens, ginger, yuzu, and bitter melon.

Another Northwest organic row crop farmer betting on unique varieties of vegetables and tree fruit is Charles Duryea at Grateful Harvest Farm in Junction City, Oregon. Charles told me he had always wanted to be a farmer, and in the 1980s he moved from Michigan to Oregon, where he went to work on Tom Denison's farm in Corvallis. Charles worked there for five years before branching off on his own.

Well known for cherries, Grateful Harvest has a small orchard with about 155 cherry trees of five sweet varieties. Charles told me that it's hard getting consistent harvests, and the quantity depends on bee pollination. He keeps a few beehives of his own but said it's difficult to keep honeybees healthy today. And if the trees bloom before bees emerge in the spring, crop pollination is down. "With pollination, it's all about timing," he explained, referring to the fact that honeybees don't fly in cold and rainy weather. "One year, winter didn't want to stop and June arrived before we could plant anything," he added.

But not many shoppers at the Eugene farmers'

Charles Duryea with his heirloom tomatoes and fig trees under cover at Grateful Harvest Farm

market think about weather patterns and honeybees as they reach for Grateful Harvest's succulent cherries and figs glistening in the sun. "It's a new, upcoming crop," said Charles about his figs.

Cultivating tree fruit can be a gamble, as farmers depend on pollination in the spring and count on favorable weather to boost their harvest. Charles covers his cherry trees with nets so birds don't feast on the crimson treats. Greenhouses shelter his 12-year-old fig trees from weather perils. Western Oregon and Washington aren't the easiest places to grow soft summer fruit, and for peaches and nectarines, soggy spring weather invites diseases.

"It's easier growing orchard fruit east of the Cascades," Liz Eggers of Grouse Mountain Farm in Chelan, Washington, told me. There, a dry climate discourages the diseases that thrive in maritime dampness.

Delectable figs from Grateful Harvest Farm at the Eugene farmers' market

Liz Eggers and Michael Hamphel moved to Washington in the 1970s. Liz was a Jersey girl, "from the Garden State." And Michael hails from near Los Angeles. They each came to the Northwest to work in the orchards, and that's where they met. For a decade they worked in eastern Washington orchards and learned all they could about growing tree fruit. They saved money, bought 10 acres of land in 1988, and planted 2 acres with organic orchard fruit. Liz said their land is remote, and most is on a steep hillside.

"We planted unusual things for ourselves like pawpaws and kiwis, and in 1995 we sold our surplus fruit at the University District farmers' market." Nowadays, they arrive at the market just as summer peaks, bringing sweet and sour cherries. "We grow 10 varieties—7 sweet and 3 sour. We also grow 15 kinds of plums, 6 types of nectarines, and 15 varieties of peaches," Liz told me. They also bring juicy mulberries, which many people believe grow on bushes because of an old childhood song. But Liz told me, "The natural state of mulberry is a tree."

Mulberries are soft and sweet when ripe, and birds are crazy about them. Liz told me they originally planted their mulberry trees as bird traps so the birds wouldn't devour all their cherries. Then she and Michael decided they liked the delicate purple mulberries so much they planted more trees for themselves. In addition to birds, bears often show up for the summer plum and pear buffet. Liz and Michael set up a motion detector with a light to discourage these unwanted guests. "Bears love the fruit but hate the light so they leave," Liz explained. Every year, more shoppers at the University District market linger over the luscious fruit and listen to stories about the bears' midnight picnics at Grouse Mountain Farm.

Another popular tree fruit farm represented at the University District market is Cliffside Orchards of Kettle Falls, 80 miles north of Spokane near the Canadian border. Farmed by Jeanette and Jeff Herman, this 40-acre farm boasts 9 acres of organic apples, pears, nectarines, peaches, apricots, and cherries. Like Liz and Michael, Jeanette and Jeff met while pruning Northwest orchards during the 1970s. They, too, saved for and bought farmland away from conventional fruit orchards to avoid pesticide drift.

"We moved onto our land the day after Mount St. Helens blew in 1980," Jeanette told me. "And we've had our share of challenges in the orchards, mostly weather." She recounted a story of how one year they were in a boat on a lake with some friends when they spotted dark clouds rolling in. "The wind began blowing and picking up speed, and by the time we got the boat to shore, the wind was blowing trees over. I kept hoping the orchard would be okay," said Jeanette. But when the wind stopped, hail started, and by the time it finished it had wiped out their entire orchard. "We made about $3,000 that year. It was depressing, but we knew the next year had to be better, and it was." A decade later, Jeanette and Jeff's farm tables are laden with the sweet fruits of their labor.

Shoppers at urban markets are all smiles when they see tables spilling over with fresh fruit from local farms. What they don't realize are the multiple risks and challenges fruit farmers face in their quest to deliver the sweet rewards of summer.

Raw Fruit Magic

Juicy, flavorful berries, cherries, peaches, nectarines, and plums as well as crisp apples and pears are transported to farmers' markets during the summer and fall. Close your eyes and inhale their subtle, enticing aroma. Raw fruit desserts are humble showcases for these sweet treasures grown locally in the Northwest.

Melon with Sweetened Lime Juice

Nothing beats the taste of a vine-ripened sweet Northwest melon. Gathering Together Farm, Ayers Creek Farm, and Mair Farm-Taki are just a few of the farms that grow juicy organic melons. I found lavender honey in Sequim, Washington, during the annual summer lavender festival, but if you can't find lavender honey at your local farmers' market, add a generous pinch of crushed fresh lavender buds to 1 tablespoon honey. Make sure the lavender is culinary lavender; other varieties of lavender are too strong and soapy tasting.

> **3 cups bite-size pieces of melon (any variety)**
>
> **¼ cup fresh lime juice**
>
> **1 to 3 teaspoons lavender honey**
>
> **Mint sprigs**

Place the melon pieces in a medium-size serving bowl. Combine the lime juice and honey in a separate small bowl, then pour over the melon. Garnish with mint sprigs. **Serves 4 to 6**

Marinated Strawberries

Strawberries fresh from the farm or garden are perfect in this easy dessert. A small amount of sugar helps pull the juice from the berries that are infused with the flavors of a liqueur, wine, or juice. You can use raspberries or blackberries, or sliced apricots, peaches, or nectarines, instead of strawberries. You can also serve these berries over shortcake or ice cream.

> **2 cups sliced strawberries**
>
> **1 tablespoon sugar**
>
> **2 tablespoons orange juice, Chambord, Grand Marnier, key lime liqueur, Malibu rum, or balsamic vinegar**
>
> **Edible flowers such as violets, Johnny jump-ups, nasturtiums, anise hyssop, calendula, squash blossoms, miniature roses, or lavender**

Combine the strawberries, sugar, and liquid of your choice and gently mix together in a bowl. Refrigerate for at least 1 hour before serving. Garnish with edible flowers. **Serves 4**

Ambrosia

This dessert combines four of my summer favorites—strawberries, apricots, peaches, and cherries. I like to use Holmquist Orchards hazelnut butter and Port Madison goat yogurt for this easy dessert, but almond butter and plain yogurt like Nancy's also work. For a dairy-free version, use 1 cup silken tofu instead of yogurt and blend the lime juice in with a hand blender for a smooth sauce with a tart zing.

- 1 cup plain yogurt
- 2 tablespoons fresh lime juice (optional)
- 1½ cups strawberries
- 1 or 2 tablespoons hazelnut or almond butter
- 1 to 2 teaspoons honey or agave nectar
- 1 cup chopped apricots
- 2 ripe peaches, peeled, pitted, and sliced
- 1 cup grapes
- 1 cup pitted cherries
- 2 tablespoons grated coconut (optional)

Combine the yogurt, lime juice, strawberries, hazelnut or almond butter, and honey or agave nectar in a blender and puree until smooth. Gently mix in the apricots, peaches, grapes, and cherries. Top with grated coconut if desired.
Serves 4

Summer Fruit with Fresh Apricot-Ginger Sauce

This easy-to-make fruit dessert uses an equally simple sauce—fruit pureed with ginger. The beauty of this fruit puree is its adaptability. You can easily substitute a few lavender buds, mint, or anise hyssop if you don't have ginger. The best choices for fruit puree are soft fruits like nectarines, apricots, strawberries, and blueberries. Raspberries and blackberries can be used, but unless you strain the puree, it will contain seeds. As for preserves, check your farmers' market. I found the best peach-nectarine preserves for this recipe from Pennington Farms at the Ashland farmers' market.

- 4 cups assorted melon balls, sliced peaches, or nectarines
- 8 ripe medium-size apricots
- 2 tablespoons apricot or nectarine preserves
- 1 tablespoon grated ginger
- 1 tablespoon grated coconut (optional)
- Edible flowers such as violets, Johnny jump-ups, nasturtiums, anise hyssop, calendula, squash blossoms, miniature roses, or lavender (optional)

1. Place the melon or stone fruit in a serving bowl. Place the apricots and preserves in a blender and puree. Squeeze the juice from the grated ginger into the mixture, discard the pulp, and blend.

2. Pour the puree over the fruit and mix gently. Garnish with grated coconut and edible flowers if desired. **Serves 6**

Autumn Fruit Delight

Nothing says autumn like succulent pears and crisp sweet-tart apples. It doesn't really matter which variety you choose; the Northwest offers many. My favorite apple is Prairie Spy, an old-fashioned variety developed in Minnesota in the 1940s and now grown and sold by Grouse Mountain Farm of Chelan, Washington.

2 tablespoons fresh lemon juice

1 tablespoon finely chopped lemon zest

1 tablespoon honey

2 sweet-tart apples, seeded and chopped

2 Bosc pears, chopped

Handful of grapes

4 ripe figs, cut in half (optional)

¼ cup chopped walnuts

1. Mix the lemon juice, zest, and honey together in a small bowl. Toss with the apples and pears in a large bowl, making sure the sauce coats all the fruit. Blend in the grapes.

2. Place in separate serving bowls and garnish with fig halves if desired and walnuts. **Serves 4**

Belle Island grapes, a Northwest native, growing at Rockridge Orchards in Enumclaw, Washington

HERBS, SPICES, LIQUEURS, AND FLOWERS TO ENHANCE FRUIT DESSERTS

If you want to substitute a different Northwest fruit in your favorite recipe, check the following list and see which flavors go along with it. You can find edible flowers at the farmers' market or grow your own.

- Apples—lemon or orange zest, cardamom, cinnamon, nutmeg, cloves, ginger, Amaretto (almond liqueur), Applejack brandy, Merlot, lilacs
- Apricots—almond or vanilla extract, cardamom, ginger, nutmeg, apricot brandy, Grand Marnier (orange liqueur), hazelnut liqueur, lavender
- Berries—coconut extract, lemon or orange zest, rose water, mint, lemon verbena, Kirsch (cherry brandy), Triple Sec (orange liqueur), Crème de Casiss (black currant liqueur), Chambord (black raspberry liqueur), key lime liqueur, Zinfandel, lavender, pansies
- Cherries—lemon or orange zest, almond extract, Cherry Herring (cherry brandy), Kirsch, hazelnut liqueur, banana liqueur, Grand Marnier, cognac, balsamic vinegar, rose geranium, violets, lavender
- Figs—cardamom, nutmeg, cinnamon, cloves, anise, star anise, almond or vanilla extract, coconut flavoring, orange or lemon zest,

- balsamic vinegar, rose or orange flower water, Malibu rum, lavender
- Melons—lime or orange zest, mint, ginger, star anise, Alize, Midori melon liqueur, key lime liqueur, Malibu rum, Japanese plum wine, sparkling white wine, nasturtiums, lavender, violets
- Nectarines and peaches—vanilla extract, maple syrup, cardamom, cloves, cinnamon, ginger, bourbon, Kahlua, peach schnapps, hazelnut liqueur, key lime liqueur, Marsala, pansies
- Pears—lemon verbena, mint, cardamom, cinnamon, cloves, ginger, balsamic vinegar, Clavados (applejack brandy), bourbon, Riesling, ruby port wine
- Plums—vanilla extract, orange or lemon zest, anise, cloves, ginger, Cointreau (orange liqueur), gin, Japanese plum wine
- Strawberries—lemon, orange, or lime zest, rose water, mint, tequila, coconut schnapps, strawberry liqueur, banana liqueur, key lime liqueur, Grand Marnier, white chocolate liqueur, hazelnut liqueur, Malibu rum, port wine, balsamic vinegar, pansies, violets, lavender

Frozen Fruit Desserts

Hot summer days and cooling frozen treats naturally go together, and Northwest fruit adds a touch of elegance. These frozen fruit desserts are dairy-free, and all but the Easy Frozen Raspberry Pops rely on churning to make them creamy. Using an ice cream maker is much easier than hand mixing and produces creamier results, but you can also mix by hand, a process that takes about three hours. To hand mix, combine all the ingredients in a large bowl and place the mixture in the freezer. Take it out every half hour to stir with a hand blender or mixer to incorporate air into the mixture. Stir until the mixture becomes cold and thick, stirring by hand when it becomes too difficult to use a hand blender.

Easy Frozen Raspberry Pops

No churning is required to make this easy fruit dessert. Get Popsicle molds at a kitchen or department store. Check the market for apple cider, and when you substitute another fruit, consider which variety of preserves will best complement the fruit. Certified organic Ayers Creek Farm of Gaston, Oregon, sells both berries and preserves at the Hillsdale farmers' market. Look for these items at a market in your neighborhood.

- 1 cup fresh raspberries
- 1 12-ounce shelf-stable package firm silken tofu, or 1½ cups plain or vanilla yogurt
- 2 tablespoons fresh lemon juice
- 3 tablespoons berry preserves
- 1 tablespoon finely chopped orange zest (optional)
- 1 teaspoon agar flakes
- 1 cup apple cider

1. Combine the berries, tofu, lemon juice, preserves, and orange zest if desired in a blender and mix until smooth and creamy.

2. In a small saucepan, sprinkle the agar flakes over the apple cider. Bring to a boil over high heat, reduce the heat, and simmer until the flakes are dissolved, about 5 minutes. Add to the raspberry-tofu mixture and puree until smooth.

3. Pour the puree into Popsicle molds and freeze until solid; or pour into small paper cups, freeze until slushy, insert a stick, and freeze until solid. To remove from plastic molds, run water over the mold, twist the handle gently, and pull. **Makes 12 pops**

Brandied Strawberry Granita

Enjoy the bursts of tantalizing summer berry flavor from the combination of fresh berries and Kirsch (a cherry brandy) in this rich-tasting Italian-style frozen ice. You need a blender and a few hours to make this delicious treat.

½ tablespoon agar flakes

1 cup apple juice or cider

¼ cup sugar

2 cups strawberries

3 tablespoons fresh lemon juice

¼ cup Kirsch (cherry brandy)

1 cup water

Pansies, lavender, or other edible flowers

1. Sprinkle the agar flakes over the apple juice in a small saucepan. Let the agar soak for a few minutes to soften. Bring the liquid to a boil over high heat, then reduce the heat to medium and cook, stirring constantly, for 5 minutes.

2. Remove from the heat and stir in the sugar. Let the mixture sit while you blend the strawberries, lemon juice, Kirsch, and water in a blender or food processor.

3. Add the apple juice mixture to the strawberry mixture. Blend on low until well mixed. Pour into ice cube trays and freeze solid.

4. At least 2 hours before serving, remove the cubes from the freezer and let them thaw for 5 minutes. Then place about a third of the cubes in a food processor or blender and pulse the machine on and off until the cubes are the consistency of coarse snow. Keep blending until the mixture is creamy looking and not runny. Process the remaining cubes in the same way.

5. Place in a glass or plastic container, cover, and freeze for a few hours. There is no need to let this dessert sit out before serving. Garnish with edible flowers. **Serves 4**

FREEZING BERRIES EFFICIENTLY

Ayers Creek Farm of Gaston, Oregon, offers this great no-fuss method for freezing whole organic berries purchased at the farmers' market: Take the berries home and place them in the freezer in the clam shell or pint box they came in. Once the berries are frozen, remove them. If any are bad, add those to the compost heap. Place the rest in a Ziploc bag or sealed container. They will keep this way for at least six months in the freezer. As for rinsing the berries first, it's a matter of taste. Running cold water over berries grown close to the ground may remove bacteria, but it doesn't disinfect them or remove pesticides, and thus the importance of buying organic or growing your own organically.

Frozen Vanilla–Fresh Fruit Delight

Add your favorite summer fruit to this great basic recipe; experiment with different fruit and flavor combinations. Agar (or agar agar) is found in natural food stores on the international aisle. While you are there, look for a shelf-stable silken tofu for this recipe; Mori-Nu makes a great organic version. If you prepare this recipe one or two days ahead and refrigerate it, the flavors marry and the churning process is easy and quick. Top this dessert with more fresh fruit or mix in your favorite dried fruit or finely chopped walnuts or hazelnuts.

2 vanilla beans or 1 teaspoon vanilla extract

1 cup plain or vanilla soy milk (rice milk is too thin)

1 12-ounce shelf-stable package firm silken tofu

½ cup sugar

⅛ teaspoon salt

Pinch of freshly grated nutmeg

2 tablespoons light olive or canola oil

2½ teaspoons agar flakes

¾ cup water

½ cup chopped dried fruit, walnuts, or hazelnuts (optional)

½ cup chopped fresh fruit (optional)

1. If you use vanilla beans, cut them in half lengthwise and scrape out the insides, then discard the pods.

2. Combine the vanilla from the beans or the vanilla extract with the soy milk, tofu, sugar, salt, nutmeg, and oil in a blender and puree until creamy. Chill for at least 2 hours.

3. Sprinkle the agar flakes over the water in a small saucepan. Bring to a boil over medium heat, then reduce the heat and simmer until the flakes are dissolved, about 5 minutes. Let cool for about 10 minutes and then add to the cold mixture.

4. Turn on the prepared ice cream maker (chilled overnight in the freezer) and add the mixture. Churn until very thick, about 35 minutes. If you add dried fruit and/or nuts, pour them in just before turning off the ice cream maker. Serve with fresh fruit on top if desired.
Serves 4

Stopping for berries and ice cream at Cascadian Home Farm, Rockport, Washington

Creamy Frozen Maple-Apricot Dessert

The flavors of apricots and maple syrup blend well in this frozen dessert, but you can substitute other local fruits if you want. Peel peaches, pit cherries, and if you want to use berries, use 1/2 cup of fruit concentrate instead of maple syrup to sweeten. With berries, try orange or lemon zest for added flavoring. Top with a sprinkling of shredded coconut or chopped nuts.

3 cups sliced apricots

1 12-ounce shelf-stable package firm silken tofu

¼ cup maple syrup

1 tablespoon fresh lemon juice

Generous pinch of nutmeg or cardamom

⅛ teaspoon salt

2 teaspoons agar flakes

1 cup apricot or apple juice

Maple syrup for topping

1. Combine the apricots, tofu, maple syrup, lemon juice, nutmeg or cardamom, and salt in a blender and mix until smooth and creamy. Pour into a container and refrigerate for at least a few hours before churning.

2. Sprinkle the agar flakes over the juice in a small saucepan, bring to a boil over high heat, reduce the heat, and simmer until the flakes are dissolved, about 5 minutes. Let cool for 10 minutes and then blend with the cold mixture.

3. Turn on the prepared ice cream maker (chilled overnight in the freezer) and add the mixture. Churn until very thick, about 35 minutes. Serve with a swirl of maple syrup on top.

Serves 6

TIPS ON USING AN ICE CREAM MAKER

- Read through the recipe before beginning.
- Experiment with flavorings and fruits but keep the same proportion of tofu, sweeteners, liquid ingredients, and agar.
- Blend all the ingredients, except the agar and liquid, 24 hours before you make the frozen dessert. Refrigerate the mixture until you're ready to make the dessert.
- Place the ice cream maker base in the freezer at least eight hours before making the dessert. If your freezer has space, simply store the base in your freezer all summer for great desserts on the spur of the moment.
- When mixing the dessert, turn on the ice cream maker first before adding the mixture; otherwise the dessert will stick to the sides of the base and freeze up, and it will freeze unevenly.
- Churn for 35 minutes and sample liberally to make sure the mixture has the right consistency before turning off the machine.
- Consume the dessert immediately, if possible. Because these desserts have a lower fat content, the water molecules begin linking up as the dessert sits in the freezer, changing the texture from creamy to hard and grainy

Easy Cooked Fruit Desserts

Many cooked or baked fruit desserts can be made easily and quickly. The most important ingredient is the fruit you use. Seek out the best quality local fruit for these sweet indulgences. Add a garnish of grated coconut or mint leaves, or a dollop of whipped cream and some edible flowers, and these simple treasures turn into decadent-tasting desserts.

Cider-Baked Pears

This easy dish is just pears and cider. Pears span a range of textures and flavors; my favorite baking variety is Bosc, a buttery textured pear that holds up well with cooking and has a mild sweet flavor. The ginger adds a bit of spice. I buy fresh ginger from Mair Farm-Taki in Wapato, Washington, and I get apple cider from Rockridge Orchards in Enumclaw, Washington.

> **4 to 6 pears (Anjou or Bosc)**
>
> **2 cups apple cider**
>
> **1 to 2 tablespoons freshly grated ginger (optional)**
>
> **Grated coconut**

1. Preheat the oven to 325°F. Cut the pears into quarters. (No need to seed the pears because the seeds are soft enough to eat.)

2. Place the pears in a shallow baking dish. Pour the apple cider over the pears and sprinkle with ginger if desired. Cover and bake until the pears soak up most of the cider, 1 hour or more.

3. When the pears are soft and done, sprinkle with coconut and place them under the broiler for a few minutes to brown lightly on top. **Serves 6**

Balsamic Poached Pears

Classic poached fruit is simmered in one part sugar and two parts water, but I haven't ever used that much sugar for poaching fruit. Most Northwest fruit needs little sweetening to improve the flavor. After you've tried this recipe once with pears, mix it up and try poaching peaches, apricots, nectarines, or apples.

> **2 tablespoons berry preserves or marmalade**
>
> **2 tablespoons sugar**
>
> **¼ cup balsamic vinegar or raspberry wine**
>
> **1½ cups water**
>
> **2 large Bosc pears, cored and halved**
>
> **Grated coconut (optional)**

1. Combine the berry preserves or marmalade, sugar, and balsamic vinegar in a small bowl. Mix well and stir into the water in a medium saucepan. Bring the mixture to a boil over high heat.

2. Add the pears, reduce the heat to low, and gently simmer uncovered for about 10 minutes. Let the pears cool in the liquid, then remove them to a serving dish and spoon the sauce over. Garnish with coconut if desired. **Serves 4**

Stuffed Baked Apples

Take your pick of apples for this recipe (good ones to try are Newton, Pippin, Granny Smith, Fuji, or Winesap), keeping in mind that the apples that work best are those that hold their shape and texture as they bake. Some apples become mushy when cooked, so it's best to ask the farmer who grew them to suggest which apples are best for baking.

¾ cup apple juice or cider

¼ cup Applejack brandy, or more apple juice

1 tablespoon arrowroot powder

1½ tablespoons maple syrup

3 tablespoons hazelnut butter

3 Medjool dates, pitted and cut into small pieces

2 large sweet-tart baking apples, cored, peeled, and halved

1. Preheat the oven to 350°F. Combine the apple juice, brandy, and arrowroot powder in a small saucepan. Stir until the arrowroot has dissolved.

2. Mix the maple syrup, hazelnut butter, and dates together in a small bowl.

3. Place the apples in a baking dish and fill their hollowed-out centers with the date mixture. Pour the apple juice–arrowroot sauce over the apples. Cover and bake until the apples are soft, about 45 minutes. **Serves 4**

Summer Fruit Compote with Lavender

Compotes are perfect for serving over plain cakes or bread pudding. Lavender is available in midsummer at most Northwest farmers' markets. Coconut milk adds a creamy texture without dairy. Use a mortar and pestle to crush the lavender buds.

3 peaches, peeled, pitted, and sliced

4 apricots, pitted and quartered

4 plums, pitted and quartered

¾ cup apple juice

¼ cup coconut milk

1 teaspoon crushed lavender buds

½ tablespoon arrowroot powder

Combine all the ingredients in a large saucepan. Mix until the arrowroot powder has dissolved. Cover and simmer until the fruit is soft, about 10 minutes. **Serves 4**

FOOD FOR THOUGHT: TREE FRUIT AND THE LOCAL ECONOMY

Northwest tree fruit producers help grow our local economy. The Washington State Horticultural Society says that in the Yakima Valley the estimated economic boost from tree fruit for the state is more than $2 billion. About 140,000 jobs are tied to this farm industry, which employs personnel from pickers to warehouse workers to delivery truck drivers and retail sales clerks. Every local apple and pear purchased helps support hardworking farmers and grows our local economy.

Winter Ginger Fruit Compote

What's a Northwest food lover to do in winter when local options dwindle? Dip into the dried fruit treasure chest, dehydrated from summer's bounty, and enjoy the sweet rewards. For this recipe, the best flavors are achieved when the dried fruit marinates in juice overnight or all day, before baking. Fruit flavors concentrate when fruit is dehydrated. Use juice or cider from the farmers' market; some farms like Rockridge Orchards sell juice and cider year-round. The quince is optional here since it has a short run in the fall and then it's gone, but it's a great addition and it blends in well with so much pectin. Many Northwest apple growers also grow quince.

> **3 cups assorted dried local fruit (peaches, nectarines, apples, apricots, pears, figs, or cherries)**
>
> **4 cups apple juice or cider**
>
> **2 tablespoons fresh lemon juice**
>
> **1½ to 2 tablespoons grated ginger**
>
> **1 quince, peeled and diced small (optional)**
>
> **Sugar**

1. Place the dried fruit in an ovenproof ceramic or glass bowl and combine it with the apple juice or cider and the lemon juice. Squeeze the juice from the grated ginger over the dried fruit and discard the ginger pulp. Let the fruit sit overnight in the refrigerator.

2. Preheat the oven to 350° F. Remove the fruit from the refrigerator and blend in the quince if desired.

3. Bake uncovered until the fruit is plump and soft, about 75 minutes, basting and sampling occasionally. Add sugar to taste. **Serves 4 to 6**

Maple-Glazed Grilled Peaches

A few years ago I was surprised to read that the best peaches in the country were grown in Grand Junction, Colorado. My first thought was that the author obviously hadn't sampled the certified organic peaches from Rama Farm, a small farm in Washington. I buy boxes of their juicy peaches every summer. When I visited the Ashland farmers' market, I tasted peaches so sweet they made my mouth tingle and so juicy I needed a napkin. Don't worry about driving to Grand Junction; local Northwest is the key for the best peaches. If you buy red haven peaches, they don't have to be blanched to peel them. Simply run water over them and pull the skin off. You can also grill apricots, nectarines, apples, and pears. Slice apples and pears so they cook a little faster.

> **3 tablespoons maple syrup**
>
> **2½ tablespoons orange juice**
>
> **½ tablespoon Grand Marnier**

TIPS ON DRYING SUMMER FRUIT

A dehydrator is fun and helpful, but you don't necessarily need one to dry summer fruit. Peel, core, and slice the fruit. To prevent discoloration of apples and pears, toss them with a mixture of about 2 tablespoons lemon juice to ½ cup water. Then lay the fruit flat on a pizza screen or parchment-lined baking sheet. Set your oven to the lowest possible temperature and put the fruit in to dehydrate. The timing depends on how thick the fruit slices are. In a dehydrator at 100°F, peach slices take about three days to dehydrate.

Pinch of nutmeg or cardamom (optional)

6 peaches, peeled, pitted, and halved

Vanilla ice cream or yogurt (optional)

Mint sprigs

1. Lightly spray the grill grid with oil to prevent sticking. Preheat the grill. Combine the maple syrup, orange juice, Grand Marnier, and nutmeg or cardamom if desired. Brush the cut side of the peaches with the mixture.

2. When the grill is ready, place the peaches cut side down on the grill. Brush the tops with the maple glaze. After 5 minutes turn the peaches and cook for another 5 minutes, until lightly browned.

3. Pour any remaining glaze over the peaches and serve with a dollop of ice cream or yogurt if desired. Garnish with mint sprigs. **Serves 6**

Ginger-Simmered Rhubarb and Nectarines

Tart rhubarb and pungent ginger are balanced by sweet nectarines and apple cider in this fruit dessert. Enjoy it over angel food cake or ice cream, or with a shortbread cookie on the side. Rhubarb is everywhere in the Northwest in the spring and summer, so take advantage. I blanch and freeze rhubarb in the spring so I'll have it on hand when nectarines appear at the market in August.

2 cups rhubarb cut into ½-inch lengths

1¼ cups apple cider

1 tablespoon grated ginger

4 nectarines, pitted and sliced

Whipped cream or crème fraîche

1. Place the rhubarb and apple cider in a medium saucepan. Squeeze the juice from the ginger over the rhubarb and discard the ginger pulp.

2. Bring to a boil over high heat, reduce the heat, and simmer until the rhubarb is fork-tender, about 10 minutes. Add the nectarines and cook until tender, 3 to 5 minutes.

3. Top with a dollop of whipped cream or crème fraîche. **Serves 4**

Baked Nectarines

I'm always amazed when I meet someone who isn't a nectarine fan, because for me, any way you slice them, juicy ripe nectarines are heavenly. Grouse Mountain Farm, Mair Farm-Taki, Rama Farm, and Cliffside Orchards are just a few farms that sell beautiful nectarines at Seattle farmers' markets. Baked nectarines are great alone, or serve them over vanilla ice cream or a coconut sorbet for a decadent treat.

4 nectarines, halved and pitted

1 tablespoon fresh lemon juice

1 cup peach, apricot, or apple juice

1 tablespoon sugar

Freshly grated nutmeg

1. Preheat the oven to 350°F. Place the nectarine halves, cut side down, in a shallow baking dish. Sprinkle with the lemon juice. Pour the peach juice over and sprinkle with the sugar and nutmeg.

2. Bake uncovered until very tender, about 30 minutes. **Serves 4**

Sautéed Balsamic Cherries

These cherries make an easy, quick dessert that is simple and elegant. Sample cherries at the market before you make your final selection. At the Eugene farmers' market, look for Grateful Harvest Farm's sweet cherries. At the University District farmers' market in Seattle, try sweet cherries from Grouse Mountain Farm or Mair Farm-Taki. For the best flavor when making these cherries, use a high-quality balsamic vinegar, not a cheap grocery store brand.

1 tablespoon ghee (clarified butter)

2½ cups pitted sweet cherries

2 tablespoons balsamic vinegar

Generous pinch of crushed lavender buds

1 to 2 tablespoons sugar

Grated coconut

1. Heat a heavy skillet over medium heat. Add the ghee and when the skillet is hot, stir in the cherries. Sauté until soft.

2. Sprinkle sugar over the cherries and stir until all cherries are coated. Add the balsamic vinegar and lavender buds. Stir and cook for another 30 seconds.

3. Remove from the heat and garnish servings with coconut. **Serves 4**

Cranberry Apple Whip

Cranberries add seasonal color and make fall more festive. Incorporate them with apples and pears into fall desserts. Check farmers' markets, because different local selections appear frequently. In Seattle, look for cranberries from Rainier Mountain Cranberries of Eatonville, Washington, at the University District farmers' market. At Northwest food co-ops look for Ladybug Brand organic cranberries, grown by small-to-medium Northwest family farms and packaged and distributed by Organically Grown Company, an Oregon-based company; look there also for organic cranberries from Stahlbush Island Farms of Corvallis, Oregon.

2 cups sliced apples

2 cups fresh cranberries

½ cup apple juice

¼ cup sugar

1 teaspoon almond extract

1 12-ounce shelf-stable package firm silken tofu

¼ cup finely chopped walnuts, hazelnuts, or pecans

1. Place the apples, cranberries, apple juice, sugar, and almond extract in a saucepan and cook over medium-low heat until the fruit is tender, 5 to 10 minutes.

2. Puree 2 cups at a time in a blender, then return the fruit to the saucepan and cook until the mixture thickens.

3. Puree the tofu with the mixture in a blender until smooth and creamy. Top servings with chopped nuts. **Serves 6**

Plums with Honey and Mint

Lemon, honey, and plums were meant to be together, and cooking enhances the sweet-tart contrast tones in this recipe. The end result depends on the plum quality; don't expect to get great results from conventionally grown plums. Look for unusual varieties of plums at your local market. Grouse Mountain Farm in Chelan, Washington, sells elephant heart plums at the University District farmers' market; Ayers Creek Farm in Gaston, Oregon, grows and sells several popular old-fashioned varieties at the Hillsdale farmers' market. These plums with honey make a decadent topping over a slice of pound cake. Garnish with a dollop of lemon yogurt or a scoop of lemon sorbet.

⅔ cup water

1 tablespoon fresh lemon juice

1 tablespoon finely chopped lemon zest

2 tablespoons honey

14 to 16 small plums, pitted and halved

Fresh mint sprigs

Pinch of salt

Lemon yogurt (optional)

Pound cake (optional)

1. Stir the water, lemon juice, zest, and honey together in a small saucepan and bring to a boil over high heat. Add the plums, mint sprigs, and salt. Reduce the heat and cook on low until the plums are soft, about 10 minutes.

2. Remove from the heat, cool, and serve over pound cake with a dollop of yogurt if desired. Garnish with fresh mint sprigs. **Serves 4**

Vanilla Baked Plums and Pears

Plums and pears can be found at any Northwest farmers' market in the fall. Seasons for the two fruits overlap, and the flavors of the two fruits enhance each other. Italian prune plums are among the most popular and abundant plums. Bosc pears add a buttery texture and a silky sweetness.

- 12 Italian prune plums (or 8 to 10 larger plums), halved and pitted
- 2 Bosc pears, cored and sliced
- ½ cup apple juice or cider
- 1 tablespoon fresh lemon juice
- 1 tablespoon arrowroot powder
- 1 vanilla bean or ½ teaspoon vanilla extract
- ½ cup whole wheat flour
- ¼ cup rolled oats
- 3 tablespoons brown sugar
- 3 tablespoons butter
- ¼ cup chopped walnuts or hazelnuts, toasted

1. Preheat the oven to 350°F. Combine the plums, pears, apple juice or cider, lemon juice, arrowroot powder, and vanilla extract in a small bowl and mix well. If you use a vanilla bean, cut it in half lengthwise and scrape the inside into the mixture, then discard the pod. Pour the mixture into a 9-by-9-inch baking dish.

2. Combine the flour, oats, brown sugar, butter, and nuts, mixing until well blended. Sprinkle over the fruit mixture.

3. Bake covered for 40 minutes. Uncover the dish and continue to bake for another 10 minutes. Place this dish under the broiler for a few minutes to brown the topping, if desired. **Serves 4**

Country farm market sign near Medford, Oregon

Quince Paste

I spotted quince on the Grouse Mountain Farm table at the University District farmers' market, and I picked up the yellow slightly pear-shaped fruit, ran my fingers over the light fuzz on the skin, and inhaled the sweet perfume. Liz Eggers from Grouse Mountain shared a favorite recipe for quince paste. This sweet-tart reddish orange confection takes time but is worth the time invested. As it cooks, the abundant pectin in quince makes it jell. To make a spread instead of a sliceable confection, cook it for only one hour.

4½ pounds ripe quinces, washed, peeled, cored, and coarsely chopped (reserve cores and peels)

5½ cups sugar

Water

1. Place the quince in a large saucepan. Wrap the cores and peels in cheesecloth, tie the packet with kitchen string, and add it to the pan. The peels contain most of the pectin, which contributes to the firmness of the quince paste.

2. Pour enough water into the pan to cover the quince. Simmer half-covered until the fruit is very soft, about 30 minutes. Remove the bag of peels and pass the quince flesh through a sieve or food mill. Don't use a food processor or the texture will be too fine. You should have about 4 cups of fruit pulp.

3. Transfer the quince pulp to a 6-quart or larger pan and add the same amount of sugar as there is pulp. Stir and cook over low heat until the sugar has dissolved. Continue cooking, stirring frequently with a wooden spoon, until the paste has a deep orange color, about 1½ hours. (If you want a spread instead of a paste, stir for about 1 hour and skip the next two steps. Store in the refrigerator.) When you draw the wooden spoon along the bottom of the saucepan, it should leave a trail, and the quince mixture should stick to the spoon.

4. Lightly oil a 9-by-13-inch baking dish, or line it with parchment paper. Transfer the paste to the baking dish, spreading it to about 1½ inches thick. Smooth the top and allow the paste to cool.

5. Bake the paste on the lowest oven setting, no more than 125°F, until dry, about 1½ hours. Allow the paste to cool completely (overnight is preferable). Slice into 1-inch squares and store the squares in an airtight container in the refrigerator for up to 7 months. The color deepens with age. **Fills a 9-by-13-inch pan to 1½ inches deep**

FOOD FOR THOUGHT: OLD-FASHIONED QUINCE

Quince is one of those foods that most people haven't tasted and don't know how to use, but in colonial England quince preserves were popular, and in the early years of the American colonies, quince enjoyed a brief moment when home gardeners cultivated the trees and made quince pies with raisins and nuts. But the sweeter flavors of apples won over the new immigrants, and the mouth-puckering quince fell by the wayside and has never returned to join the favored fruits in America. At Northwest farmers' markets, some farmers know the value of quince and are trying to revive this lovely ancient fruit. If you see quince, buy one or two and peel, slice, and enjoy them with cooked apples in recipes.

The baked desserts in this section are simple comfort foods that bring back memories of my grandmother's apple and cherry pies. Everyone raved about her flaky, tender piecrusts, but Grandma's real secret was the fruit tucked inside. It was local and perfectly ripe. Mom used to tell me, "Use the best fruit and even your mistakes taste like winners." Cook up some seasonal comfort of your own with these old-fashioned recipes.

Sour Cherry Bread Pudding

I freeze cherries in the summer so I can make this sweet dessert for Valentine's Day. The farmers' market is the only place to look for pie cherries in the Northwest because they are so perishable. My favorite pie cherries are called North Star and are available from Grouse Mountain Farm in Chelan, Washington, but I'm sure you can find your own favorite at your local market. Unlike sweet cherries, pie cherries are a snap to pit. Serve this pudding warm with a little vanilla soy milk poured over it, or top it with whipped cream or ice cream.

> 5 cups artisan bread cubes, crusts removed
>
> 1½ cups pitted sour cherries
>
> ½ cup sugar
>
> 1½ cups milk or vanilla soy milk
>
> 3 eggs, separated
>
> 2 tablespoons rum or ½ tablespoon vanilla extract
>
> ½ teaspoon salt

1. Preheat the oven to 325°F and lightly oil a 9-by-9-inch baking dish. Combine the bread cubes, sour cherries, and sugar in a large bowl and mix well.

2. Heat the milk in a small saucepan over medium heat. When warm, stir in the egg yolks, blending well. Add the rum or vanilla and the salt. Stir and cook for a few minutes until the mixture thickens. Remove from the heat, pour over the bread cubes, and mix well.

3. Whip the egg whites until soft peaks form, and then fold into the bread mixture. Turn the mixture into the prepared baking dish and bake until the pudding is set, about 45 minutes.
Serves 6

Cherry Upside-Down Cake

Pineapple upside-down cake was the inspiration for this recipe that uses pie cherries available at many Northwest farmers' markets in the summer. Look for sour pie cherries early in the summer and buy enough to pit and freeze for winter. If cherry season is gone, try nectarines, peaches, or blueberries for this cake. Serve with ice cream or just plain.

3 cups pitted sour pie cherries

½ teaspoon finely chopped lemon zest

¾ cup sugar

1 tablespoon arrowroot powder

3 tablespoons fresh lemon juice, divided

⅓ cup milk or vanilla soy milk

1 cup whole wheat pastry flour

½ tablespoon baking powder

½ teaspoon baking soda

½ cup sugar

⅓ cup butter

1 egg, beaten

Edible flowers (optional)

1. Preheat the oven to 350°F and lightly oil a 9-inch cake pan. Combine the cherries, lemon zest, sugar, arrowroot powder, and 2 tablespoons lemon juice in a saucepan. Heat over medium heat until the liquid is clear and thick, about 10 minutes. Remove from the heat.

2. Mix the milk and remaining 1 tablespoon lemon juice together in a small bowl. Combine the flour, baking powder, and baking soda in another bowl. Cream the sugar and butter together in another bowl until soft and creamy. Add the egg and stir until creamy.

3. Make a well in the dry ingredients. Stir in half of the milk, then add half of the egg-butter-sugar mixture. Repeat. The consistency should be on the thick side.

4. Place an even layer of cherries on the bottom of the cake pan. Spread the cake batter on top.

5. Bake until the cake lightly springs back when touched, about 40 minutes. Cool, then cut the cake and flip it over to serve. Sprinkle with edible flowers if desired. **Serves 6 to 8**

Sweet Baked Rice Pudding with Nectarines

When you have leftover cooked rice, it's time to make rice pudding. I've made this homey old-fashioned dessert many times and often used blueberries, peaches, or apricots instead of nectarines. Cherries would probably work, too, but they'd need more sugar. Cashew cream makes a great thick nondairy addition to the pudding; you can also pour some over the top when serving.

2 tablespoons fresh lemon juice

Zest of ½ lemon, finely chopped

2 cups cashew cream (see the following recipe)

⅓ cup arrowroot powder

¼ cup maple syrup

½ teaspoon freshly grated nutmeg

¼ teaspoon salt

2 cups cooked rice

2 ripe medium-size nectarines, pitted and sliced

2 tablespoons sugar

½ teaspoon cardamom

1. Preheat the oven to 325°F and lightly oil a 9-by-9-inch baking dish. Combine the lemon juice and zest, cashew cream, arrowroot powder, maple syrup, nutmeg, and salt in a blender and mix until foamy.

2. Combine the cashew cream mixture with the rice in a large bowl and mix well. Pour into the prepared baking dish and bake until thick, about 35 minutes.

3. Remove from the oven and spread the sliced nectarines over the top. Combine the sugar and cardamom in a small bowl and sprinkle over the nectarines. Return to the oven and bake until the nectarines are tender, another 15 minutes. The pudding thickens as it cools. **Serves 6**

Cashew Cream

Use this decadent-tasting nondairy topping over any fresh Northwest fruit. This topping makes cobblers, crisps, and rice or bread puddings sublime.

1 cup water

1 cup cashews

½ teaspoon vanilla extract

1 tablespoon maple syrup

1 tablespoon fresh lemon juice

Salt

Soak the cashews in the water for an hour. Then puree the cashews and water in a blender with the vanilla extract, maple syrup, lemon juice, and salt. Sweeten to taste with additional maple syrup. Top desserts immediately or refrigerate to use later. Store in a covered container for about 1 week in the refrigerator. **Makes 2 cups**

Apple Cobbler

This dessert brightens the rainy days of autumn. I prefer Golden Delicious from Cliffside Orchards in Kettle Falls, Washington, but ask your local apple growers which apples they recommend for cobbler. This recipe is easy to adapt to other seasonal fruits like blackberries or cherries. Just use more arrowroot powder when the fruit is soft and juicy. Some fruits like pie cherries, cranberries, and the tart quince require at least ½ cup of sugar. Whichever fruit you choose, pair it with a complementary herb, spice, or liqueur.

4 cups peeled, cored, and thinly sliced sweet-tart apples

¼ cup fresh lemon juice

¼ cup agave nectar

½ teaspoon cinnamon

2 tablespoons arrowroot powder

1¼ cups unbleached flour

½ tablespoon baking powder

3 tablespoons brown sugar, divided

¼ cup cold butter

⅓ cup milk

1 tablespoon melted butter (optional)

1. Preheat the oven to 350°F. Combine the apples, lemon juice, agave nectar, cinnamon, and arrowroot in a 2-quart casserole dish and toss to mix.

2. In a separate bowl, blend the flour, baking powder, and 2 tablespoons brown sugar, and mix well. With a pastry blender or fork, cut in the butter until the mixture resembles coarse meal. Stir in the milk until a dough forms.

3. Turn the dough out onto a board and knead about three turns, then pat the dough into an 8-inch round, or large enough to cover the fruit in the casserole dish. Lift and place the dough over the fruit.

4. Cut about five slits into the dough, radiating out from the center. Brush melted butter onto the top if desired and sprinkle with 1 tablespoon brown sugar. Place the cobbler on a baking sheet and bake 35 to 45 minutes or until the top is golden brown. Cool 10 minutes before serving.
Serves 6

Apple harvest time at BelleWood Acres in Lynden, Washington. Photo by Dorie Belisle.

Peach Kuchen

This homey version of the old-fashioned German coffeecake glistens with peach slices on top. Make the cake with eggs and it will turn out more cakelike, or make it with tofu and the crust is heavier. I've made this cake with blueberries, cherries, and apples. Substitute another flavoring for cardamom when changing fruits.

3 medium peaches, peeled, pitted, and sliced

1 tablespoon fresh lemon juice

1 tablespoon arrowroot powder

1¼ cups flour (whole wheat pastry or barley)

½ cup sugar

1 teaspoon baking powder

1 teaspoon baking soda

1 teaspoon cardamom

4 tablespoons butter, divided

2 eggs or ½ cup silken tofu

⅓ cup milk or vanilla soy milk

2 tablespoons powdered sugar (optional)

1. Preheat the oven to 350°F. Lightly oil a 14-inch pizza pan. Combine the peaches, lemon juice, and arrowroot in a bowl and mix gently until the arrowroot has dissolved.

2. Combine the flour, sugar, baking powder and soda, and cardamom in a medium-size mixing bowl and mix well. Cut in 3 tablespoons butter with a pasty blender or fork until the mixture resembles coarse crumbs.

3. Combine the eggs or silken tofu and milk in a blender or mix with a hand blender until smooth. Pour into the dry ingredients and stir to combine until the batter has a consistency between a thin cake batter and a brownie mix—a little too stiff to pour and a little too sticky to pat out.

4. Scrape the batter onto the pizza pan and spread with a knife or bowl scraper to about an inch from the edge. The crust will be thin.

5. Place the peach slices one at a time on the crust, radiating out from the center. The crust should be completely covered with peaches. Distribute dots of the remaining 1 tablespoon of butter over the peaches; then drizzle the juice left in the bowl over the peaches.

6. Bake until the crust is browned around the edges, about 25 minutes. Remove from the oven and let sit for 5 minutes. With a large, wide spatula, carefully remove the kuchen from the pan and place on a cooling rack. Sprinkle with powdered sugar if desired before serving. **Serves 4 to 6**

FOOD FOR THOUGHT: CHANGING FRUIT ORCHARDS IN SOUTHERN OREGON

The first fruit trees in southern Oregon traveled by covered wagon across the plains in the mid-1800s, and by the early 1900s about 400 growers were harvesting apples in the Rogue Valley. Cherries, peaches, plums, and walnuts were also grown. In 1914, Harry and David Rosenberg started Harry & David and exported Comice pears to restaurants and hotels in Europe. Many of the pear orchards today have changed to high-density orchards, and some have been replaced by wine grapes and housing developments.

Northwest Berry Crisp

Berries are everywhere in the Northwest during the summer, and many people have their favorites. Mix and match yours in this recipe. Blueberries, blackberries, loganberries, marionberries, and raspberries all work here. Culinary lavender expert Kathy Gehrt says to crush lavender before adding to recipes to disperse the flavor. If you want to use this recipe to make apple crisp, use 6 cups of the same sweet-tart apple slices that you would use for a pie or cobbler. Try a teaspoon of cinnamon or cardamom instead of lavender. While this cobbler is still warm from the oven, get out the serving dishes and vanilla ice cream. Then sit down and enjoy it.

- **5 to 6 cups berries**
- **2 tablespoons fresh lemon juice**
- **¼ cup arrowroot powder**
- **½ teaspoon crushed lavender buds**
- **1 cup unbleached or whole wheat pastry flour**
- **1 cup rolled oats**
- **½ cup sugar**
- **½ teaspoon baking soda**
- **½ cup butter**
- **½ cup maple syrup**

1. Preheat the oven to 350°F. Combine the berries, lemon juice, arrowroot, and crushed lavender buds in a 2-quart casserole dish and stir gently.

2. Combine the flour, oats, sugar, and soda in a medium mixing bowl and mix thoroughly, making sure there are no small lumps.

3. In another bowl, combine the butter and maple syrup with a fork, mashing and mixing until smooth.

4. Mix the butter and maple syrup into the dry ingredients and stir until all particles are coated. Sprinkle the topping over the berries and pat down. Bake until the filling bubbles up, about 45 minutes. **Serves 6**

Signs at Pennington Farms near Grants Pass, Oregon, beckoning shoppers to the bakery and farm store during berry season

Cranberry-Raspberry Slump

A slump is an old-fashioned New England fruit dessert simmered on the stovetop. Here, a tantalizing blend of cranberries and raspberries creates an amazing deep ruby color and a sweet-tart flavor that leaves you hungry for more. I use raspberries frozen from summer's harvest because the season for them is over by the time cranberries arrive. Orange dumplings add citrus tones. I have also used lemon in place of orange with a little more sugar and had great results. For seasonal slump variations, try strawberries and rhubarb, peaches and blueberries, or pears and plums. Serve the slump with whipped cream, cashew cream, or ice cream.

2 cups fresh cranberries

2 cups frozen raspberries

⅓ cup orange juice

½ cup sugar

1 tablespoon arrowroot powder

1 tablespoon Grand Marnier or orange zest

⅓ cup milk (dairy or soy, plain or vanilla)

1 tablespoon fresh lemon juice

1 cup whole wheat pastry flour

2 tablespoons sugar

2 tablespoons baking powder

½ teaspoon baking soda

½ teaspoon salt

1 tablespoon finely chopped orange zest

2 tablespoons cold butter

1. Heat a heavy skillet (not cast iron) over medium heat. Combine the cranberries, raspberries, orange juice, sugar, arrowroot powder, and Grand Marnier or orange zest in the skillet, lower the heat, and simmer for 5 minutes. While the fruit cooks, prepare the dumplings.

2. In a small bowl, combine the milk and lemon juice and set aside. In a medium-size mixing bowl, combine the flour, sugar, baking powder and soda, salt, and orange zest. Mix well, making sure there are no small lumps of baking soda. Cut in the butter until the mixture has a mealy consistency. Add the milk and lemon juice and stir until a fairly thick but still sticky batter forms.

3. Drop the batter from a heaping teaspoon onto the simmering fruit, going around the outside of the pan until you reach the middle, covering almost all of the fruit.

4. Cover and simmer until the dumplings are done, about 40 minutes. Serve in individual dishes with the simmering fruit ladled over the dumplings. **Serves 6**

White Chocolate Raspberry Silk Pie

A decadent-tasting raspberry and white chocolate filling tucked into a chocolate cookie crust makes this pie suitable for special occasions. Making it is a three-step process—crust, filling, refrigeration. Prepare and bake the crust one day; blend the filling another; make the pie, then refrigerate for a few hours before serving. Coconut oil tends to hold the crust together better, but butter works. Get extra virgin oil if you choose coconut oil.

- 1 8-ounce package plain chocolate, vanilla, or lemon cookies
- 3½ tablespoons melted coconut oil or butter
- 1 tablespoon water
- 1 teaspoon vanilla extract
- 1 12-ounce shelf-stable package extra-firm silken tofu
- 2 tablespoons white chocolate liqueur or 2 teaspoons vanilla extract
- 1½ tablespoons honey
- 1 cup fresh raspberries, plus ½ cup for garnish
- 2½ cups grated white chocolate, plus 2 tablespoons for garnish (about 6 ounces)
- 2 tablespoons chocolate syrup

1. Preheat the oven to 350°F. Lightly oil the bottom of a 9-inch springform pan.

2. Crush the cookies into crumbs in a blender or food processor. Blend the crumbs with the coconut oil or butter, water, and vanilla extract until completely mixed. Press the crust into the prepared pan and bake for 10 minutes. The crust will be soft but will get firm as it cools. Let the crust cool completely before filling.

3. Place the tofu, liqueur or vanilla extract, honey, and raspberries in a blender and process until smooth and creamy.

4. Heat the white chocolate in a cup in the microwave on high for 1 minute or melt it in a double boiler, 8 to10 minutes. Stir the chocolate and then combine it with the tofu-raspberry mixture in the blender. Blend for 1 minute.

5. Pour the filling into the cooled pie shell and refrigerate for at least 2 hours before serving. The pie will harden as it cools. Garnish with raspberries and grated chocolate and drizzle chocolate syrup in a decorative pattern over the pie. **Makes a 9-inch pie**

Blueberry Cheesecake

My husband's friend Hoby Jergens makes this delectable cheesecake with pie cherries. This is my blueberry version. I like using fresh blueberries from Cascadian Home Farm, but you could use sweetened sour pie cherries, peaches, or nectarines. A springform pan works best for this recipe.

- 1 8-ounce package shortbread cookies
- ¼ cup melted butter
- 2 8-ounce packages cream cheese, softened
- 2 eggs
- ⅔ cup sugar
- 2 tablespoons white chocolate liqueur or 1½ teaspoons vanilla extract
- ½ cup sour cream
- 1½ cups blueberries
- ¼ cup sugar
- 1 tablespoon arrowroot powder

1. Preheat the oven to 350°F. Crush the cookies into crumbs in a blender or food processor. Mix with the melted butter and press firmly into the bottom of a springform pan and 1½ inches up the sides. You can use a glass pie pan that has been lightly oiled, but it may be hard to remove a slice without leaving some of the crust in the pan.

2. With an electric mixer, beat the softened cream cheese until fluffy. Beat in the eggs, one at a time, and gradually add the sugar. Add the liqueur or vanilla extract and finally the sour cream. Mix until well blended. Spread the mixture evenly over the crust. Bake until the cheesecake is firm, about 60 minutes. Prepare the topping while the cheesecake bakes.

3. Combine the blueberries, sugar, and arrowroot powder in a small saucepan. Cook over medium-low heat, stirring frequently, until the color changes from opaque to clear. Keep stirring until it thickens, then remove from the heat and let cool.

4. When the cheesecake is done, turn off the oven, open the door, and let the cake sit for another hour. Remove from the oven and gently release from the springform pan onto a serving platter. Spread the cooled topping over the top. Chill for a few hours before serving. **Makes a 9-inch pie**

A Treasure Trove of Berries

Berries lured me to the Northwest in the summer of 1972. I was on vacation in Oregon when I impulsively purchased a pint of blueberries at a grocery store in Medford. A few miles down the highway I pulled into a rest area near the Rogue River and sat on a picnic bench eating one sweet berry after another as the river rushed by. The flavor and sounds triggered memories of family camping vacations to the Northwest a decade earlier when I'd picked wild berries. Rushing water, warm summer sun, and the fresh scent of pine all mingled with the best fruit I'd ever tasted to create a memory that I've treasured for decades.

Intrigued by the idea of fresh berries growing close to home every summer, I moved to Bellingham, Washington, where I drove to U-pick farms and bought flats of berries. Abundant wild berries grew just outside our door. Later, when I moved closer to Seattle, I planted raspberries in our yard and bought all kinds of berries from farmers at Pike Place Market and later at neighborhood farmers' markets. In the summers I sometimes foraged for huckleberries when hiking.

Wild berries thrived in the Northwest long before raspberries and high bush blueberries came along. Native Americans gathered berries, and in 1853 Reverend David Blaine wrote letters home to his parents about dewberries, salal berries, whortleberries, salmonberries, cranberries, and wild grapes that Northwest natives shared with settlers. Huckleberries, native blackberries, thimbleberries, currants, and gooseberries were also part of the treasure trove. Everyone who passed

through here, it seems, picked wild berries in the summer, even the late James Beard, who foraged for them near Gearhart, Oregon, where his family vacationed.

Domesticated varieties of berries arrived by wagon in the mid-1800s. Although we have a native blackberry, Oregon explorers brought the evergreen blackberry into the area around 1850. Raspberries, high bush blueberries, and Himalayan blackberries appeared in the late 1800s. Wilson strawberries traveled from the East Coast to the Willamette Valley in 1846, and by the 1920s Marysville, Washington, had become the strawberry capital of the world. Then in the 1950s a freeze destroyed the crops, and California took over the lead in commercial strawberry production in the 1960s.

Despite competition from California, Northwest berry cultivation continued to thrive. Many Northwest row crop farms started out growing berries in the 1970s. Longtime local residents recall riding buses out to pick berries on farms as their first job when they were teenagers. Roadside stands dotted the landscape, and U-pick farms offered fields of ripe berries.

Today, farmers' markets offer all kinds of berries, including the more familiar strawberries, raspberries, blueberries, and blackberries. Many tables also offer berry products such as jam, syrup, vinegar, soda pop, juice, and wine. Berry pastries and shortcake have become popular, and in Corvallis, Wilt Farms sells dehydrated organic blueberries, a great trail snack. Grateful Harvest Farm processes apples and berries into fruit leather; Pennington Farms bakes them into mouth-watering turnovers.

Word travels fast about the best berries at the market. In Seattle, at the University District farmers' market, people line up for the giant, sweet blueberries from Rent's Due Ranch. In Oregon, at the Hillsdale farmers' market, loganberries, pink currants, and Chester blackberries attract customers to the Ayers Creek Farm booth. Farther south, at the Medford farmers' market, Pennington Farms sells nine kinds of berries throughout the season—tayberries, olallieberries, raspberries, blueberries, loganberries, marionberries, strawberries, and two kinds of blackberries. They also cultivate goumi berries, small tart red berries that grow on trees and taste like a cross between cherries and cranberries.

The Penningtons, Cathy and Sam and their five children, moved from Colorado to southern Oregon in 1994 to live what they thought would be a simpler life. They had had a flower farm in Colorado, and when they purchased a 90-acre hay farm in the Applegate Valley, just south of Grants Pass, they started out growing flowers and sold them at area farmers' markets. When I caught up with Cathy Pennington, tan and blond with a big smile, at the Medford market in the summer of 2008 she was selling fresh blueberries and raspberries as well as luscious berry turnovers, cookies, jams, and syrups.

"Sam likes berries, so we grew them and I

The Country Bakery at Pennington Farms in the Applegate Valley near Grants Pass, Oregon

started bringing them to the market along with flowers, and people wanted more berries. One year we planted seven acres of berries, and suddenly, we had so many berries that we started making jam. The pies and turnovers came later," Cathy told me. The Penningtons transformed an old barn into a rustic bakery where they bake pies, turnovers, and cookies, and make jam and syrup. They sell pies and turnovers at the bakery, but take most to three farmers' markets (Grants Pass, Medford, and Ashland), where they sell out long before the market ends.

A big challenge for berry growers in southern Oregon is "keeping up with the weeds," said Sam. "It's hard when you use organic methods."

Another berry farm that uses organic methods is Wilt Farms, a 75-acre certified organic blueberry farm near Corvallis, Oregon. I'd tasted Wilt blueberries at the Corvallis farmers' market, and the intense sweet flavor enticed me back after visiting Pennington Farms. At Wilt Farms, I met Diane Wilt, who told me about their farm, passed down from her husband Bob's grandfather.

In 1912, Bob's grandfather started with dairy cows, vegetable crops, and hops. In the 1950s through '60s, they switched to seed crops, and later, Bob's father raised sheep, clover, and string beans. The first blueberry bushes were planted in 1970, and when Bob and Diane took over the farm, they added blueberry plants every year. In 2006 the farm became a certified organic blueberry farm.

"Our goal is to have the most flavorful, nutrient-dense blueberries around," Diane told me. "We add minerals to the soil and we harvest the berries only when they are perfectly ripe, not green. Our berries were tested for nutrients and tests revealed our berries were higher in nutrients than conventional, sustainable, and wild organic berries." What they don't sell fresh, they freeze and sell to local stores under their own Sunset Valley Organics label. Sunset Valley Organics also offers an expanding product line that includes blueberry spread, dried blueberries, and freeze-dried blueberry powder, as well as chocolate-covered dried blueberries.

The big bags of frozen blueberries in the freezer at the Wilt farm reminded me of bags of frozen plump blueberries at the Cascadian Home Farm roadside stand in Rockport, Washington. Cascadian Home Farm is a picturesque 28-acre organic farm and popular berry stop about a hundred miles northeast of Seattle, on Highway 20, next to the foothills of the Cascades.

Follow the Skagit River past small towns and farms through luxuriant greenery, and three

The sign to follow to find blueberries at Wilt Farms just outside of Corvallis

miles past Rockport a vista opens up to a breathtaking view of mountains. The rustic Cascadian Home farm stand is just across the highway from the Skagit River.

The farm stand belongs to the nationally known Cascadian Farm Organic company, and since 1993, Cascadian Home Farm has been farmed and managed by Jim and Harlyn Meyer, who moved to the Northwest from Colorado. The Meyers arrived with many years of organic farming experience and now grow five kinds of blueberries, all handpicked, sorted, and packaged under the brand Many Hands. You can find these blueberries at food co-ops in Seattle and Mount Vernon and at the farm stand that also sells frozen berries and homemade berry ice cream.

"Blueberries take from 3 to 5 years to start producing, but they keep producing for 50 years," Jim told me. The hand-weeded rows of blueberry bushes at this farm are picture perfect, each on a raised row of compost and sawdust. Jim also relies on organic farming techniques and says that pesticides upset the natural balance of nature.

Every summer I visit this farm stand and can't resist a pint of blueberries. The picturesque river lures me across the highway. There aren't any picnic tables, but a rock will do. I sit and close my eyes, enjoy the berries, and think about my first taste of Northwest blueberries by the Rogue River.

The Cascadian Home Farm roadside stand in the foothills of the Cascades, in western Washington's Upper Skagit Valley

Glossary of Ingredients

agar (or agar agar) A vegetarian gelatin from a red seaweed. Agar is available in natural food stores in bars, flakes, or powder. It sets like gelatin as it cools and can be substituted for gelatin in recipes.

agave nectar A natural sweetener from agave, a cactuslike plant native to Mexico. The sugar in agave nectar is more slowly absorbed than sugar, yet it tastes 25 percent sweeter than sugar. It adds little flavor to recipes compared to honey or maple syrup. Look for agave nectar in natural food stores.

aioli A mayonnaise-like spread flavored with garlic, traditional in the south of France. Look for aioli in natural food stores.

arrowroot powder A starchy thickener from a tropical plant native to South America and the West Indies. Arrowroot is less processed than cornstarch and lacks the chalky aftertaste. Arrowroot is high in calcium and can be used like cornstarch to thicken sauces and puddings. Mix it into cold water before adding to simmering sauces. Do not overcook arrowroot-thickened sauces past thickening or they may break down. Look for arrowroot in natural food stores.

flaxseed, flaxseed oil The seed of the annual flax plant, and the oil expressed from the seed, a rich source of omega-3 essential fatty acids. Flaxseed and flaxseed oil are an important addition to any healthy diet, but the oil is fragile and is damaged by heat, so use the oil only in dressings and marinades. Look for flaxseed oil in natural food stores. Some farmers grow and sell flax seeds; I found some beautiful golden flax seeds from Heavenly Harvest farm at the Wednesday Corvallis farmers' market. Ground flaxseed can be combined with water to replace eggs as a binding agent in baking; blend together 1 tablespoon ground flaxseed and 3 tablespoons water to replace each egg. You can also add a tablespoon of ground flaxseed to smoothies.

ghee Butter that has been clarified or slow-cooked with the foam skimmed off so it is free of all milk solids. Ghee can be stored without refrigeration, but I generally refrigerate homemade ghee. Look for ghee in specialty food stores, Asian markets, and natural food stores, or make your own ghee by letting butter simmer over a low flame for about 45 minutes. The milk solids will turn brownish and cling to the sides of the pan or drop to the bottom. Strain the ghee through triple layers of cheesecloth, then discard the solids.

kombu A sea vegetable that can be cut and added to beans to help tenderize them. Kombu is filled with minerals and is also an excellent addition to soup stocks. Some people harvest their own from the Pacific Ocean; look for it in natural food stores or Asian markets.

mirin A sweet Japanese rice wine related to sake. Mirin starts with rice koji, rice that has been cooked and then injected with mold spores and incubated for a number of weeks. The koji, a catalyst for making many fermented

Japanese foods, is blended with water and aged to result in mirin. Mirin adds flavor depth to marinades and salad dressings, where its mild sweetness shines. Look for mirin in Asian markets and natural food stores.

miso A paste made from fermented soybeans or other beans and grains; a traditional staple in Japan. With an intense winelike taste, miso can be used for flavoring a wide variety of dishes from soup to salad dressings. A concentrated protein, miso contains eight essential amino acids, B vitamins, calcium, and iron. Miso is low in fat but contains a lot of salt, so use it sparingly. Sweet and light-colored misos are high in enzymes and simple carbohydrates. Red and brown misos are higher in protein and salt, and contain more essential fatty acids from the soybeans. Dark miso has been fermented for a longer period of time and has a bold, assertive flavor. Look for miso in natural food stores and Asian markets.

nutritional yeast A yellow powder that adds a cheeselike flavor to foods; a living organism that is grown on mineral-rich molasses or wood pulp. The yellow powder is rich in B vitamins that come from synthetic vitamins fed to the culture during the growth stage. The end product is also fortified. It can be found in natural food stores.

tahini A smooth, creamy paste made from hulled, ground sesame seeds. Some commercial tahini is more processed and made from seeds have been soaked in chemicals to remove the hulls, then neutralized and bleached. This type of tahini tastes bitter and slightly soapy. The best-quality tahini comes from mechanically, not chemically, hulled seeds. Tahini is available in grocery stores, specialty markets, and natural food stores.

tamari A natural variety of soy sauce. To make most common soy sauces sold today, soybeans are broken down chemically and then blended with caramel coloring, salt, corn syrup, water, and a preservative. Higher-quality, traditionally processed tamari is fermented with a koji (mold spore) starter that uses only soybeans. Shoyu, another natural soy sauce, uses koji made with equal parts cracked wheat and soybeans. Containing more glutemic acid than shoyu, tamari is a better choice for cooking because glutemic acid enhances flavors. Tamari also retains a deep rich taste, even in long-simmering liquids. Look for tamari in natural food stores.

tempeh An ancient Indonesian food made by splitting, cooking, and fermenting soybeans. A white threadlike mycelium mold binds the beans after they are pressed. This mycelium mold makes tempeh quite easy to digest. The protein and minerals are easily assimilated. Tempeh also contains very little fat, and at 19.5 percent protein, it contains 50 percent more protein than the equivalent amount of hamburger. Look for tempeh in natural food stores.

A Guide to Northwest Produce

FRUIT

Washington is famous for apples and Oregon is renowned for pears, but many people might be surprised to learn these are only a fraction of the fruits from gardens and orchards that fill farmers' markets in the Northwest. Our parade of seasonal fruits includes apricots, cherries, peaches, nectarines, plums, melons, and grapes. Some of our less well-known Northwest-grown fruits to watch for at markets include figs, currants, kiwis, persimmons, and even a few citrus fruits. Berries form their own procession, starting with strawberries in the spring and ending with coastal huckleberries and cranberries in the fall. Read about your favorites or discover something new in the following list. Then go forth and enjoy the sweetest gifts of the season.

Apples Members of the rose family, apples originated in Central Asia. Today, Washington produces more than half of the apples grown in the United States. One of America's most popular fruits, the apple comes in many sizes and flavors from supertart to very sweet. Thanks to farmers' markets, we have access to many old-fashioned varieties of apples. Apples are convenient and easily pack into lunches, and are superstars in baked desserts. They can be grated and added raw to salads and desserts or cooked to enhance their sweetness. Combine raw grated apples with lemon or lime juice so they don't turn brown before using. Remember that apples ripen too quickly at room temperature, so keep them in the refrigerator and store them for up to four weeks. When apples begin to soften, it's time to make applesauce.

Apricots Apricots originated in China thousands of years ago, and most of the nation's commercial apricot crop is grown in California today, but Northwest apricots are sweeter and juicier than any shipped in from elsewhere. More farms in Washington than Oregon advertise apricots, and they're available at most farmers' markets. Grouse Mountain in Chelan, Cliffside Orchards in Kettle Falls, and Rama Farm along the Columbia River are a few Washington farms that sell delectable perfectly sweet-tart organic apricots at the University District farmers' market. Always select local apricots because they don't travel well, and apricots from California are picked green and can never develop as much flavor as a tree-ripened Northwest apricot. Aside from enjoying them fresh and pureeing them into smoothies and ice cream, you can bake, stew, or grill apricots. Make an apricot crisp, cheesecake, or tart. Fresh apricots can be stored at room temperature for only a day or so. In the refrigerator, they can be stored for up to a week. Slice, toss with a little lemon juice, and freeze in a covered glass or plastic container for the winter.

Asian pears Asian pears are very popular in Japan, where more than 100 kinds are grown. They are about as big as an apple, and their colors range from light yellow to golden to brown. Their juicy flavors vary; some have sweet honey tones, some taste like butterscotch, and others may be reminiscent of rum, so sample different varieties and savor the flavors. Rockridge Orchards in Enumclaw, Washington, grows a wide variety of sweet, crisp Asian pears. Try them diced in fruit salads. Ginger, honey, dates, and walnuts pair well with Asian pears. Sliced Asian pears spread with hazelnut butter are a great Northwest treat. If unbruised, they can be stored loose in the produce bin in your refrigerator for up to a month. These are also great dehydrated.

Blackberries Like apples, blackberries are members of the rose family and originated in Asia. They now grow wild and are cultivated in temperate climates all over the world. On the West Coast, these berries grow in backyards in San Francisco as well as fields in British Columbia. Their harvest season is late summer and early autumn. Pick them before a rain because after they get wet, many of the soft berries quickly mold. Some varieties are flavorful and sweet, while some types of wild blackberries simply taste like water with lots of seeds. Blackberries don't keep well, so use them within a day or two. Freeze them in the same container they came in, then remove, discard bad berries, and place the rest in a bag. Defrost the berries in the winter for a blackberry slump or crisp.

Blueberries North American natives, blueberries once only grew wild. Domestic cultivation began in the early 1900s, and blueberries now grow in 30 states and are the nation's second most popular berry, after strawberries. America and Canada produce 95 percent of the world's commercial blueberry crops. Our Northwest blueberry season lasts from midsummer through early fall. Not all blueberries taste the same, so sample one before buying. Before storing, sort through the berries and discard any crushed or moldy

ones. Store in the refrigerator in a glass or plastic container and use within a few days. Freeze them as you would blackberries.

Cherries Cherries were cultivated in China more than 3,000 years ago. Most of our nation's commercial crop now comes from the western states—Washington, Oregon, Utah, Colorado, and Idaho. These stone fruits are fragile and are better when purchased from the farmer who grew them. Vans and Lamberts are known for their great sweet flavor, while pie cherries make mouths pucker and are very perishable. Cherries need a cold temperature for storage, so keep them in the coldest part of your refrigerator, either in plastic bags or in a container, and store for about four days. Sour cherries should be used or pitted and frozen the day you get them. Cherries are also excellent dehydrated and added for color to pilafs and whole-grain salads.

Cranberries Native to the United States, cranberries were first cultivated in natural bogs in Massachusetts by Native Americans, and today cranberry bogs are also harvested in Oregon, Washington, and British Columbia. Since these berries grow in bogs that wildlife may travel through, always wash these berries before using. Like rhubarb, currants, and gooseberries, cranberries require the addition of sweeteners. However, if you combine them with sweet fruit like raspberries or apples, you can cut back on the amount of sweetener called for in a cranberry recipe by one-third or more. Look for plump, firm berries with no bruises or brown spots. Because the damp bogs where cranberries grow are perfect environments for fungus and weeds, organic crops must be continually monitored and hand weeded, which means that organic berries cost more to bring to market. Store cranberries for three weeks in a plastic bag in the refrigerator or freeze in a plastic bag or container for up to a year.

Currants Currants and gooseberries include about 150 varieties that grow nearly all over the world—North America, Europe, Asia, and Africa. Black currants were used for wine in medieval England, and Native Americans used them as a medicine for a variety of ailments. Very tart, they are often used in jams and jellies. Red and pink currants aren't as intense as the black ones, and they make a great addition to sparkling water, or use them in pilafs or whole-grain salads. Grouse Mountain Farm in Chelan, Washington, sells red and black varieties at the University District farmers' market in Seattle. In Oregon, Ayers Creek Farm sells red and pink currants at the Hillsdale farmers' market. Store currants for a few days in the refrigerator, or freeze them as you would blackberries.

Figs Native to southwestern Asia, figs were one of the first cultivated fruits. Because most of our nation's domestic fig crop comes from California, most people don't think of the Northwest when figs are mentioned, but a number of farmers grow them, especially in Oregon where the weather is more favorable. You can find them at farmers' markets from Ashland to Portland. Grateful Harvest Farm in Junction City sells the most delectable figs at the Eugene farmers' market. In Washington, Rockridge Orchards in Enumclaw grows yellow-green Desert King figs, although in 2009 a severe winter freeze destroyed many of the Bennetts' fig trees and many Seattle pastry chefs, well known for local fig-filled pastries, mourned the loss. Figs taste like candy when dehydrated, but you need a dehydrator to dry them at 100°F. Take

them out when they are still slightly soft and store them in the freezer for an exceptional winter treat. Fresh figs can range from light green to orange to deep purple, and all have different flavors. Store figs in a covered container in the refrigerator and use within a few days.

Ginger Not really a fruit, ginger is distantly related to bananas, and some Northwest farmers grow it. Ginger is a rhizome, or an enlarged underground stem, that has a pungent, assertive flavor and is known for its digestive properties. Dried ginger, most often used in baked goods, is not interchangeable with the fresh variety. When fresh ginger is young, there is no need to peel it before using. Mair Farm-Taki in Washington sells fresh ginger at the University District farmers' market. Dice or finely grate fresh ginger before adding it to recipes. Fresh ginger lasts about a week in the refrigerator.

Grapes Grapes have been cultivated since biblical times, and two-thirds of the grapes cultivated in the United States are processed into wine. You can find a variety of table grapes, with and without seeds, at farmers' markets in late summer and fall. Rockridge Orchards is cultivating Belle Island grapes, a Northwest native grape, and Mair Farm-Taki is still harvesting tasty heirloom Concord grapes from 70-year-old vines. Along with apples and strawberries, grapes are one of the most chemically treated fruits, so ask farmers about their farming techniques before purchasing grapes. To select grapes, pick up a stem of grapes and gently shake it. If many fall off, the grapes are overripe. Store grapes in the coldest part of the refrigerator either in a bag or container. They will keep for about five days.

Huckleberries Huckleberry plants have been

around since prehistoric times and are said to be one of the oldest living plant forms on earth. Available at farmers' markets and along hiking trails in the Pacific Northwest, huckleberries are a seasonal treat. Red huckleberries are tart, and deep blue huckleberries have a more pronounced flavor than the blueberries they resemble. Blue huckleberries are sometimes mistaken for wild blueberries, but true wild blueberries are rarely found in the Northwest. Mountain huckleberries have a better flavor than the blue coastal and tart red huckleberries that require a sweetener like sugar or agave nectar when cooked. Stored in the refrigerator in an uncovered bowl, the berries will keep for a few days. Freeze them as you would blackberries.

Kiwifruit A China native, kiwifruit is now widely cultivated in New Zealand, Australia, Italy, France, and the United States. Most of the commercial kiwis in the United States are grown in California, but they also grow well in the Northwest, especially the tiny hardy kiwis. This is a fall fruit, so look for kiwi from September through November. Select plump, fairly firm, unblemished fruit. There is no need to peel the skin when eating them raw, but the skin of the fuzzy varieties can be distracting in a salad or dessert. Many Northwest gardeners grow hardy kiwis, and in Seattle, Grouse Mountain Farm sells them in late September at the University District farmers' market. Eaten whole, these tiny green kiwis are the perfect blend of tart and sweet tones. Leave kiwi out at room temperature to ripen, then store in the refrigerator for up to one week.

Lemons The most useful of all fruits, lemons originated in Southeast Asia and are now grown in tropical and temperate regions around the world. Lemons that we use in the Northwest are mostly imported from California and Arizona, but at the Portland farmers' market in the spring, check out the Meyer lemons from Raynblest Farm, which specializes in unusual citrus varieties. And in Washington, Raintree Nursery in Morton recommends Meyer lemon trees for Northwest gardeners. However, for most of us, it's lemons purchased from natural food stores that add zing to Northwest dishes. Lemon season is late summer and fall. Select lemons that are firm and heavy for their size. Meyer lemons have thin skins and an intense lemon flavor. Stored loose in the refrigerator, they should last for up to three weeks. Cut lemons can be stored on a small plate, cut side down, and used within a few days. Read about yuzus below for a great Northwest lemon substitute.

Loganberries Considered a natural hybrid between raspberries and dewberries, commercial loganberries are mostly cultivated for winemaking. They are soft and have a flavor like raspberries and blackberries. Look for them at farmers' markets during July and August. At the Medford farmers' market, Pennington Farms is known for its fresh loganberries, loganberry jam, and berry turnovers. Cooked loganberries need a little more sweetener than other berries. Store loganberries unwashed in the refrigerator in an uncovered container for one or two days at the most. Freeze them as you would blackberries.

Melons Related to cucumbers and squash, melons most likely originated in Africa or Asia. Wild melons still grow in Africa, but they are not as sweet as cultivated melons. The melons available in grocery stores in January are shipped from foreign countries and are usually without flavor or sweetness. In the Northwest, melons make an appearance in late summer or early autumn. Eat your annual fill at this time because melons don't freeze like berries or peaches. Heat makes melons get sweeter—that's why you find some of the sweetest organic melons grown where it gets very hot. Many small farms grow melons for maximum flavor, checking the sugar content of their melons before they harvest. Some Northwest varieties include cantaloupe, butterscotch, casaba, Charentais, Crenshaw, honeydew, and watermelon. You can store whole melons for a day or so at room temperature; keep cut melon in the refrigerator in a covered container for a few days.

Mulberries Black and white mulberries are native to China, and red mulberries originated in North America. These are not commercially grown berries and just a few farmers sell them at Seattle farmers' markets. Farmer Michael Hamphel of Grouse Mountain Farm says mulberries are difficult to harvest (they lay a tarp under the tree to catch the ones that fall), and the tiny stems are better eaten than tediously removed. Mulberries have a deep sweet flavor and a different texture from other berries; they retain softness when they freeze, making them the most delectable treat right from the freezer. Add mulberries to fruit salads, blend with peaches for smoothies, or simply enjoy them fresh. Refrigerate and eat mulberries within a few days. Freeze them as you would blackberries.

Nectarines Sometimes referred to as a fuzz-free peach, the nectarine is a totally separate species and has been around for at least 2000 years. But nectarines from the past bear little resemblance to the supersweet versions available today. Big and juicy, white or pinkish-orange fleshed, nectarines don't need peeling. Mid to late summer is nectarine season, so slice and freeze some in containers for an autumn or winter treat. Add a little lemon juice to help maintain the color. Select nectarines with a sweet fragrance. They should be firm, giving just slightly to a gentle touch. Store at room temperature for a few days. Refrigerate in a perforated plastic bag, and they will last up to five days.

Pawpaws North American natives, pawpaws ripen in autumn and are related to South American cherimoyas. Also called wild banana custard apples, pawpaws grow on trees and are 3 to 5 inches long when ripe. Brown on the outside with a sweet custardlike flesh inside, pawpaws are a rare treat at farmers' markets. Grouse Mountain Farm brought a few to the University District farmers' market one autumn, but they only have one or two trees, and most of their pawpaws never make it to market. Enjoy pawpaws raw, and if you must store them, keep them in the refrigerator for only a day or two.

Peaches Another stone fruit like cherries and plums, peaches originated in China. They are classified as freestone or clingstone because the pit either breaks free of the flesh easily or clings to it. Like other stone fruit, peaches picked too early get softer but never sweeter. Northwest peach season arrives slightly before nectarines ripen, late spring through summer. Carry peaches carefully from the market because these peaches are ripe with flavor and bruise with the slightest impact. These Northwest gems make the perfect dessert. You don't have to do a thing other than wash, pit, slice, and sprinkle with a few edible blossoms or lavender buds. Before using peaches for a cobbler or pie, remove the skin; this is more easily done for some varieties than for others. Peaches taste best at room temperature. Store them at room temperature for a day or two or for three to five days in the refrigerator. If you have a dehydrator, slice and dehydrate for three days at 95°F. Slice and freeze in pint containers for winter desserts and smoothies; sprinkle with lemon juice before freezing to help maintain the color of the flesh.

Pears Grown in Europe and Asia since prehistoric times, pears are nearly as ubiquitous as apples today. Mention pears, and Harry & David in Medford, Oregon, comes to mind, but 360 different Oregon growers harvested 800 million pears in 2008. Most of the nation's commercial pear crop comes from Oregon, Washington, and California. Like apples, pears come in numerous varieties, and the season begins in late summer and continues into winter, depending on the variety. Unlike soft fruits and apples, pears are harvested early when the fruit is still hard, and they ripen off the tree. The sugar content has increased by the time they are soft enough to eat. One way to tell if a pear is ripe is to gently squeeze it near the stem and look for a slight give, and to inhale for a sweet pear aroma. Left out at room temperature, pears will ripen in five days. Store ripe pears in the refrigerator for three to five days.

Persimmons Some sources say persimmons originated in Japan, while others claim they are North American natives, but no matter where they originated, persimmons are grown by a few Northwest farmers today. Persimmons are a red-orange fall fruit that look a little like fake tomatoes. The flavors of persimmons vary, depending on whether the variety is astringent or nonastringent. Astringent varieties such as Hachiya are mouth-puckeringly sour when hard; when soft and perfectly ripe, they taste like a combination of

stone fruit, honey, and pumpkin. Nonastringent varieties such as Fuyu are crisp and taste almost like cantaloupe when ripe. If you find these Northwest treasures locally, simply enjoy them raw.

Plums Originating in Asia more than 2,000 years ago, plums can be found today in more than 2,000 varieties. In the Northwest, a few of our varieties are Italian prune plums, violet plums, golden and transparent Gages, cherry plums, and tiny wild mirabelle plums. Unlike cherries, nectarines, or apricots, unripened plums can be picked and will get sweeter and ripen at room temperature. Cooking enhances their sweet-tart flavor. Plums combine well with strawberries, peaches, nectarines, and apricots. Their season is late summer to midfall. If the plums are very firm, leave them out at room temperature for a few days; otherwise, store them in the refrigerator for up to five days.

Quince Native to the Middle East, quince is an autumn fruit that can be found on market tables near apples because many apple growers also have quince trees. Quince is not edible raw but must be cooked, and even then it is very dry and sour and needs sugar. Ginger is a natural partner for quince, and fruit compotes are a good way to combine the two flavors. Quince can also be used in apple recipes alongside apples, and in chutney fruit combinations, quince adds character. One of the best things about quince is its ability to perfume an entire room with a seductive apple-pear aroma. Even if you don't want to eat quince, it's worth buying a few and setting them on a table just for the seasonal scent. The aroma lasts for a month or two.

Raspberries A delicate, fragile berry, the raspberry is a member of the rose family and has been around since prehistoric times. In addition to the familiar red raspberries, there are light yellow, deep amber, and black raspberries (called black caps). Black raspberries grow wild and should be picked in the morning because the warm sun softens them. Their season in midsummer is shorter than that of red and yellow raspberries. All raspberries have a coating of natural sugar on the outside that is easily rinsed off. If your berries come fresh from your own pesticide-free backyard, resist washing them and taste the sweetness. Because they spoil quickly, use raspberries within a day or so, or place unblemished berries in a single layer on a baking sheet to freeze, then store in a container or plastic bag in the freezer until you are ready to use them.

Rhubarb Originating in northern Asia, rhubarb is not a fruit but a vegetable related to buckwheat. A hardy plant, it grows well in many areas of the country and fills tables at Northwest farmers' markets. Peak season is May and June. The leaves are very high in oxalic acid and are poisonous, so if you grow them, plant them away from pets that might eat them. The stalks also contain some, and because oxalic acid blocks calcium absorption, eat rhubarb in moderation. Rhubarb is generally treated like a fruit, makes an excellent addition to baked goods, and can be incorporated in tarts, jams, pies, and compotes. Combining with other fruits such as apples or strawberries can be helpful if you want to cut down on the amount of sugar added to a rhubarb recipe. Try it with spring vegetables such as asparagus and sugar snap peas. Fresh rhubarb stalks can be stored in a plastic bag in the refrigerator for about five days. Slice and freeze for longer storage.

Strawberries As early as Roman times, people cultivated strawberries, but the perfect flavor and size of the strawberries we enjoy today weren't attained until the 19th century. Today, strawberries—along with grapes, apples, and peaches—are among the fruits most contaminated with pesticide residues and should always be purchased from organic growers or grown in your own garden. Grateful Harvest Farm in Junction City, Oregon, grows some of the sweetest organic strawberries in the Northwest and sells them at the Eugene farmers' market. Don't purchase strawberries in large containers where you can't see most of the berries, because some underneath may be crushed, and berries mold quickly. Local strawberries can be obtained at farmers' markets from spring until fall with a small break in between. Store unwashed berries in a covered container in the refrigerator for a few days. Freeze them as you would blackberries.

Yuzu A frost-hardy yellow citrus fruit that originated in China, yuzu can be large like an orange or quite small like large walnuts. It is rarely eaten like a fruit, but the juice and zest are used like lemons'. Yuzu juice and zest are great in salad dressings or added to vegetables with butter and a pinch of salt. Mair Farm-Taki in Yakima and Rockridge Orchards in Enumclaw, Washington, grow them, but most of Rockridge's yuzus are sold to local chefs and never make it to markets. Northwest gardeners should look for yuzu trees at nurseries. Yuzu stores like lemons.

SALAD GREENS

We are fortunate to have a long season for salad greens in the Northwest. Lettuce and other greens like it cool and damp, and they get plenty of that here. In the spring, foragers gather miner's lettuce, and summer through fall, greens spring up in abundance in gardens and on market tables. Following are descriptions of a few greens I have seen at Northwest farmers' markets to consider for salads.

Arugula Also called rocket, arugula is a member of the family Cruciferae and is related to radishes, turnips, cabbage, and watercress. Spicy with a peppery flavor, this green has long been a favorite in Italy. Refreshing in salads, arugula is often paired with goat or blue cheese or citrus. The white blossoms are also excellent additions to salads. Arugula can also be used in soup or added to pasta with lightly sautéed vegetables. Store arugula in the refrigerator wrapped in a damp towel in a produce bag and use it within a few days.

Belgian endive, curly endive, escarole, and chicory Technically, these are all varieties of the pungent-flavored dark green chicory. Chartreuse curly endive and frisée with loose heads and crinkled leaves are the easiest to spot at markets. Belgian endive has yellow-green crispy leaves and is grown in darkness to keep the leaves pale. Escarole has broad curly-edged green leaves that appear pale yellow in the center. Look for wild and cultivated chicory at the markets. The thick, solid leaves add a slightly bitter tone to salads and pair well with blue cheese, hazelnuts, and pears or apples. Blanching can take the edge off the bitter taste of the leaves. Belgian endive is also good gently braised with a little citrus juice and water. Store chicory or endive in a perforated bag in the refrigerator for up to a week.

Butterhead and bibb lettuce Loose-leaved heads of butterhead or bibb lettuce are sweet with buttery, tender leaves. Gathering Together Farm sells a number of old-fashioned types, and you can purchase seeds for some of these varieties through the Wild Garden Seed Web site (www.wildgardenseed.com). Wash bibb lettuce gently just before serving. Store the loose heads wrapped in a light towel and placed in a perforated bag in the refrigerator. This type of lettuce will store for about three days.

Iceberg lettuce Crisp and unassertive, this slightly bitter lettuce has been labeled a nutritional wipeout, but according to the Wild Garden Seed catalog (from Gathering Together Farm), crisp-head lettuce is a rich source of choline, a nutrient that feeds the brain. It also feeds the soul nostalgic for salads of yesterday. This lettuce stores for a week in a plastic bag in the refrigerator. Tear rather than cut this lettuce or the leaves will start to turn brown. I like this one with shredded carrots, and avocado and tomato slices.

Leaf lettuce Red or green, these loose-leaved heads are the essence of summer salads. The leaves are generally sweet and tender. Oakleaf lettuce is one of the most popular and tastiest varieties of the leaf lettuces. This is a mild green lettuce to use if you want other ingredients to take center stage in the salad bowl. Store leaf lettuce for a few days in the refrigerator, wrapped in a light towel to absorb excess moisture.

Mâche Also called corn salad or lamb's lettuce, mâche is a cold-weather lettuce. Native to Europe, mâche thrives in the Northwest climate and is a popular salad green at farmers' markets. The small green leaves, tender with a tangy lemonlike flavor, make a great addition to spring salads. Use mâche by itself or mix it with spinach or another mild salad green. These young greens can be stored for up to a week in a bag in the refrigerator.

Miner's lettuce This refreshing, slightly

lemony-tasting green shows up toward the end of winter and the beginning of spring. Look for it at farmers' markets or forage for the wild version yourself. Use a simple lemon-honey vinaigrette to dress the small, round leaves. I like to add tiny wild violets or arugula blossoms in the spring. Store these greens in a plastic bag in the refrigerator for a few days.

Mizuna Pungent with delicate-looking dark green leaves, mizuna originated in Japan. This vibrant spring green belongs to the cabbage family. Look for it at farmers' markets when other greens are scarce. Mizuna is often blended with other greens in salads and can also be braised, steamed, or used as a substitute for spinach in recipes. Store mizuna in a bag for a few days in the refrigerator.

Mustard greens Crisp and refreshing, these greens can be found in any season but are most abundant from late November through early spring. Many varieties of mustard greens are available in the Northwest, and the distinguishing characteristic is the peppery flavor. Some are wasabi hot and others are milder tasting, but just about any young mustard green can be used to spice up Northwest winter salads. These greens go well with bread-and-butter pickles, chopped apples, or pears. Puree raspberry vinegar with blue cheese in the blender and drizzle over these hearty greens, or finely chop and add them to a pilaf or a stir-fry. These greens can be stored for a week in a perforated bag in the refrigerator.

Purslane More recognized in Europe than here, purslane has a long history as an edible wild plant. Gathered and cultivated by foragers and farmers, purslane is a rich source of antioxidants and is higher in omega-3 fatty acids than any other green. With small, crisp green leaves and a light lemony flavor, purslane is a nutritious, attractive addition to salads. Look for wild and cultivated purslane at farmers' markets from spring through late summer.

Radicchio In Italy, *radicchio* refers to all the members of the chicory family, but in the United States, *radicchio* triggers images of small, loose-leaved, red-striped heads that resemble small cabbages. Though the red variety is the most popular, radicchio can also be green, cream, or burgundy-marbled and white. The bittersweet leaves, whether raw or braised, add pizzazz to summer salads. Pair them with hazelnut oil, vinegar, and honey in salads, or sauté in olive oil with peppers and zucchini and toss with pasta. Store for a week in a bag in the coldest part of the refrigerator.

Romaine Nothing beats the crunch of this popular salad green on a hot summer day. Romaine has crisp, long, sturdy leaves, with a slightly bitter flavor and succulent inner leaves. While other more exotic greens have appeared at farmers' markets, romaine lettuce remains a popular choice for summer salads in the Northwest, and it's *the* lettuce for Caesar salad. Another bonus is that it stores well; keep it for up to a week in a perforated bag in the refrigerator.

Spinach Native to the Middle East, spinach was brought to the United States by Spaniards. This popular leaf vegetable has an appealing sweetness that blends well with other greens. Look for different varieties at farmers' markets during the summer. Some farms, like Whistling Train Farm in Kent, Washington, grow a hardy variety for winter; these little winter spinach plants are pulled from the ground, and the base of the plant is especially sweet and tender. While baby spinach is more popular at the market, the leaves aren't as flavorful as those of some larger heirloom spinach varieties. Depending on the variety and time of year, spinach will keep for up to a week in a bag in the refrigerator. When it rains in the fall, eat damp baby spinach within a day.

Watercress With a pronounced bitter taste, watercress is reminiscent of mustard greens and has been popular in Europe for decades. You can find wild varieties of watercress around streams or from foragers and some farmers at some Northwest farmers' markets. The small, vibrant dark green leaves add zest to salads and are great for garnishes or tucked into sandwiches. Try a watercress, cucumber, tomato, and avocado sandwich for a taste treat. You can also substitute watercress for parsley and stir it into tabouleh-like salads or blend it into cooked soba noodles with lemon juice, hazelnut oil, honey, and diced radishes. Watercress keeps for a few days in a perforated bag in the refrigerator.

VEGETABLES

The most popular vegetable in America today is the potato, usually eaten as French fries, but if potato lovers sampled some fresh locally grown produce, they might discover that it's easy to fall in love with Northwest vegetables. And with so many seasonal gems to choose from, it's a breeze to increase your vegetable intake. Choose a new variety each week and learn what you can about it. Try it in a couple of easy recipes. For Northwest vegetable ideas, peruse the following list and gather the seeds of inspiration for your next meal.

Amaranth With edible multicolored leaves and beautiful burgundy-colored tassels that droop, amaranth was once considered a weed. Now gardeners grow it for fall color and flowers, and farmers cultivate it for greens and seeds. Amaranth greens are tender young leaves found in some farm salad mixes. Cookbooks also place amaranth greens in sautés and soups, where a squeeze of lemon and a dash of crunchy sea salt completes them. Use the leaves within a few days. Store wrapped in a lightweight towel in a bag in the refrigerator.

Artichokes A Mediterranean native, the artichoke found in stores is mostly grown in California's midcoastal region. California's artichoke season is spring, but you can find Northwest-grown artichokes at markets throughout the summer. DeNoble's Farm Fresh Produce of Tillamook, Oregon, sells a variety of great-tasting artichokes on stems at Portland farmers' markets. Tom DeNoble says the soil near the Oregon coast is great for growing artichokes. A number of Northwest row-crop farms like Whistling Duck Farm in Grants Pass, Oregon, and Rent's Due Ranch in Stanwood, Washington, also grow artichokes and sell them at Northwest markets. When selecting artichokes, look for heavy, compact heads with good color. Pressure cooking is a quick and easy way to prepare artichokes in just 15 minutes. Baby artichokes can also be cooked quickly, and JoanE from Rent's Due Ranch says you can eat the entire artichoke when it's small. Cut in half and sautéed, braised, or simmered in liquid, these babies take 15 to 20 minutes to cook. Big artichokes can simmer for 50 to 60 minutes on the stovetop. Store artichokes wrapped in a damp towel in the coldest part of the refrigerator and cook within a few days.

Asparagus Native to North Africa, asparagus dates back to the dinosaur days when ferns were the dominant plant. Asparagus was cultivated as early as 200 BC. In Europe today, much of the asparagus grown and served in restaurants is white, not green. White asparagus is cultivated in the dark so pigment doesn't form, and though most Northwest farms grow green asparagus, Rockridge Orchards in Enumclaw, Washington, also grows a white variety especially for Seattle chefs. Many farmers bring their asparagus crops to markets in Seattle and Portland in the spring. The season lasts a month, maybe two. By the time summer is in full swing, local asparagus is a memory. Skinny or fat stalks? It doesn't really matter, but look for bunches with firm spears that are tightly closed. A rubbery stalk is an old vegetable. Often cheap asparagus advertised in grocery stores or commercial fruit stands is of poor quality; it tastes inferior and is a waste of money. To prepare asparagus, snap the base off at its natural break and feed it to the dog or add it to the compost. Rinse the asparagus, then blanch, steam, sauté, roast, or even grill it. It also makes a nice addition to soups or casseroles. Sometimes you can find a vendor at the market who pickles it, like Woodring's at various farmers' markets in Seattle. Store asparagus upright in a little water in the refrigerator and use within a few days.

Bamboo shoots Bamboo has been used in China for more than 5,000 years, for food and medicine and in making books and furniture. There are more than 1,200 species of bamboo and most have edible shoots, usually found fresh only in Asian markets. Rockridge Orchards in Enumclaw, Washington, cultivates a number of bamboo varieties that are available in early spring. New bamboo shoots are tender and taste a little like asparagus. Choose heavy, solid shoots that have no soft spots or cracks. Cut away the outer layers and discard. The white core can be cut into lengths and used in a stir-fry, or roast the shoots, cut into 2-inch lengths, with asparagus and extra virgin coconut oil for an exotic flavor. Store fresh bamboo shoots for a week in a plastic bag in the refrigerator.

Beets Beets have been around since prehistoric times, and centuries ago they grew wild near the coast in Europe. While many Americans have encountered only pickled beets in salad bars, Northwest farmers cultivate a wide variety of beets. Albino, golden, candy-striped, and Chioggia beets (pronounced kee-OH-ja) are unique varieties that don't bleed purple over everything. Among the red varieties you can choose baby, red, and cylindrical beets. Look for bunches with firm roots and deep-colored fresh greens attached. The leaves should be cooked within a day or two. In the winter, the greens aren't available. The roots will keep for weeks in the refrigerator, stored in a plastic perforated bag in the vegetable bin.

Bok choy A member of the cabbage family, bok choy (also called pak choi) has been popular in China since the fifth century. Northwest farmers bring it to market in late spring and summer. Thick white stalks with green leaves make it an excellent addition to salads, a great scoop for dips, and an added attraction in a pilaf, soup, or sauté. Crunchy bok choy stalks can easily replace celery in many dishes. Tat soi is a tiny version of bok choy with dainty leaves on slender stems. The sweet-tasting leaves can be torn, and the stems chopped or minced and added to any salad, or sauté the entire plant with baby carrots for a great spring side dish. Store in a perforated bag in the refrigerator for up to a few days.

Broccoli Another cabbage family member, broccoli was cultivated by the ancient Romans, and was mostly grown by Italian immigrants in this country until the 1920s. In grocery stores broccoli is available year-round, but if you enjoy broccoli, don't bother with the grocery store variety because the sweetest-tasting specimens come from farmers' markets. Willie Green's Organic Farm in Washington grows broccoli so sweet even the stems are a treat. Broccoli stores for only a few days in the refrigerator.

Broccoli rabe Originating in the southern Mediterranean, broccoli rabe (also known as broccoli raab or rapini) was brought to America by Italian immigrants and was widely cultivated in California in the 1930s. Many Northwest farmers grow this assertive leafy green with a mustardlike bite to it. Blanch it briefly in salted water to tame much of the bitterness before using in casseroles, sautés, and soups. Broccoli rabe is more perishable than it looks, so refrigerate it in a perforated plastic bag and use it as soon as possible. The stalk, leaf, and flower of the plant can be used.

Brussels sprouts No one knows if their origin is really Brussels, but Brussels sprouts were originally cultivated in Europe. The miniature cabbage heads are sweeter after the first freeze in autumn. Choose firm, compact heads. I prefer to buy the sprouts still attached to stalks because they taste a little sweeter. When steaming, cut the larger ones in half and begin testing for doneness at 4 minutes. When a fork pulls out easily, they are done. Stored Brussels sprouts deteriorate rapidly, losing their sweetness, so use them within a few days. You can store loose sprouts in a perforated bag in the vegetable crisper.

Burdock Also known as gobo, this humble brown Japanese root has a unique earthy artichoke-like flavor. In the Northwest, look for burdock in late summer and fall and through the winter. Winter Green Farm in Noti, Oregon, and Mair Farm-Taki in Yakima, Washington, are known for growing and selling organic burdock. Choose firm roots about as big as medium-to-large carrots. If burdock has a thin skin, there is no need to peel it. Instead, scrub it, cut it, and cook it like you would a carrot. Think soups and stews with burdock. Pair it with carrots, leeks, mushrooms, and lemon juice or wine; try sliced burdock, leeks, and mushrooms braised with apple cider or wine with a squeeze of lemon juice. Another idea for burdock is to make thin diagonal slices and sautée them on low heat in safflower oil until crisp, then sprinkle these chips with fleur de sel (a crispy sea salt) or tamari. Store fresh burdock in the refrigerator wrapped in a damp paper towel inside a plastic bag.

Cabbage Native to the northern European coast, cabbage has been cultivated for about 4,000 years. Though green or red cabbages are the most familiar varieties, you can also find savoy and napa in many markets. Select fairly compact heads, heavy for their size. Some cabbages, such as napa, have looser leaves but should feel crisp and have a vibrant light green color. Sliced cabbage is good raw in salads, lightly steamed, or braised. If you want to make the red stand out when cooking red cabbage, add lemon juice or vinegar to the water. Store cabbage in a perforated plastic bag in the refrigerator for about a week. If you leave it loose, it dries out and becomes rubbery.

Cardoons Used in ancient Greece, cardoons are popular in Italy, France, and Spain. Like a giant artichoke, a cardoon is a thistle with prickly flowers that aren't eaten. The stalks are usually blanched, and the stringy fibers must be peeled before it is sliced and then cooked. Blanching takes the bitterness out, leaving a taste similar to artichokes. Some Northwest farmers grow them, but they are not often prominently displayed at farmers' markets. Precook cardoons in salted boiling water for 15 to 25 minutes, then cool, slice, and use in gratins, pair them with baked potatoes, or try a creamy cardoon soup flavored with hazelnut butter, lemon juice, and rosemary. Store them in a plastic bag in the refrigerator for one week.

Carrots Native to Afghanistan, carrots were cultivated as early as 500 BC. The familiar orange carrots were originally purple or yellow, and the root was more woody than sweet, but after centuries of breeding, the preferred color changed to bright orange in the 1600s. Nowadays, you can find tables at Northwest farmers' markets filled with carrot colors—orange-purple, yellow, and red. Color and texture are the best indicators of freshness when selecting carrots. Attached greens are also a sign of freshness, but remove them as soon as possible because carrots store better without them. Use the greens in a stir-fry or add to soup or stock. Smaller carrots can be steamed or roasted whole with a small part of the greens attached. Larger carrots can be sliced and sautéed in a little butter. Most carrots found in grocery stores have been stored for months and have lost their sweet flavor and probably many of their nutrients. Carrots keep for about a week, sometimes longer, in a perforated bag in your refrigerator.

Cauliflower Cultivated in the Mediterranean for more than 2,000 years, cauliflower is an evolved variety of broccoli and a member of the cabbage family. Now cauliflower is available in three basic colors—white, green, and purple. The size of the head doesn't matter when it comes to taste, and basic white varieties often prove the sweetest choice. Look for solid, compact heads with few blemishes and healthy green leaves. In Seattle, Rent's Due Ranch sells some of the sweetest cauliflower at the University District farmers' market and at PCC Natural Markets. Steam or sauté cauliflower, mash it with potatoes, or puree it into a creamy soup. Cauliflower leaves can also be cooked, but they take a little longer; add chopped leaves to soups and stews. Refrigerate cauliflower in a perforated plastic bag in the vegetable bin for up to a week. In late summer and early fall you can find Romanesco cauliflower, also sometimes called Romanesco broccoli, a chartreuse, cone-shaped, spiraling head with turrets. Romanesco can be eaten raw or lightly steamed, and it keeps for at least a week in the refrigerator.

Celeriac Celeriac is a kind of celery grown for its edible root; the plant's stalks and leaves aren't edible. Hundreds of years ago, farmers in the Mediterranean region grew both celery and celeriac. Both were common vegetables in this country until the 1940s and then celeriac fell out of fashion and practically disappeared, but now it's making a comeback at Northwest farmers' markets in late summer and fall. The root has a concentrated celery taste with a potato-like texture when cooked. Peel it and steam or mash it with potatoes, garlic, and butter. Select small, firm roots that are fairly round for easier peeling. Slice off the root end and peel with a sharp knife. Then cut it into slices or chunks and plunge it into lemon water to prevent discoloration. Many people enjoy celeriac raw, grated in mayonnaise-based salads. Celeriac can also be steamed, boiled, or braised, or added to a potato gratin. Use it in casseroles, soups, or vegetable medleys with a sauce. For storage, trim the stalks, wrap in plastic, and refrigerate for one week.

Celery With ties to the carrot family, stalk celery has been cultivated since ancient Greek and Roman times but was consumed solely as a medicinal herb until the 16th century. Today, commercial celery is grown under soil or paper so it has very little color, but celery found at Northwest farmers' markets has a more pronounced green color and better flavor than grocery store celery. When selecting celery, go for crisp, rigid stalks with few blemishes and fresh-looking leaves on top. When celery gets soft and rubbery, it's still good for soup stock, but when leaves turn yellow, discard it. Celery generally plays a supporting rather than starring role and is good in pilafs, salads, soups, and casseroles. Store celery in a perforated plastic bag in the refrigerator for about one week.

Chard Also referred to as Swiss chard, this beet family member originated in the Mediterranean. In the Northwest, chard is available for most of the year, and during the summer, look for white, red, and rainbow chard. Chard leaves look best in summer months; look for bright-colored leaves with no yellowing or blemishes. Chard tastes mild and cooks quickly, like spinach. It's good steamed or braised with onions and peppers. Tiny raw leaves are added to salad mixes, and bigger leaves make a good addition to soups, stews, risottos, and casseroles. Store chard in a perforated plastic bag in the refrigerator for up to a week.

Collards One of the oldest cultivated forms of cabbage, collards are popular in southern cooking and are available most of the year in the Northwest. Sweet and mild tasting compared to kale, collard leaves should be deep green when you buy them. Some farms, like Stoney Plains Organic Farm in Tenino, Washington, sometimes sell collards with smaller leaves that are tender and crisp with a sweet, mild taste. Other farms add baby collard leaves to bags of braising greens. To prepare leaves for cooking, remove large leaves from their tough stems. Holding the stem of a washed leaf with one hand, push the leaf off with the other. Discard the stems, lay the leaves flat, roll them into a fat cigar, and finely slice into thin ribbons before adding to cooked dishes. Store collards in perforated plastic in the refrigerator for a few days.

Corn Originating in Mexico more than 8,000 years ago, corn is available in many varieties. Fresh corn is considered a vegetable and is plentiful at markets in the summer. Colored flint corn grown for popcorn and polenta is available at the Hillsdale farmers' market from Ayers Creek Farm in Gaston, Oregon. During the summer, the best place to find sweet corn is the farmers' market. Husks should be green, and the cobs filled with firm-looking kernels. When pressed, fresh kernels should spurt juice. Store corn in a plastic bag in the refrigerator for a few days.

Cucumbers One of the oldest food crops, cucumbers probably originated in Thailand and were later transported to India and China. From there they spread around the world. Most Northwest cucumbers are available during the summer. They seem to appear at farmers' markets spontaneously and disappear just as quickly six to eight weeks later. Japanese cucumbers have a longer season, and surprisingly, some hearty cucumbers may be available at markets as late as December. Select firm specimens without any soft spots and buy organic if you want to eat the skin; otherwise peel. Slice and eat them raw on salads or make pickles with them. In some countries, cucumbers are cooked. One French cream of cucumber soup recipe included stock, herbs, cucumbers, butter, cream or sour cream, and potatoes to thicken it. For storing, one authority says to wrap cucumbers in a towel and store in a plastic bag in the refrigerator for a few days, but you can also leave them loose in the refrigerator produce bin and they are fine for two days.

Dandelion greens Look for tender young cultivated organic or wild foraged dandelion greens in the spring at farmers' markets. Donna Weston, a forager who sells dandelion greens at the University District market, says you can harvest this one from your own pesticide- and pet-free yard in the spring. Tangy with a bitter bite, these greens should be used sparingly in salads. They can also be lightly braised with shallots and a little ginger or garlic. Store dandelion greens wrapped in a damp towel inside a bag for a few days in the refrigerator.

Eggplant Originally cultivated in India or Burma, eggplant was transported by Arab caravans to Europe in the 13th century. Like its relatives potatoes, tomatoes, and peppers, eggplant can be found at local markets from Ashland to Bellingham in the summer. For a treat from the Corvallis farmers' market, look for Fairy Tale eggplant from Gathering Together Farm. At the Ashland farmers' market, check out the Japanese eggplant from the Fry Family Farm. Each variety has a slightly different taste and texture. You can bake, roast, grill, or sauté it. Eggplant is a summer crop, so enjoy it while the sun shines. Don't waste your money on eggplant during the winter, because off-season grocery store varieties have bitter tones and keep miserably. Store your eggplant in the refrigerator and use it within a week.

Fennel Cultivated since ancient Roman times, fennel is a parsley relative and is quite popular in the Mediterranean region. Today many Northwest farmers grow and sell it. The best time to look for fennel is summer through autumn. Select specimens with firm, white bulbs and vibrant green feathery leaves. With a texture like celery and a sweet licorice flavor, fennel is a great choice for tomato-based dishes and can be used in almost any recipe that calls for celery. The bulb is often used, but you can also use the thin stalks in soups and stews and the leaves for garnish. Fennel can be steamed, braised, sautéed, or even grilled. Offer it raw, cut in wedges and served with dips. Store fennel in a plastic bag in the refrigerator for up to a week.

Garlic A member of the lily family, garlic has been used for centuries as an herb, vegetable, and medicine. Northwest market shoppers welcome green garlic to the markets in the spring. Many farmers sell bundles of these green shoots that can be sliced and added to stir-fries and pasta dishes for a milder flavor than mature garlic. Crushing the shoots can release more of garlic's essential pungent oils. Green garlic can be stored in a plastic bag in the refrigerator for a week. In summer and fall, look for varieties like Spanish roja, Korean red, elephant, and California early. Some kinds, like elephant garlic, are mild, and others quite hot. Garlic can also become sweeter or more pungent according to how it is handled, cut, and used. Whole roasted garlic and sliced sautéed cloves are remarkably sweet. Pressing or mincing makes garlic more pungent. Elephant garlic is more closely related to leeks than garlic. Select firm dry garlic heads. Avoid garlic with black spots or green sprouts growing out of the top. Fresh garlic purchased or harvested during autumn months can be stored in a cool, dry cupboard through the winter. The key is keeping the bulb dry.

Green beans Originally from Central America, green beans are one of the most extensively cultivated garden vegetables in the United States today. In midsummer, they are everywhere at Northwest farmers' markets, and so are the crowds that love them. Though green and shell beans are related, fresh green beans are eaten in their pods. Green bean varieties at farmers' markets include Romano, yellow wax, and the skinny green haricots verts. For the tenderest green beans, choose smaller firm specimens with good color and no blemishes. When the pods are broken, the seeds inside will be small. Green beans keep for a few days enclosed in a paper towel and stored in a plastic bag in the refrigerator. Cook them as soon as possible.

Jerusalem artichokes These odd-shaped tubers aren't from Jerusalem and aren't even related to artichokes. Cultivated along the East Coast by Native Americans long before Europeans arrived, the homely, humble Jerusalem artichokes (sunchokes) aren't supermarket stars today, but many Northwest farmers grow them, and many Northwest foodies love them. The flavor is uniquely wild and earthy with nutty tones. Peak harvest is fall, making them perfect candidates for gratins with potatoes, carrots, and mushrooms. Look for firm, unblemished tubers and use them within a week.

Once cut, they must be plunged into acidulated water (water with a little lemon or vinegar added) or they turn brown. One of the easiest things to do is sauté them in butter with caramelized onions and then sprinkle with sugar and add a squeeze of lemon juice and a pinch of salt. Store Jerusalem artichokes in a perforated paper or plastic bag in the refrigerator and use within a week.

Kale An ancient relative of cabbage, kale is sometimes called the king of vegetables because it contains so many nutrients. Kale has fiber, folic acid, potassium, vitamin C, vitamin K, beta-carotene, and a good amount of calcium. Like parsnips, kale is best in the cold winter months because the flavor sweetens after a frost, but you can buy it year-round at Northwest farmers' markets. When selecting kale, look for crisp, brightly colored leaves. Limp or light-colored leaves might mean it has been stored too long. To remove any bitter tones, blanch kale for a few minutes in boiling water before adding to soups or stews. You can also braise the blanched kale with caramelized onions and white wine or apple cider. Add a squeeze of lemon juice and a pinch of salt and you've got an excellent side dish. Store kale in a perforated plastic bag in the refrigerator for a week.

Kohlrabi Kohlrabi is a member of the cole or brassica family, which started with the wild cabbage and now includes cauliflower and broccoli. A cross between a cabbage and a turnip, kohlrabi is not a very popular vegetable, but it grows well in the mild Northwest climate and many farmers offer it at farmers' markets. Kohlrabi season is spring through fall and into the winter, so give it a chance and try it raw, cut into sticks, or grated into a salad. Kohlrabi is also delectable cooked, and in India it is seasoned with curries. In *The Victory Garden Cookbook*, Marian Morash has recipes for simple sautéed kohlrabi with butter, salt, pepper, and lemon juice, and whipped kohlrabi and potato for a lighter version of mashed potatoes. To prepare kohlrabi, cut the leaf stems off. Wash and carefully peel off the tough skins with a paring knife. A kohlrabi globe keeps for up to one month in a plastic bag in the refrigerator.

Mushrooms A mushroom is the edible fruit of a fungus and is not really a vegetable. Some varieties are cultivated and some are wild, found in damp soils in meadows or forests. They are found in shades of yellow, tan, gray, brown, and orange; some are shelflike and live on trees, some are subterranean, and others have gills and cluster in forests, meadows, and on decaying tree stumps. Black trumpets, chanterelles, morels, cremini, portobello, porcini, and shiitake are some of the varieties you can find at farmers' markets. If you're interested in foraging, check out *All That the Rain Promises and More: A Hip Pocket Guide to Western Mushrooms* by David Arora, but go with an expert a few times to be certain about what you're picking. You can keep sturdy mushrooms like porcini for up to a week in a paper bag in the refrigerator. Cook more fragile mushrooms like chanterelles within a few days; store these types in a basket in the refrigerator, in a single layer covered with a cloth.

Nettles Although many people consider nettles a lowly weed with nasty thorns, nettles have been cooked and eaten as a vegetable since ancient Rome. Nettles grow abundantly in the Northwest, and harvesting is done in the spring when the new leaves appear. Foragers like Jeremy Faber at Foraged and Found sell these healthy greens at Seattle markets in the spring. Some farmers also put them on tables, so look for them at your local market. The tiny new leaves are the preferred leaves to gather and cook, just in case you want to forage for your own. Make sure you know which plants are nettles, wear gloves, and strip the leaves from their stems, discarding the stalks. At home, use gloves to place nettles in liquid and cook until limp. Nettles are especially good in a pureed spring green soup with a twist of lemon and a dollop of yogurt.

Okra Originating in Ethiopia, okra is most well known in the southern United States, where it is often found in gumbo. The gelatinous texture thickens gumbo and transforms tomato-based dishes. Okra season in the Northwest is midsummer. If you aren't an okra fan, try tiny young okra rather than the large specimens. I love the tiny okra from Alvarez Farms in the Yakima Valley sold at various Seattle markets. Okra pairs well with tomatoes, peppers, fennel, garlic, sweet onions, corn, and peas. Select small firm and fresh-looking specimens with a uniform color. Okra doesn't store well, so keep it for only a few days in a perforated bag in the refrigerator.

Onion Another Middle East native, the onion is a bulb, not a root vegetable, and can be sweet, pungent, or hot, with many shades of flavor in between. The onion family includes chives, green onions, leeks, shallots, and sweet, red, pearl, and storage onions. The latter are found fall through winter in the Northwest. Sweet onions like Walla Wallas show up at farmers' markets in the spring as young green onions, then they mature and finally fade away in the fall. When selecting onions, look for firm bulbs with no flaws; the green of scallions and chives should be vibrant.

Keep green and sweet onions in the refrigerator for about a week. Like garlic, onions want to grow in the spring, and if they begin to sprout, remove the green sprouts before using them. Store dry onions in a cool, dark place (not the refrigerator), away from potatoes. Thick-skinned yellow or red onions will keep for a few weeks.

Parsley Parsley has been used since ancient times when the Greeks wore parsley wreaths to stimulate appetites. A well-recognized herb, flat or curly-leaf parsley brings salads and pilafs to life. Finely chop about a cup or more, blend in with rice, add a little lemon juice and honey and salt, and garnish with toasted chopped hazelnuts or walnuts. Bean, pasta, and grain salads also benefit from parsley's vibrant color, sparkling flavor, and concentrated nutrients. Flat-leaf parsley keeps for about a week and curly-leaf parsley stores for up to two weeks in a bag in the refrigerator.

Parsley root A European native, parsley root has long flavored German, Polish, and Hungarian dishes. This pale root looks like an anemic carrot or a parsnip. Americans cultivated it in the early 1800s and a few Northwest farmers grow it today, but it hasn't really caught on as a popular vegetable. The flavor is an assertive combination of celeriac and parsley, with a hint of carrot tossed in. Choose solid, uniformly colored roots. Ideally, it will have greens attached, which is a sign of freshness. A few slices of the root add earthy tones to soups and stews. Store parsley roots for up to a month wrapped in paper towels in a plastic bag in the refrigerator.

Parsnips Though parsnips have been cultivated since ancient times, their popularity hasn't spread much beyond the Midwest today. Many Northwest farmers grow parsnips, and a number of market shoppers have become converts to this nutty-flavored root. A carrot relative, the parsnip tastes sweeter when harvested after the first fall frost. Select medium-size, firm roots; larger parsnips often have tough cores and require longer cooking. Steam or sauté parsnips or use them in soups or casseroles. They are also good pureed with a little butter, salt, and pepper. Store them for up to 10 days in a perforated plastic bag in the refrigerator.

Peas Though peas are an ancient vegetable, it wasn't until the 17th century that eating fresh green peas (not dried) became popular. You can sometimes find pea shoots in the early spring, and when summer produce is at its peak you can buy English shelling, sugar snap, and snow peas. Peas begin to lose their sweetness soon after they are picked, so buying locally and using peas immediately is your best bet. Store them in an open plastic bag in the refrigerator and use them within a few days.

Peppers Originating as a New World crop, peppers are now incorporated into cuisines all over the world. Pepper varieties can cross-pollinate each other, creating new kinds of peppers. Ranging from sweet to very hot, peppers can be red, green, yellow, orange, or chocolate. Peak season is July through October. Bake, roast, grill, sauté, or steam them. Use peppers in salads, pureed in sauces, grilled on sandwiches, or added to soups and stews. They store well in a perforated plastic bag in the refrigerator for about a week.

Potatoes Another New World native, the potato is popular all over the world, and the Northwest is no exception. There are two types of potatoes: dry-textured potatoes like russets, for baking, and thin-skinned, waxy potatoes like Yellow Finn or Yukon Gold that make excellent mashed potatoes and potato salad and that are great in soups and gratins. Northwest farmers grow a wide variety, and some farms specialize in unique-tasting types. Though the different potatoes are fun to sample, if you are budget conscious you can save money by sticking to the basic garden variety. Select firm, unblemished potatoes. If dropped, potatoes become damaged even if they don't show it, so use them soon after. Organic potatoes might grow sprouts if you don't eat them within a week or two. Sprouts and green spots contain solanine, which can be toxic, so cut the sprouts out before cooking and don't eat potatoes that have turned green. Store potatoes in a cool, dark place (a cupboard, not a refrigerator) away from onions.

Radishes Members of the mustard family, radishes are edible roots that are spicy and come in white, red, purple, and even black. Many people are familiar with the usual garden variety of radishes used for salads or set on fancy plates with appetizers, but the long white daikons are more commonly seen in Asian markets. Daikons are 6 to 15 inches long; some exceptional varieties are even longer. Though most radishes are eaten raw in the United States, in China they are cooked and in Korea, Japan, Thailand, and India radishes are pickled. Radish greens should not be discarded, because they are also good in sautés and braising mixes. Wash the greens and lightly sauté in butter. When done, gently blend with a little yuzu or lemon juice, a drizzle of agave nectar, and a sprinkling of salt. Radishes keep for about a week in the refrigerator. Use the leaves within a few days.

Rutabaga Developed in the 17th century, rutabagas were often thought of as a turnip hybrid. However, a rutabaga is a mutant, not a hybrid, since the rutabaga contains 38 chromosomes while turnips contain 20. Yellow-fleshed, the rutabaga is sweeter than the turnip. The season is October through March. Use them as you would turnips. They are great sliced for dips and perfect additions to casseroles. Look for firm, unblemished specimens. Store them unwrapped in the refrigerator for one week.

Salsify, black salsify Though these vegetables are cooked frequently in European kitchens, salsify and black salsify (also known as scorzonera) are not common vegetables at Northwest markets. A dark brown carrot or parsniplike root, black salsify can be found from June through February in the Northwest. When cooked, it imparts hints of artichoke flavor. To prepare it, scrub the root and trim the neck and tips, cut it in lengths, or leave it whole and soak it in water with a little lemon juice added. Then remove from the water and steam or simmer until just tender, but avoid overcooking because it can easily go from cooked to mush. Toss it raw with vinegar or lemon juice and add a little diced raw celery and salad greens for a salad. Keep salsify for up to two weeks wrapped in a perforated plastic bag in the vegetable bin of the refrigerator.

Shell beans Less well known than their green and yellow cousins, shell beans are mature beans that have remained longer in the pod. Black turtle, cannellini, cranberry, flageolet, and garbanzo are some varieties spotted at Seattle farmers' markets. In Corvallis, Oregon, Tom Denison grows some of the best-tasting favas, so if you stop at the Corvallis farmers' market, be sure to pick up a few pounds. At Ayers Creek Farm near Gaston, dried favas are a specialty crop, and these dried beans have a more intense flavor and a different texture from the fresh variety. They are great cooked with garlic. For fresh or dried shell beans, look for smooth surfaces and few cracks or blemishes. Fresh shell beans keep for about a week in the refrigerator's vegetable crisper. Store in the freezer for longer storage. Dried beans will keep for about a year in a closed glass container on a pantry shelf. Leaving jars out, exposed to light, can cause loss of some B vitamins.

Sorrel Acidic with a strong lemony taste, sorrel is one of those vegetables people claim to either love or hate. Blanching can transform it from bitter to sour, and many add it in moderation to raw and cooked dishes. Recipes for cream of sorrel soup are passed around at farmers' markets. Sorrel is also good wilted in grain and white bean dishes. Pair it with champagne or white balsamic vinegar. Green onions, lemon, cream, and nutmeg are creamy soup ingredients to try with sorrel.

Soybeans Also known as sweet beans or edamame, these tasty treats can be found in mid to late summer at farmers' markets. Look for bright green pods. Some farmers sell them still attached to the branches of the bushes they grow on, but a better buy is to purchase loose pods by the pound. Steam or boil the pods for three to five minutes and then drain. Place the steaming pods in a bowl and squeeze the small, creamy-textured beans out to eat. Alternatively, remove the beans from the cooked pods, and cook as directed in your recipe. Store edamame uncooked in the pods for a day or so in a plastic bag in the refrigerator. Cooked edamame keeps for a week in the refrigerator.

Squash Native to the New World, squash cross-pollinates like peppers do, producing an endless variety of hybrids. Squash can be divided into two groups: summer and winter. Both can be found in abundance at Northwest farmers' markets. Summer squash contains more water, and the most well known is zucchini, but pattypan, yellow crookneck, sunburst, and other varieties are available. When selecting summer squash, look for firm, colorful specimens with no blemishes. Keep them in a perforated bag in the refrigerator and use within a few days. They can be grilled, braised, sautéed, or added to other dishes. Winter squash has tougher skin with a colorful yellow-to-orange creamy flesh. Select winter squash that is heavy for its size, firm, and without soft spots or blemishes. Store it in a cool dry place, not touching other squash, for up to five months. Check stored squash frequently because sometimes bruises turn into bad spots. Squash can be steamed, boiled, or baked. It can also be stuffed with whole grains, beans, and vegetables or mashed and used in quick breads or muffins.

Sweet potatoes (and yams) Cultivated in South America and throughout the Pacific islands, sweet potatoes were a dietary staple in the Americas by the time Columbus arrived in the West Indies. Sweet potatoes require 8 to 11 months of very warm weather to mature, but farmers are discovering some varieties that grow well in the Northwest. Look for them in late autumn. The so-called yams in grocery stores are actually varieties of sweet potatoes, while true yams are a large, bland, starchy tuber from Africa similar to potatoes in texture. The sweet potatoes known as yams are sweeter and moister and have more vibrant color than those called simply sweet potatoes. Select firm specimens with no soft spots and use them within a few days. Store in a cool, dark cupboard for a few weeks.

Tomatillos Used by the Aztecs in pre-Columbian

times, tomatillos grow abundantly in the Southwest. Homestead Organic Produce in Quincy grows and sells them at Seattle's University District farmers' market. Wrapped in a thin, paperlike husk, these green and chartreuse tomatillos can be the size of a cherry tomato or an egg. They are traditionally cooked but can also be used raw. They are usually added to salsas and then incorporated into tacos, enchiladas, and burritos. Look for tomatillos in the heat of the summer. Choose firm, dry specimens with husks that fit the tomatillo. Store in a paper-lined container in the refrigerator for several weeks.

Tomatoes A South American native, tomatoes are members of the nightshade family, along with potatoes, eggplants, and peppers. There are three basic shapes of tomatoes: round, plum or roma, and cherry. Heirloom tomatoes have a unique deep rich tomato taste. Brandywine, Yellow Pear, Yellow Plum, Stupice, and Zebra are examples of heirloom tomatoes you might find at farmers' markets in the summer. Though tomatoes are often enjoyed raw, they are also great additions to casseroles and soups. Select tomatoes heavy for their size that are firm with no soft spots or blemishes and that have a slight give when you gently press them. Store them on a kitchen counter or in a fruit bowl until ready to use; most keep for about a week. Refrigeration drains them of flavor and changes the texture, but when tomatoes are very ripe, they should be refrigerated or blanched and frozen for soup in winter.

Turnips Turnips have been around since prehistoric times. They grow in poor soil, store well, and are inexpensive. Nutritional all-stars, turnips contain anticarcinogenic phytonutrients. The taste is slightly pungent, earthy, and sweet. Mash them with potatoes, puree them with other root vegetables, add them to soups and stews and casseroles, or roast them with other vegetables. Young, fresh turnips are excellent grated on fresh green salads. You can cook the greens like beet greens. Buy firm, unblemished specimens with vibrant leaves. Store larger turnips in the refrigerator for about a week. Young turnips with greens keep for a few days. Use the greens first.

SEASONS FOR LOCAL FRUITS AND VEGETABLES

In the Northwest, the seasons for vegetables and fruits vary slightly from region to region and from year to year. For example, strawberries show up in the Willamette Valley weeks earlier than those in the Skagit Valley, north of Seattle. And each year the weather is a little different so some crops come late and others show up a little early. Michaele Blakely of Growing Things Farm in Carnation, Wade Bennett of Rockridge Orchards in Enumclaw, and Liz Eggers of Grouse Mountain Farm in Chelan, Washington, helped me compile the following dates for seasonal produce availability.

CROP	SEASON
Apples	late July–October
Apricots	June–August
Artichokes	April–July
Asian pears	August–November
Asparagus	May–June
Bamboo shoots	April–July
Beans, green	July–October
Beans, shell (dried)	August–October
Beets	May–November
Blackberries	August–September
Blueberries	June–September
Bok choy	year-round

CROP	SEASON	CROP	SEASON
Boysenberries	July–August	Mulberries	July–August
Broccoli	year-round	Mushrooms, wild	June–November
Brussels sprouts	November–February	Nectarines	July–August
Cabbage	year-round	Nettles	early spring
Cardoons	April–June	Okra	July–September
Carrots	May–February	Onions	June–November
Cauliflower	year-round	Parsley	May–September
Celeriac	September–October	Parsley root	October
Celery	August–November	Parsnips	October–early spring
Chard	year-round	Pawpaws	October
Cherries	June–July	Peaches	July–August
Collards	year-round	Pears	August–October
Corn	July–October	Peas	June–fall
Cranberries	October–November	Peppers	June–fall
Cucumbers	July–September	Persimmons	October–November
Currants	August	Plums	August–September
Dandelion greens	March–April	Potatoes	July–November (winter storage)
Eggplant	July–August		
Fava beans	throughout harvest season	Pumpkins	October–November
		Purslane	June–September
Fennel	July–October	Quince	October–November
Figs	Late June–July and September–October	Radishes	year-round
		Raspberries	June–October
Garlic	June–October	Rhubarb	May–September
Grapes	August–October	Romanesco cauliflower	late August–November
Greens, specialty	year-round	Rutabaga	October–throughout winter
Greens, wild	March–June		
Herbs	June–September	Shallots	August–September
Huckleberries, blue	August–October	Soybeans, green	July–October
Huckleberries, red	July	Spinach	year-round
Jerusalem artichokes	fall through winter	Squash, summer	June–frost
Kale	year-round	Squash, winter	September–November (storage)
Kiwis	September–October		
Kohlrabi	year-round	Strawberries	June–October
Leeks	year-round	Sweet potatoes	November–December
Lettuce	year-round	Tomatillos	July–September
Melons	August–November	Tomatoes	July–September
		Turnips	year-round

Northwest Beans and Grains

In the Northwest, grains and beans can provide a year-round food base. In the past few years, a number of farmers in Oregon and Washington have started growing grains and bring them to markets. So look for whole grains and beans at farmers' markets.

Whole Grains

Cultivated for at least 8,700 years, grains are a staple in every cuisine around the world. Ancestors of barley and wheat were originally grown almost 9,000 years ago in the Tigris-Euphrates Valley in what is now Iraq. Corn and amaranth were New World crops, and quinoa sustained Andean civilizations for centuries before Spanish colonization. Our list of available grains has expanded, and some Northwest farmers are now growing specialty grains to sell at markets. Ask farmers at your market or chefs who specialize in local food for grain growers in your area.

Amaranth An ancient grain cultivated by the Aztecs in Mexico, amaranth was also known in ancient China and has been found growing wild on five continents. Though the burgundy flowers are common and some farmers sell the greens at markets, not much amaranth grain is available locally. With a glutinous texture, amaranth imparts a sweet taste slightly reminiscent of corn.

Barley Originating in either western Asia or the Ethiopian highlands, barley was a grain staple in Europe before being replaced by wheat and rye. Most of the barley found in stores is pearled barley, which means the outer hulls and an inner layer have been mechanically removed, leaving it similar to refined rice in nutritional quality. Ayers Creek Farm in Gaston, Oregon, sells naked or hull-less barley at the Hillsdale farmers' market.

Emmer or farro An ancient wheat that predates durum wheat, emmer is grown by Bluebird Grain Farms, a sustainable organic farm in the Methow Valley, east of the Cascades in Washington. They sell through their Web site, www.bluebirdgrain-farms.com, and can be found at the University District market. The flour doesn't have as much gluten as wheat, but the grains are chewy and taste a little like wheat berries.

Rye Developed from a species of a northeastern European grain, rye can sustain itself in severely cold climates and thrives in damp, cold climates. In the Northwest, rye is used as a cover crop to help build healthy soil. In cooking, rye is generally used as a bread grain. Rye is nutritionally similar to wheat, but the flavor is a little stronger. Rye berries are quite chewy and are rarely cooked by themselves. Use a handful of them in place of rice, spelt, or wheat berries in recipes. Bluebird Grain Farms and Nash's Organic Produce sell rye at the University District farmers' market.

Wheat American colonists from Europe brought wheat with them, and later wheat grains were carried west with the pioneers. Eastern Washington still has commodity wheat farms today. The most frequently eaten grain in the

United States, wheat is the basis for nearly every bread and cookie in America today. Whole wheat contains 12 B vitamins, vitamin E, protein, and a number of important minerals such as zinc, iron, and magnesium. Cooked wheat berries have a chewy texture. A number of farms in the Northwest are bringing wheat back, and some, like Bluebird Grain Farms and Nash's Organic Produce, are carting it to markets.

Wild rice The seed of an aquatic grass, wild rice is native to the Great Lakes region of the United States. It grows along streams in shallow water in Minnesota. In the Northwest, Freddy Guys in Oregon grows hazelnuts and wild rice. They sell their wild rice at the Saturday Portland farmers' market.

BUYING AND STORING

Whole grains contain natural oils, and the shelf life is much shorter than for refined grains. Purchase whole grains where the turnover is rapid and buy in small quantities that can be used in a few months. Label and store grains in containers away from the light, and use them within six months, or store them for up to a year in the freezer.

PREPARATION

Whole grains are minimally processed and may contain small stones, sticks, and dirt. Place all but very tiny whole grains in a double-mesh strainer, pick out any rocks, and rinse them. If you want to rinse tiny grains like amaranth, place them in a mason jar with a piece of cheesecloth covering the opening, then rinse them before using them in recipes.

Soaking grains before cooking is often recommended for better digestibility, but you don't really have to do this for most grains. If you do soak grains before cooking, discard the soaking water and use fresh water to cook the grains.

COOKING

Cooking whole grains doesn't always go according to instructions because there are many variables. Use a grain-cooking chart as a guide, not an absolute, because the age of the grain, the weight of the pot, the fit of the lid, and the stove's temperament all affect cooking times. Find out what works on your stove with your pans. For best results, write down exactly how you cook the grain each time. I start with less water than most cooking charts call for because it's easier to add hot water to undercooked grains than to simmer too much water off fully cooked grains. A rice cooker is another option for cooking grains.

For a sticky grain, start the grain in cold water. Bring the water to a boil, reduce the heat, cover, and simmer for the specified time. To get a perfect, fluffy dinner grain, add dry grains when the water is already boiling. Toss in a pinch of salt for taste and digestibility. Once the grains are cooking, resist the urge to stir, because air pockets are formed between the grains as they cook, and when these air pockets are disturbed, the starch molecules on the outside of the grains move together, creating a sticky grain. The texture can become quite gluelike if you continue to stir the grains. To check and see if there is still liquid in the pan before the grains are done, gently move the grains on one side with a fork. Add a little hot water or stock if necessary. Check again in 5 to 10 minutes.

The following table indicates how to cook a variety of grains seen on market tables in Oregon and Washington.

GRAIN (1 CUP)	LIQUID	TIME	YIELD
Amaranth	2 cups	30 minutes	2 cups
Barley, whole or hull-less	2 cups	60 to 75 minutes	3½ cups
Emmer or farro	2 cups	60 minutes	2½ cups
Rye	2 cups	60 to 75 minutes	2 cups
Wheat berries	2 cups	60 to 70 minutes	2½ cups
Wild rice	2 cups	60 minutes	2½ cups

Legumes

The world of legumes includes peas, lentils, and beans. First mentioned in the Bible, the legume family has more than 14,000 members. Of those, about 700 are listed by the Seed Savers Exchange as edible varieties. Many are heirloom or old-fashioned varieties that have been handed down within families for generations.

Along with grains, legumes are the cornerstone of protein in vegetarian cooking. An inexpensive protein source, beans are often called "a poor man's protein" because they can be grown in relatively poor soil, they give a high yield per acre, and they can feed people for less than it costs to eat meat. Legumes range from 17 to 25 percent protein, significantly higher than whole grains and vegetables. Soybeans contain about 35 percent protein. Beans contain a wide range of B vitamins as well as minerals—calcium, potassium, magnesium, iron, and zinc. They also contain complex carbohydrates and soluble fiber, which has a stabilizing effect on blood sugar imbalances.

Beans are also healthy for the earth and known for putting nitrogen back into the ground and building up the soil. Farmers rotate legumes with other crops to enrich their soil. A good example is alfalfa, an amazing legume with a root system that can penetrate up to a hundred feet and bring up trace minerals that other root systems can't reach. Alfalfa is often alternated with wheat for a number of years to enrich farmland in eastern Oregon and Washington.

Following are descriptions of a few varieties of beans grown in the Northwest.

Black beans A native of Mexico, the black bean is earthy and sweet. It can be substituted for other beans, but the liquid tends to turn things black. Use black beans in salads, soups, stews and side dishes. They are widely available in grocery stores, but try the varieties at farmers markets to see how good local beans can be. Alvarez Farms of the Yakima Valley and Stoney Plains Organic Farm of Tenino, Washington, sell dry black beans at Seattle and Olympia farmers' markets.

Cannellini beans A large white bean with a creamy texture, the cannellini bean was originally cultivated in Argentina. Cannellinis are favorites in Italian recipes like *pasta e fagioli*. Longer and bigger than navy beans, cannellini beans are good in salads or soups. Look for these white beans from Willie Green's Organic Farm at Seattle farmers' markets.

Cranberry beans About the size of a pinto bean with the same creamy texture, the cranberry bean is grown by a number of farmers in the Northwest. Growing Things Farm of Carnation, Willie Green's Farm of Monroe, and Stoney Plains Farm of Tenino, Washington, sell these beans in the autumn. When you purchase cranberry beans fresh from the farmers' market and cook them, they have a wonderful buttery texture.

Fava beans More ancient than most other legumes, fava beans are widely used in cuisines throughout the world. Fresh favas demand more preparation than other legumes—shelling, blanching, and then peeling the outside skin—but they offer a distinct flavor and personality, best savored on their own and not hidden in soups or stews. According to the late Bob Meyer of Stoney Plains Farm, when fava beans are fresh they don't require a second peeling, and Tom Denison of Denison Farms in Corvallis says some favas pods are also edible. Dried favas impart a deep, rich flavor. These specialty beans are available from Ayers Creek Farm at the Hillsdale farmers' market. Dried favas can be cooked, then squeezed from the skins and pureed with garlic and onions and a little olive oil.

Flageolets Immature kidney beans, flageolet beans are often mentioned in French cooking. Pale green, delicate, and tender, these small buttery beans can make any dish shine. Look for fresh flageolet beans during late summer at the farmers' market. Willie Green's Organic Farm offers these wonderful treats in the fall at Seattle markets. Cook them with a little ghee, salt, and pepper.

Garbanzos Though they have Old World origins, garbanzos (chickpeas, ceci beans) and other legume crops are extensively grown and alternated with wheat in eastern Washington.

Garbanzos are round beans with wrinkly skins and a distinctly nutty taste. The texture is firm. You can also find black or split baby garbanzos, but the beige variety is more common. Garbanzos are also ground into a flour that adds a nutty flavor to baked goods. The beans need to be soaked, then simmered for a long time. When pressure-cooked, they are creamy and delicious. Some of the best garbanzos in Seattle come from Alvarez Farms in the Yakima Valley. Look for these at farmers' markets.

Great Northerns, navy, and small white beans Also referred to as haricot beans, Great Northerns are similar to cannellini beans, only smaller in size. Navy beans are the small white beans that put baked beans on the culinary map. They are also the main ingredient in navy bean soup. Small white beans include anything that tastes and looks similar to navy beans. In 2009, Alvarez Farms, which sells many varieties of organic dried beans at an affordable price at Seattle farmers' markets, added white beans to their dried bean parade.

Lentils Idaho, eastern Washington, and parts of Oregon are considered the best region in the world for growing lentils, peas, and chickpeas. More are cultivated and harvested here than anywhere else, and they are exported worldwide. Per ounce, compared to beef, they contain more protein and also have vitamins, minerals, and iron. A "Persian" variety, French lentils hold their shape well when cooked and have a sweet, subtle earthy flavor. Whitman County in Washington produces more lentils than any other county in the country, so lentils are bound to show up at farmers' markets in the Northwest. Unlike other legumes, lentils don't contain sulfur and are more easily digested than beans.

Pinto beans A small common bean from South America, the pinto can be bought in big bags in warehouse stores, but you won't find the quality that is offered from small farmers who cultivate these beans locally. Though pink speckled when dried, these beans like cranberry beans turn a boring beige color when cooked, so spice them up when you cook them. Use Northwest-grown chiles and sweet onions to enhance their bland flavors. Think of these beans as a culinary canvas with savory possibilities.

Red beans These beans are similar in color to kidney beans but closer in texture to white or Great Northern beans. Along with black beans, they are popular in Cuban cooking. Red beans are also the peas in Jamaican peas and rice. A good all-occasion bean, this should be a staple in the pantry. Alvarez Farms of the Yakima Valley grows and sells large red kidney beans and small red "lava" beans.

BUYING, STORING, AND SOAKING

Some varieties of legumes are eaten fresh, in or out of the pod, but the beans more familiar to most of us are the dried varieties. Except for lentils, dried legumes should be soaked and rehydrated before cooking.

The optimal shelf life for dried beans is about a year. They dry out on the shelf and after a year, they don't cook very well; trying to tenderize and cook very old beans can be like attempting to tenderize gravel on a country road. Besides, eating old beans isn't kind to your digestive system. Buy dried beans at farmers' markets for a fresher product. Look closely at beans before buying them, and if they are in bags, choose one without moldy, broken, chipped, or split beans. Uniformity of shape and color is not important. Some farmers have them on tables in the summer, but many sell more dried beans in the spring before most of their fresh crops come up and in the fall when summer crops are winding down.

Store beans in covered glass containers away from the light. If beans are left out in the light, pyridoxal and pyridoxine, two natural forms of a B vitamin, deteriorate rapidly. Cooked beans should be refrigerated as soon as they cool. They will keep for about one week in the refrigerator. You can also store cooked beans in the freezer for about six months.

Before cooking legumes, spread them out on a tray and pick out any stones or small sticks. Discard any shriveled, split, or obviously damaged beans. Rinse all legumes except red lentils, which can stick together like cement after rinsing. To soak, place the beans in a pot and cover with three times the amount of water. Soak overnight. Long soaking is ideal, but use the quick soak method if pressed for time.

To quick soak, place the beans in a pot and cover with three times the amount of water. Bring to a boil on the stovetop. Boil for about 10 minutes and remove from the heat, then let the beans sit for another 10 to 20 minutes. To check if your beans have finished soaking, cut a bean in half. If there is a dark spot in the middle, continue soaking. If it is uniform all the way through, the beans have finished soaking. Discard the soaking water and cook according to directions.

COOKING

Pour off the soaking water, cover the beans with three times the amount of water, and bring to a boil over high heat. Add a 1-inch strip of kombu, a sea vegetable, to make the beans more digestible. Reduce the heat and simmer until the beans are done, usually 1 to 1½ hours. To determine if the beans are done, gently mash one against the roof of your mouth. It should crush easily. Some beans such as garbanzos have a firm grainy texture when done and are more crumbly than buttery.

Beans are delicious when slow-simmered all day in a Crock-Pot. A pressure cooker is another option if you want beans without waiting. See the table below for cooking times both on the stovetop and in a pressure cooker. For quick release, run water over the pressure cooker at the end of the cooking time until the pressure drops. You can cook the beans for a few minutes less if you let the pressure come down naturally (natural release).

DRIED BEANS (1 CUP)	SOAK?	TIME ON STOVETOP (BEANS:WATER 1:3)	TIME IN PRESSURE COOKER (BEANS:WATER 1:1¼)	YIELD
Black	Yes	1½ hours	6 to 9 minutes	2½ cups
Cannellini	Yes	1½ hours	10 to 12 minutes	2 cups
Cranberry	Yes	1¼ hours	9 to 12 minutes	2¼ cups
Fava	Yes	2 to 3 hours	18 minutes	2 cups
Flageolet	Yes	1 hour	12 minutes	2 cups
Garbanzo	Yes	2½ hours	18 minutes	2½ cups
Great Northern or white beans	Yes	1 hour	12 minutes	2 cups
Lentils, brown French	No	40 minutes	6 to 10 minutes	2 cups
Pinto	Yes	1½ hours	8 to 10 minutes	2¼ cups
Red	Yes	1 hour	12 minutes	2 cups

MAKING BEANS DIGESTIBLE

All around the world, you can find tips on how to make beans more digestible. In India, *asafetida*, a resin from a giant fennel, is said to lower gas-producing tendencies. In Mexico, *epazote*, a tropic native, is added to bean dishes to enhance digestion. In Japan, kombu, a sea vegetable, helps speed up cooking time, enhances flavor, and helps de-gas beans. The digestive problems with beans stem from their complex sugars (stachyose and raffinose). The human digestive system can't break these sugars down, and they end up in our large intestines. To enhance digestibility and decrease the possibility of having gas, try any of the following tips.

- Soak beans overnight to leach out the indigestible sugars responsible for causing gas. When you soak beans, pour the soaking water off and use fresh water to cook your beans. If gas is a problem, change the soaking water frequently.

- Cut a strip of kombu into small pieces and cook it with the beans. Kombu also adds vitamins and minerals to the cooking water.
- Do not add salt until the beans are thoroughly cooked. Salt retards the cooking process and toughens the beans.
- Eat small portions of beans on a regular basis to build up your body's tolerance level and develop the digestive enzymes needed to break down and absorb beans.
- Sprout beans to reduce gas, increase protein content, lower the starch, and reduce the cooking time.

The Farms

Here is basic contact information for the farms that appear in this book. Visiting them on the Web is a great way to confirm details and check on their current offerings.

Oregon

Ayers Creek Farm
Gaston, Oregon
Anthony and Carol Boutard
aboutard@easystreet.net

Columbia Gorge Organic Fruit
Hood River, Oregon
Cheryl, Jimmy, and Ronny Stewart
www.cogojuice.com

Deep Roots Farm
Albany, Oregon
Aaron, Kimberly, Kaia, and Arissa Bolster
www.deeprootsfarm.com

Denison Farms
Corvallis, Oregon
Tom Denison and Elizabeth Kerle
www.denisonfarms.com

Fry Family Farm
Talent, Oregon
Suzanne and Steven Fry
www.fryfamilyfarm.com

Gathering Together Farm
Philomath, Oregon
John Eveland and Sally Brewer
www.gatheringtogetherfarm.com

Grateful Harvest Farm
Junction City, Oregon
Charles and Jesse Duryea
www.gratefulharvestfarm.com

Pennington Farms
Grants Pass, Oregon
Cathy and Sam Pennington
www.penningtonfarms.net

Whistling Duck Farm
Grants Pass, Oregon
Vince and Mary Alionis
www.whistlingduckfarm.com

Wilt Farms (Sunset Valley Organics)
Corvallis, Oregon
Diane and Bob Wilt
www.buyorganicberries.com

Winter Green Farm
Noti, Oregon
Jack Gray, Mary Jo Wade, Jabrila and Wali Via,
    Chris and Shannon Overbaugh
www.wintergreenfarm.com

Washington

Bellewood Acres
Lynden, Washington
Dorie and John Belisle
www.bellewoodapples.com

Cascadian Home Farm
Rockport, Washington
Jim and Harlyn Meyer
www.cascadianfarm.com

Cliffside Orchards
Kettle Falls, Washington
Jeanette and Jeff Herman
www.cliffsideorchard.com

Grouse Mountain Farm
Chelan, Washington
Liz Eggers and Michael Hamphel
hamneggs@nwi.net

Mair Farm-Taki
Wapato, Washington
Katsumi Taki
www.mairtaki.com

Nash's Organic Produce
Sequim, Washington
Nash Huber
www.nashsorganicproduce.com

Rama Farm
Bridgeport, Washington
Rick and Marilyn Lynn
ramafarm@nwi.net

Rent's Due Ranch
Stanwood, Washington
JoanE McIntyre and Michael Shriver
rentsdueranch@verison.net

Rockridge Orchards
Enumclaw, Washington
Wade and Judy Bennett
www.rockridgeorchards.com

Rosabella's Garden Bakery and Merritt Farm
Bow, Washington
Rose and Allan Merritt
www.rosabellasgarden.com

Stoney Plains Organic Farm
Tenino, Washington
Patricia and Patrick Meyer
stoneyp@comcast.net

Tahuya River Apiaries
Hood Canal, Washington
Roy Nettlebeck
www.hiveharvest.com

Whispering Winds Farm/Freshly Doug
   Vegetables
Stanwood, WA
Doug and Charlene Byde
www.freshlydougvegetables.blogspot.com

Willie Green's Organic Farm
Monroe, Washington
Jeff Miller
www.williegreens.org

Recommended Reading

Ableman, Michael. 1998. *On Good Land: An Autobiography of an Urban Farm*. San Francisco: Chronicle Books.

———. 2006. *Fields of Plenty: A Farmer's Journey in Search of Real Food and the People Who Grow It*. San Francisco: Chronicle Books.

Arora, David. 2004. *All That the Rain Promises and More: A Hip Pocket Guide to Western Mushrooms*. Berkeley, CA: Ten Speed Press.

Ballister, Barry. 1987. *The Fruit and Vegetable Stand: The Complete Guide to the Selection, Preparation and Nutrition of Fresh Produce*. Woodstock and New York: The Overlook Press.

Cooper, Ann, with Lisa M. Holmes. 2000. *Bitter Harvest: A Chef's Perspective on the Hidden Dangers in the Foods We Eat and What You Can Do About It*. New York: Routledge.

Costenbader, Carol W. 2002. *The Big Book of Preserving the Harvest: 150 Recipes for Freezing, Canning, Drying and Pickling Fruits and Vegetables*. North Adams, MA: Storey Books.

Gartenstein, Devra. 2008. *Local Bounty: Seasonal Vegan Recipes*. Summertown, TN: The Book Publishing Company.

Harrington, John (editor), and Ingrid Dankmeyer (writer). 2005. *Renewing the Countryside—Washington*. Minneapolis, MN: Renewing the Countryside.

Hawkes, Alex D. 1968. *A World of Vegetable Cookery*. New York: Simon & Schuster.

Henderson, Elizabeth, with Robyn Van En. 1999. *Sharing the Harvest: A Guide to Community Supported Agriculture*. White River Junction, VT: Chelsea Green.

Jackson, Wes. 1994. *Becoming Native to This Place*. Lexington: University Press of Kentucky.

Jones, Doug. 1999. *My Brother's Farm: Reflections on Life, Farming and the Pleasures of Food*. New York: Putnam's.

Kimbrell, Andrew (editor). 2002. *Fatal Harvest: The Tragedy of Industrial Agriculture*. Sausalito, CA: Foundation for Deep Ecology.

Kingsolver, Barbara. 2007. *Animal, Vegetable, Miracle: A Year of Food Life*. New York: HarperCollins.

Kurzweil, Jenny. 2005. *Fields That Dream: A Journey to the Roots of Our Food*. Golden, CO: Fulcrum.

Lappé, Francis Moore, and Anna Lappé. 2002. *Hope's Edge*. New York: Penguin Putnam.

Madison Area Community Supported Agriculture. 2004. *From Asparagus to Zucchini: A Guide to Cooking Farm Fresh Seasonal Produce*. Madison, WI: Jones Books.

Madison, Deborah. 2002. *Local Flavors: Cooking and Eating from America's Farmers' Markets*. New York: Broadway Books.

Masumoto, David Mas. 1995. *Epitaph for a Peach: Four Seasons on My Family Farm*. New York: HarperCollins.

———. 1998. *Harvest Son: Planting Roots in American Soil*. New York: Norton.

McClure, Susan (editor), and the staff of the Rodale Food Center. 1998. *Preserving Summer's*

Bounty: A Quick and Easy Guide to Freezing, Canning, Preserving, and Drying What You Grow. Allentown, PA: Rodale Books.

Morash, Marian. 1982. *The Victory Garden Cookbook.* New York: Knopf.

Morgan, Lane. 1990. *Winter Harvest Cookbook: How to Select and Prepare Fresh Seasonal Produce All Winter Long.* Seattle: Sasquatch Books.

Nabhan, Gary Paul. 2002. *Coming Home to Eat: The Pleasures and Politics of Local Foods.* New York: Norton.

——— (editor). 2008. *Renewing America's Food Traditions: Saving and Savoring America's Endangered Foods.* White River Junction, VT: Chelsea Green.

Nestle, Marion. 2007. *What to Eat.* New York: North Point Press.

Onstad, Dianne. 1996. *Whole Foods Companion: A Guide for Adventurous Cooks, Curious Shoppers, and Lovers of Natural Foods.* White River Junction, VT: Chelsea Green.

Parsons, Russ. 2008. *How to Pick a Peach: The Search for Flavor from Farm to Table.* New York: Houghton Mifflin.

Pitchford, Paul. 1993. *Healing with Whole Foods: Oriental Traditions and Modern Nutrition.* Berkeley, CA: North Atlantic Books.

Pollan, Michael. 2006. *The Omnivore's Dilemma: A Natural History of Four Meals.* New York: Penguin Books.

———. 2008. *In Defense of Food: An Eater's Manifesto.* New York: Penguin Books.

Rex-Johnson, Braiden. 2003 (second edition). *Pike Place Market Cookbook: Recipes, Anecdotes and Personalities from Seattle's Renowned Public Market.* Seattle: Sasquatch Books.

Robinson, Francis. 1998. *Purslane: The Incredible, Edible Weed.* Tacoma, WA: Columbia Media.

Robinson, Jo. 2004. *Pasture Perfect: The Far Reaching Benefits of Choosing Meat, Eggs and Diary Products from Grass-Fed Animals.* Vashon, WA: Vashon Island Press.

Rothenberg, Daniel. 1998. *With These Hands: The Hidden World of Migrant Farmworkers Today.* New York: Harcourt.

Schneider, Elizabeth. 2001. *The Essential Reference: Vegetables from Amaranth to Zucchini.* New York: William Morrow.

Smith, Alisa, and J. B. Mackinnon. 2007. *Plenty: One Man, One Woman and a Raucous Year of Eating Locally.* New York: Harmony Books.

Vileisis, Ann. 2008. *Kitchen Literacy: How We Lost Knowledge of Where Food Comes From and Why We Need to Get It Back.* Washington, DC: Island Press.

Williams, Jacqueline. 1993. *Wagon Wheel Kitchens: Food on the Oregon Trail.* Lawrence, KS: University Press of Kansas.

Wilson, Duff. 2001. *Fateful Harvest: The True Story of a Small Town, a Global Industry, and a Toxic Secret.* New York: HarperCollins.

Wood, Rebecca. 1989. *The New Whole Foods Encyclopedia.* New York: Penguin Books.

Index

DEBRA DANIELS-ZELLER learned how to roll a pie crust and enjoy the simple pleasures of food in her grandmother's kitchen. After being lured to Washington by Northwest berries in the 1970s, Debra became enchanted with the diverse bounty of local fruits and vegetables. She has taught seasonally inspired vegetarian cooking classes in Seattle since 1990, and has been a regular contributor to *Vegetarian Journal* for over a decade. Her recipes and articles have also appeared in *Delicious Living*, *The Sound Consumer*, and *Veggie Life*. An avid farmers' market shopper, Debra continues to develop recipes and blog about local foods at http://foodconnections.blogspot.com/. She lives in Edmonds, Washington, with her husband, two basset hounds, and a barn cat adopted from Mair Farm-Taki, an organic farm near Yakima, Washington.

MORRIE CARTER